RONNY GOODLASS

BLUE NOSE

ON THE **TERRACES** IN THE **DRESSING ROOM** ON THE **RADIO**

MY FOOTBALL STORY FROM EVERY ANGLE

RONNY GOODLASS

BLUE NOSE

ON THE	IN THE	ON THE
TERRACES	**DRESSING ROOM**	**RADIO**

MY FOOTBALL STORY FROM EVERY ANGLE

RG PUBLISHING

First English edition
Published in Great Britain in 2018

ISBN: 978-1-5272-2692-0

Copyright © Ronny Goodlass, 2018

Published and produced by: RG Publishing

A CIP catalogue record for this book is available from the British Library.

Cover design and typesetting by Thomas Regan at Milkyone Creative
Cover photography by Liam Deveney

Photographic acknowledgments:
Ronny Goodlass Collection/ Liverpool Echo / Everton FC / Reach plc
Blackpool Gazette/ Ken Coton / Liam Deveney

Printed and bound by CPI Group (UK) Ltd, Croyden, CRO 4YY

THIS BOOK IS DEDICATED TO:

My wife Denise, a Spartan Warrior, for her patience
throughout these many years.

My children – Christopher, Gary, Stacey and Mark.

My grandchildren Ava-Ruby, and Cole.

My Dad and Mum who helped inspire my football dream.

Nan and Granddad Goodlass.

Nan and Granddad Hunt.

My brother John – he has been there from the start
and I have always appreciated his support.

Evertonians and Bluenoses everywhere of which I am so proud to be one.

CONTENTS

FOREWORD

MY MATE RONNY...
BLUE NOSE WHO GREW UP
TO FULFIL HIS DREAM

JOE ROYLE

I FIRST remember Ronny as a shy apprentice at Everton's famous old Bellefield Training Ground, a shyness he soon got over I might add!

He would come into the first team dressing room after training each day to collect the used, sweaty kit from the morning session which would then be replaced by the fresh kit for the afternoon work-outs.

Ronny would linger, smiling at the senior conversation with ears pricked as the dressing room comedians,

Brian Labone and Gordon West, began their daily routine of winding up one of the younger players in the room. It might be over a mistaken word in the papers or a misplaced pass in training. The camaraderie was strong and Ronny embraced it.

He had joined Everton as one of the elite crop of his year, a route that several young players starring for Liverpool schoolboys had taken, myself included. Ronny was living the dream, he was in the confines of Everton's training ground every day, playing football for a living and rubbing shoulders with players that he had idolized from the terraces, none more so than Alan Ball.

Ronny's reputation at the club was growing after sterling performances in the A and B teams, plus occasional call-ups to train with the first team and reserves. He had a wonderful left foot, plus a willingness to cross the ball into dangerous areas. This earmarked him as a young man who was certainly going to make a living in the game.

The early years of Ronny's career crossed with my own in a period when I was recovering from injury. Competition for the left wing position was strong and while the vastly experienced Johnny Morrissey had now departed, Ronny found himself with the slightly older Gary Jones in front of him and the emerging George Telfer behind him. He would meet this challenge to ultimately win the coveted number 11 shirt at Goodison Park.

Ronny finally made his debut against Manchester United at Goodison Park, and played in the Wembley League Cup Final against Aston Villa and the controversial FA Cup Final semi-final that same 1977 season against Liverpool.

There was still a football dream to fulfil though, so Ronny took up his own version of "going Dutch" and went to the Netherlands for three years – the home of 'Total Football' - to further his career and football education.

Regular football during the European phase of his career satisfied Ronny's professional challenge, but his family needs and a lust to still make it in the country of his birth brought him back to the UK for a spell in London with Fulham.

After another foreign adventure, playing for South China in Hong Kong, Ronny found himself back on Merseyside with Tranmere Rovers and while he then drifted into non-league football with Barrow, his enthusiasm and love of the game never diminished.

When I returned to Goodison in 1994 as manager, our paths soon crossed again. Ronny had started coaching kids locally, and when an Everton coaching position arose at Bellefield I asked him to come and work with our Academy prospects.

I had never forgotten Ronny's enthusiasm and perpetual smile. The phone conversation was short, and the answer succinct… "I'm coming!"

There was no haggling over wages, contracts or agents. Just an instinctive 'yes' to the club he had supported all his life. I did find out later that he had taken charge of Runcorn at the time and had just prepared a dossier for their board about the way forward.

However, a new Everton challenge was just what he needed. Ronny, along with John Hurst, worked tremendously hard to develop our young players. Richard Dunne, Danny Cadamarteri and Michael Ball, all went on to play for the first team.

When I left in 1997, Everton sadly pursued the all too common practice in football of changing the staff at all levels, and two close friends and very capable coaches, John and Ronny were out of work.

By the time that I had returned to Liverpool from Ipswich, Ronny was deeply involved with his Health Through Sport project and he kindly asked me to be a Patron of the charity, an honour that I was proud and willing to accept.

He had also become 'Radio Ronny', working for BBC Radio Merseyside and giving out his only slightly biased view of all things Everton while never being afraid to criticise, if required, in a positive way.

Well done Ronny. You have had many facets to your life in football and been successful with them all. I can only wish you all the best with this book my friend, and one thing is for sure. I'm certain that the next time we meet, at a football match, in a radio station or at one of your charity dinners…we will both be smiling.

THAT RARE BREED: EX-PRO WHO PUTS HIS HEART AND SOUL INTO HELPING OTHERS

JOHN BLAIN
CHAIRMAN, EVERTON FC SHAREHOLDERS ASSOCIATION

RONNY started playing first team football, his lifelong passion, in 1975. That was the year I began my working life too and I can attest that it was a long time ago, especially for an ex-player like Ronny who still claims he's only about 40 now!

Football has changed a lot since then, but what has not changed is the excitement generated by a fast, tricky winger who can go past his man, remain calm and fire in an early and pinpoint cross to the near or far post that invites a striker or a midfield player to finish off the job.

That's all Ronny did really, but what a skill. It's a simple game and his simple and highly effective skills would today have him valued in the tens of millions of pounds.

Today Ronny uses that same uncluttered and direct approach to great effect in his radio punditry. Like his playing style, it is delivered with passion and commitment. He really does bring his passion and insight to the fore during his commentaries.

As much as his playing style was simple and direct, so are his comments. He doesn't shrink from the issues, and his forthright words are rightly welcomed by all true blue Evertonians.

It's over 22 years since he started broadcasting for the BBC and he shows no sign of slowing down. Indeed, the advent of social media and Twitter has given him another outlet for his larger than life personality.

Alongside the work he does commenting about our beloved Everton, his tenacity and interpersonal skills continue to encourage support for his successful Health Through Sport charity.

I really don't know where he gets the time and energy from as he's forever pushing and cajoling people into either supporting the charity or attending one of his hugely popular dinners. Like many, I avidly look forward to these events, usually after encouragement from Ronny to "take a table" at the Devonshire Hotel that is always packed out with everyone having a terrifically enjoyable time.

Like most people who make a difference, Ronny seems

to be everywhere. Indeed, he was also the narrator of the critically acclaimed stage play 'Ball of Fire' that depicted the life and times of the late great Alan Ball. This played out to packed theatres, was attended by Everton legends from the past, and was even recommended by Manchester United and England's record goalscorer, the former born again blue Wayne Rooney.

As ever, this huge success donated its proceeds to Health Through Sport and proved yet again that Ronny's significant contribution really does make a difference.

The serious side of the charity though is the great work that flows from Ronny's fundraising efforts. I know he has people who help, but much of what happens is driven by his infectious personality, tremendous stamina and tenacity.

The outcomes over the 10 plus years since Ronny founded this project have been superb. The charity's record at working locally with ex-offenders and addicts, giving them the best opportunity for a successful rehabilitation into society and full-time employment, is quite fantastic.

In short all his attributes, and his fabulous personality, dodgy timekeeping apart, mean he's as much a pleasure to be around today as he was when he was scoring goals from the half-way line, skinning full-backs and entertaining us with his wing skills.

Ronny was born a blue and has always been a blue and it shines through in everything he does as he strives to live up to our famous 'Nil Satis Nisi Optimum' motto.

'BALL OF FIRE' LEFT ME
SPEECHLESS AND MADE
ME PROMISE TO FULFIL MY
DREAMS

THREE days before Christmas 1971 I was a young 17 years old professional on the Everton FC ground staff, hoping and praying that Father Christmas might come down the chimney that year wearing blue and white instead of his traditional red as the definitive sign that my dreams of playing for the club I had idolised all my life might soon come true.

I was at the old Bellefield training ground in West Derby where, to date, my greatest honour had been operating as

'Boot Boy' to the legend that was Alan Ball. I can't tell you how proud I had been to see him walking out at Goodison Park on match days in pristine boots that I had lovingly cleaned.

These were the days when we young pros would start the day with a brush in our hands rather than a ball at our feet, ready and willing to sweep out the dressing rooms and jump when our senior pros needed something doing.

It wasn't a chore. It was a source of pride, and no one had been prouder than me to look after the 'Ball of Fire'.

He was a great talent and he always wanted to get even better. His view was that everyone can improve. I'm sure if he was coaching the world's greatest player at the moment, someone like Barcelona's Lionel Messi, he would be telling him that he could improve – and Messi would be listening.

Equally, people have told me that when he was managing at clubs like Exeter City, his training regimes and determination to get the very best out of players who, in all reality, were not fit to lace his boots, was equally inspiring. He would work long and hard on the Exeter training ground, educating young strikers on free-kicks, corners and every aspect of player development. This is why it is so frustrating – and surprising – that this great football talent never really made it as a manager. Perhaps you have to be in the right place at the right time.

As a player he trained like he played, giving 120 per cent in every situation, and I never expected to see him anything other than upbeat in the familiar confines of

Bellefield.

On the day he finally left Everton, I was absolutely stunned. I just couldn't believe it. I instinctively knew the day was different. I saw him coming across the small dining room that was just a few yards from manager Harry Catterick's office. Bally was clearly in a state of shock, but not half as stunned as I was when he suddenly said: "Make sure whoever is cleaning those white boots of mine give them a special cleaning today Ronny. The next time I'll be wearing them it won't be at Goodison. I'm on my way."

I was speechless like thousands of Evertonians would be when they bought that night's Echo and realised that their hero had joined Arsenal for £220,000.

I'll repeat: £220,000, pin money in today's game in which £200million has now become the new benchmark. Alan Ball, at his peak, is one of the few who would have justified such a fee, WORLD CLASS in capital letters.

What would the supporters be thinking of when they heard this terrible news? What was Harry Catterick thinking of and why did he make this decision?

"We have had six years and doubled our money on him and it's good football business," Catterick would say. Was it good football business?

I felt a special affinity with Alan, having been the apprentice charged with the task of looking after him. It was more than that. It was an honour, a dream come true. Now he was leaving us, declaring: "Once Everton has touched you, nothing will ever be the same'.

On this day of days, it would have been easy for him to jump into his car and head out the Bellefield gates without a backwards glance. I shook his hand, struggling to get any meaningful words out.

Typical of Bally, he had no such problem. "Ronny," he said. "Make me proud, son, by achieving all of your Goodison dreams. One day you will be pulling on that first team jersey and when you do, think of me and play your heart out for this club."

I looked at Bally and I swear that, just for a second, Father Christmas WAS standing in front of me and his suit really was blue and white. I knew that very moment that I would work doubly hard, if that was possible, to make the breakthrough that I yearned for.

It would take a few more years, but I had a promise to fulfil to a legend and an icon, one that would now dominate my heart and soul as I set out to achieve my own football dream.

I would never be an Alan Ball, but I would play for Everton and when an Evertonian does that, every game is the local equivalent of a World Cup Final.

Some years later when I played for Everton against Arsenal at Highbury, Bally was in the opposition. I was doing my warm-up near the halfway line when somebody shouted my name and, as I turned around, it was Alan. "Ronny, keep getting those crosses in," he said with a beaming smile across his face. Even though I was playing against him, he was still encouraging me to play well and I never forgot that.

When he spoke about Everton there was a passion in is voice that underlined his sheer love for all the club stands for. He has left me and many supporters around the world with fantastic memories of his Everton, Arsenal, Southampton and England playing days.

He was not just a great player, but was also a great man who had set very high standards and values for himself, which he would go on to achieve. I would never be an Alan Ball, but I tried to live every day by his professional winning mantra.

Little did I know that 46 years after Bally left Everton for Arsenal, I would still have the great man very much in my thoughts, narrating a hugely successful play in his honour in theatres across the North West, fittingly entitled 'Ball of Fire'. But more of that later.

For now I want to tell you where my Everton FC dreams all began and take you on a personal journey that might sometimes surprise you, but which will, if you are a true blue, make you as proud to be a Blue Nose as I am.

PROUD TO BE AN INNER CITY BOY AS FOOTBALL DOMINATES MY EARLY LIFE

I WAS born in Mill Road Hospital to Ronald and Margaret Goodlass. Mum was known as 'Norma'. My parents lived close by with our grandparents in Canton Street, off Everton Road with the original Red Triangle gym at the end of our Street.

Almost three years later my brother John arrived, but this time he was delivered in the Canton Street house and from my recollection he was put in the chest of drawers, used as a make shift cot and bed!

Both mum and Dad worked and I was placed into the Adam Cliff Day Nursery on Everton Road before I went to Steers Street School in Everton. Later I attended the nearby Heyworth Street with its fenced off playground yard overlooking Netherfield Road where I played my first organised football.

We actually had a swimming pool in the basement which was unusual for such an old building and so we were able to have swimming lessons. It's remarkable that an inner city school, built at the start of the 1900s for a 100 per cent working class community, had the vision to include a pool in its plans. I know that the nearby Major Lester Primary close to Everton Valley, built at the same time, also had a basement pool although this was later boarded over to create an area for school dinners. Stew and semolina before swimming lessons was perhaps not quite so visionary, although it was clearly a necessity.

We had a teacher who was very keen on playing chess and she encouraged me and the kids to learn the game. I eventually went on to win the school Chess Championship. Thanks Miss!

During these early years all I was really interested in was football, whether it was in our street, at school or at the nearest green space – Grant Gardens. As the years went by the venues started to change. We had to look for better facilities because there was no leisure centres or state of the art 5-a-side pitches in our day.

We would bunk in over the walls of St Margaret's School at the back of Grant Gardens or go to the SFX School off

Shaw Street, known as the Wembley of Everton because of its size and the fact that the pitch was marked out.

Lads would turn up in their droves, but you always got a game. "Puddin' or Beef" would be the shout as another lad climbed over the wall who wanted to join in. This is how we chose which team he would play for.

What a schooling that was, playing with and against the older lads with no prisoners taken. We all wanted to win and had some great times with not a referee to be seen. We played until it was dark or until the 'Cocky Watchman' chased us.

It was a close knit community, but on 12th July (Orange Lodge Day) and 17th March (St Patrick's Day) there was suddenly real hostility between neighbours in our street. They would argue on those days, but 24 hours later be back to normal as the best of mates!

With no computers, laptops or games consoles in our day, we had to improvise or invent games to play, most of them no longer heard of. For the younger readers of this book, Ollies (Marbles) and the Yo-Yo kept us busy for hours. Coloured glass marbles were rolled or flicked. You would try and hit your opponent's marble to win it, or if it was a bigger and more colourful version, you had to hit it a certain number of times to win it. Are you still paying attention!

A 'steely' (large silver ball-bearing) was the one everyone wanted and that was the hardest one to win. These days I sometimes go to the Taxi Club in Walton after an Everton game where I usually bump into Ronnie Cleary, a former neighbour of ours who lived in Gleave Square. He always reminds me and the lads that I was a champion Ollies' star in the area and what a player I was.

We used to go to the local picture house, the Royal Hippodrome, using an empty jam jar to get in for free, yes for free, and the place was always packed out on a Saturday morning. Oh how times have changed for my grandchildren.

At the start of the 1960s, streets and rows of terraced houses were starting to get knocked down in the neighbourhood. It was sad to see, although it created an adventure playground for a young lad of my age. In the 'Bombdies' – named after the houses bombed in the Second World War – everything was ripped out, not just kitchens, baths and pipes but even the staircases. We would climb and jump, or drop, from floor to floor with no health and safety in our day.

'Bommy Night' was something else. A lorry would leave our street with about 30 kids on the back to go around collecting wood from around the area. It was hard work, but your street always wanted the biggest 'bommy' in the area.

We knew Canton Street would soon be up for demolition, called 'slum clearance' by the local council and city planners.

I had a happy childhood with lots of family and friends around but sadly my Mum and Dad separated and when I was five years old, they got divorced. Me and my younger brother John lived with my Dad and my paternal grandparents came to live with us and they played a massive part in bringing us up. Many people didn't want to leave their houses or the area because it would separate families, friends and neighbours who had been together for generations. I hated and still hate it that they described our homes as slums. We were a very hard working and proud community that did its best to raise families as best they could.

Skelmersdale, Kirkby, Cantril Farm, and Halewood, were amongst the new estates to be built on the periphery of Liverpool, so there was a wider district over which people were dispersed and communities broken up. Contact with each other would be more difficult and friendships built over many years would be lost.

I don't know if the local council gave families a choice as to where they could move, but mine went to the former Cantril Farm, just off Deysbrook Lane. We suddenly had a garden at the front, back and side of the house, four bedrooms, bathroom and an indoor toilet. No need to walk down the backyard with a candle to use the toilet in the dark.

We had six trees in the side garden, one that rained conkers down while Lord Derby's estate, with miles of trees, fields and the River Alt, was within walking distance of the house. First impressions of our new home for me were very good. Over the next few weeks it was getting to know the lads in the roads (not streets) by the house and playing football on the backfield, as it was known. Then jumping over the River Alt from one side of the river bank to the other and as it got wider as you walked further along you hoped that you would not be one of the lads who fell in and got soaked.

The first homes on the large and emerging Cantril Farm estate were still five years away from being occupied. Ultimately, 6,000 people arrived to take advantage of the facilities. Improved public transport, shops and schools would be a further two years away, but it was a fresh community in the making.

The next thing for my Dad was to find a school for me and our John. I don't think it was a hard choice really. Cantril Farm primary school was a couple of minutes away and we went to see the headmistress. It was all positive and everything looked fine, not least because the school was very sports orientated and that suited me fine.

They had football and athletics teams and I enjoyed taking part in most sports. I played for the school football team when I was 8, 9 and 10 years old.

We won the Cup twice in my time there, first beating Granby Street in the final at Penny Lane, which was the Liverpool Schoolboys headquarters and the place all Liverpool lads wanted to play.

Opponents Granby Street were fairly local to Penny Lane and so they had a large following at the final, but we took two coach-loads of supporters, including family and friends who made their presence felt with their noise, encouragement and the banners they had made. We played in black and gold stripes and our nickname was the 'Bees '. With the help of the teachers, our school mates created a huge bee. You couldn't miss it when we jogged out and the team was lifted when we saw it. Granby Street fielded a big team and played the ball long while we were a smaller team who liked to pass the ball on the floor and play more football.

It worked well because we won 1–0 and it was my first football trophy and medal.

The following year the football team had another great Cup run and we went on to reach the final again to play Knotty Ash. This time though the game would be held at Bellefield, Everton FC's training ground. This was a fantastic venue for the final with a lovely pitch to play on. We were impressed by the massive building that was built in 1945 to accommodate the dressing rooms. There were also big sunken baths which I plunged into.

With both teams local to Bellefield in nearby West Derby, there was a massive crowd and both teams had good support. We played really well on the day and we ran out 4–0 winners and it was an honour for me to receive the shield as captain. It was a great feeling to score two goals, assist in the other two and to captain a Cup winning team at Bellefield. It doesn't get much better at that time for a 10 year old Evertonian.

WHY I LIVE BY THAT FAMOUS BANNER SENTIMENT: 'BORN NOT MANUFACTURED'

HAVING been being born into a long-standing Evertoni-an family stretching back to my great granddad and with all of my family dedicated Toffees, 'Born Not Manufac-tured' certainly applies to me and I'm proud to say that.

That's how you become an Evertonian. It's through your family. I had no choice because it's in your blood and there's nothing you can do about it. From a very early age you get to learn our history and then you realise what a very special club we are.

My Dad and granddad always went the game. They had season tickets, but the first match I went to see was with my uncle Tommy, my mum's brother, and what an occasion that was.

I couldn't wait for the game to come around on 27 December, 1960, and was counting down the days. The opposition would be a very good Burnley team. They had won the Championship the previous season and their team would feature Blacklaw, Pointer, McIlroy, Adamson and John Connelly, who would later be included in the 1966 World Cup squad.

Horace Yates of the Liverpool Daily Post wrote: "At the biggest league gate any ground has housed this season, the 75,667 crowded into Goodison Park yesterday, the majority of the spectators were eager to see Everton complete a double over the champions Burnley."

I can vouch for the packed ground. We were in the Gwladys Street End very early to get a good spec, right behind the goal where the barriers used to be. I was able to sit on one and get a better view. For me there were more supporters in the ground than the official attendance stated because a couple of thousand young kids like me were being lifted out so we wouldn't get crushed. It wouldn't happen today because of the health and safety issues. I was on the grass to the right of the goal and in touching distance of Albert Dunlop, the Everton goalkeeper.

What took my breath away that day was how big the stadium seemed. The stands looked like they were touching the sky. The terraces were packed and I was so near the pitch I could almost reach out and touch the white pitch markings. The nets, corner flags, the noise, players, kits, boots... I soaked everything up and then there was the game!

These are the things I will never forget. Oh yes, we lost 0–3, but it was too late. I was already in love with Everton. I dreamed that one day I would play for the Blues. Most kids have that dream, but it never comes true. Would it for me?

Being Evertonians, win, lose or draw, you always want to be at the next game. I got my first season ticket when I was eight years old, sitting with my Dad and granddad in the Upper Bullens Road stand. At first I used to think I was in Vatican City because sitting behind us were always about 30 priests. That's when I knew we were God's Club! The Blues had attracted many Catholic fans in the 1950s when we had many Irish stars on our books like the great Peter Farrell.

One game I will always remember from this period was when we played Leeds United on the 9th December 1964. The game was known as the 'Battle of Goodison' and it was the most violent ever played at the stadium. Leeds had a reputation of being a tough team and they were promoted the previous season with a terrible disciplinary record.

After only four minutes, Johnny Giles did a chest-high tackle on Sandy Brown that left six studs in his chest. Sandy reacted to this, punched him, and was sent off. Giles, who was no shrinking violet, wasn't even booked in this incident.

The referee, Mr K Stokes, decided that something drastic was needed to cool down both the players and the crowd, so in the 38th minute he took both teams off the field. It was the first time in League history that a referee had taken the players off for violent play. Ten minutes later they came back out, but nothing changed much.

Tackles were still flying in and the only player booked was Norman Hunter for a foul on Roy Vernon. Leeds won the game 0–1, but the crowd were still angry and it needed mounted police to clear the streets. This was the start of a bitter rivalry between Everton and Leeds United that would last for a long time.

After a few years of being a season ticket holder in the Upper Bullens Road, I was starting to get a bit of independence and so started to go in the 'Boys Pen' with my mates. Looking from the pitch, it was situated in the top right hand corner of the Lower Gwladys Street End. The area of the 'Pen' wasn't very large, maybe 20 x 30 yards with railings and wire mesh. It had its own entrance and was like a massive cage.

It was named the 'Boys Pen' because you were literally penned in. To enter, you had to be Under 16 and it was cheap and supposed to be safe, but I saw more fights in there than at the Liverpool Stadium.

You couldn't get out every week, but the lads I was with used to go the back of the Pen, climb up and go along the girders and bunk into Gwladys Street.

The Park End accommodated the away supporters in

those days, but the only place you wanted to be was in the Gwladys Street End. The atmosphere at games was fantastic, masses of swaying chanting supporters getting behind the team.

The big difference with today's football is the all-seater stadia and trying to create an atmosphere as good as it was. Remember the rattles, flags and banners? We used to make the rattles at school in woodwork lessons and then drive the family up the wall practising how to us them.

They used to generate some noise, but think how loud it would be now with hundreds used at the same time.

You couldn't take rattles to a game these days because they would be classed as weapons and would break health and safety rules. Fashions change, but memories live on.

SIX OF THE BEST AND I'M NOT TALKING ABOUT SCORING GOALS

AS we started to take our 11-Plus exams, desperately hoping to pass, our parents had to make a list of possible schools in preferred order – assuming we were successful of course. My Dad put John Hamilton at the top because it had a good name for education and sport.

I passed and was accepted to attend. At the end of assembly on day one the teachers were asking which of the new boys had played football for their previous schools and who were the captains.

I thought this was great because they were clearly not waiting around to get the football team sorted. The only drawback I could see was that there were no grass pitches at the school. We had to get a double decker bus to the Cottage Homes in Fazakerley for PE lessons once a week and for games on the Saturday, but being lads, laughs were never far away.

I enjoyed most sports and would have a go at everything, entering as many events as I could on Sports Day. We did Cross Country around Aintree Canal for which I held the record. Sports Day was held at Long Lane that had a big running track and I won a number of events on the day.

I had a good group of lads to progress with through the years for the football teams. It was a good school where discipline was always high on the agenda for the teachers. I was a typical teenager growing up, joking and having a laugh, but I remember one time in assembly, when the headmaster made a real impression on me, literally.

Me and my mate where joking in the playground and he just carried on talking when we went into the school hall. I told him to stop in case we got detention. The teachers were looking around the hall because they could hear someone talking and were trying to spot who it was. The headmaster was on the stage and shouted: "Goodlass, go and stand outside my office for talking." For once, it wasn't me talking, but I couldn't say it was my mate, so off I went.

After 30 minutes, my mate came to stand with me and then the headmaster called me into his office. I will keep this brief because he clearly did. I got six of the best with the most flexible and supple cane you have ever seen in your life. He was practising a few swings and I could hear it going whoosh. He dished out the punishment and said I could go back to class. There was nobody about so I went to the toilet to see the damage, dropping my trousers to look. Oh my, what a sight. I was looking at a 6 bar electric fire on my backside and boy was it hurting. I never got sent out of assembly again!

I would like to mention Mr Walker, our PE teacher, who always gave me encouragement and was a good influence. Mr Sellars, our form teacher, was also great and just how a teacher should be, especially with what he had to put up with in our class. He deserved a medal.

When I was 14 years old I played for Liverpool Juniors but then I was promoted to the Liverpool Schoolboys team and played for them for two years. The first year I played 13 games and scored 7 goals and I really enjoyed my second year playing when we had a very good all round team that was competitive, strong in defence, hard to beat, played good football and could score goals.

The first opponent in the English Schools Trophy was Huyton at Penny Lane and this was just a few days after we beat them 6–0. This game though was more difficult and we struggled to win 2–1. The next round was a 6–0 home victory over St Helens before we drew 1–1 at Lancaster and Morecambe where their goalkeeper had an exceptional game. Happily, we won the replay at Penny Lane 4–0.

It was then we played Burnley at Barden Secondary

School where it was cold and windy, but we did the job and won 6–1.

We then faced one of the favourites to win the trophy, South Northumberland, a big and powerful team that had a 6ft 2ins centre-forward in Chris Guthrie who later had a good career at Newcastle United. He would become a good friend and team mate of mine when we played for England Schoolboys.

There was a nationwide freeze on, but it was particularly severe up North and we travelled to Whitley Bay to stay on the Friday. It had been snowing so bad that we didn't arrive at the hotel until 12.30am. We didn't get to bed until 1.30am and the game kicked off at 10.30 the following morning.

It was so bitter when the game started that Mr Cassidy, our manager, said we could wear a T-shirt under our football shirts. With three inches of snow on the pitch, I wanted to wear my sheepskin coat!

If we hadn't travelled so far and stayed overnight the game would have been postponed. We were up against a big Geordie crowd that had their team pumped up, but we wanted to win it. We took the lead through Gerry Edmondson and then I had a run from the halfway line and drilled it into the far corner, 2–0. We needed that goal because the aforementioned Chris Guthrie scored for them and also hit the bar from 25 yards. We deserved the win and showed a lot of character that day.

Next up in the quarter-finals was Plymouth at Home Park on the Saturday night. The previous evening we were taken to see a James Bond film. Over 7,000 turned up for the game and that was more than Plymouth Argyle had secured for their previous home game. We had a lot of chances that night and should have scored more, but a Kenny Pritchard goal took us through 1–0. In the Plymouth line up that night was a certain Trevor Francis, ex-Nottingham Forest and Man City, who I see often through our media work. He still mentions the game.

We now faced a tough semi-final against Barnsley at Oakwell, the clash inspiring another big crowd. We got off to a really good start and went 2–0 up after a quarter of an hour. Kenny Pritchard and Paul Johnson got the goals, but they pulled one back just before half time.

The Barnsley boys had a real go at us second half and Kenny Pritchard says he can still hear me shouting down his ear to get out of the way to score our third goal in a 3–1 win. That was five away games, but we still got to the final against Swindon.

The first leg was played at Anfield on a Friday night and we were not flattered by the 3–0 scoreline. Kenny Pritchard and Gerry Edmondson scored two of the goals. The second leg was the following Saturday at Swindon and Stan Harland, their captain, came into the dressing room to wish us all the best. He was an ex-Liverpool Schoolboy who signed some autographs and programmes for the lads.

Swindon won the game 1–0 with a very dodgy penalty. If VAR was in use then, the decision would have been overturned!

We eventually won 3–1 on aggregate and Liverpool Schoolboys were now English Schools Trophy winners. Get in there!

For the previous two years I would walk down from school to catch the number 46 bus on Netherfield Road to get to Penny Lane for training on Tuesdays and Thursdays. At least twice a week for the next two years I would look up at the Prince Rupert Tower on Netherfield Road South and think: "Will I ever play for my beloved Everton Football Club?"

AN ENGLAND BOYS WEMBLEY DOUBLE INSPIRES MY EVERTON DREAMS

WITH my growing success with Liverpool Schoolboys, I was coming to the attention of the England Schools selectors and I won my first cap against Scotland at Turf Moor, Burnley on 22 March, 1969. We had eight England internationals that season and I am proud to say I played in every one of them.

When I went to school on the Monday, our form teacher said the headmaster wanted to see me immediately in his office. Walking out of the classroom on the way to the head's office, I was thinking: "What have I done now?"

I arrived and the secretary told me to go in. The Headmaster, Mr Baxter said: "Morning, sit down," and I'm thinking: "Good start. I'm sitting down and there's no cane in his hand!

He said: "On behalf of myself, the teachers and the school, congratulations on gaining your first England Schoolboy cap on Saturday and we hope you go on to gain even more. You should be proud of your achievement."

I thanked him and Mr Baxter added: "I want you to bring your England cap in to school and I will present you with it on the stage during assembly."

Going on stage in front of everybody to get my cap presented was strangely daunting. I thought: "Oh sugar!"

A couple of days went by and I brought the cap in and gave it to the Headmaster. In the middle of assembly, he asked me to come onto the stage and told the school about me winning my first cap, congratulating me again. But he then started to tell a story, not just to the school but to me also.

He said: "I have presented one other England Schoolboys cap to someone when he was at my school and that boy was David Pegg," and he went on to explain about David and his football career.

David was an ex-England and Manchester United player, one of the legendary Busby Babes who sadly died in the Munich Air Disaster on 6th February 1958. Twenty three people lost their lives when the plane crashed on take-off as the team returned from a European game. The death toll included the great Duncan Edwards and seven other players, three club officials, eight journalists, two crew members and two passengers. United had played in Yugoslavia and had eliminated Red Star Belgrade to go through to the semi-final of the competition.

On 6th February 2018 a memorial was held to mark the 60th anniversary of the tragedy.

Since the headmaster told me this story, every year on this date, I think of David and everyone who lost their lives. RIP all of you.

When I reflect on my England Schoolboys days, there were four internationals that I remember vividly, two played at home and two away.

I was selected against Wales at Wembley Stadium which I was obviously delighted with and my mum hired a 52 seat coach to take family and friends. My Nan was really poorly and in a wheelchair at this time with Multiple Sclerosis, but she was determined to be there and see me play under the old Twin Towers. What character she had. I know she was proud of me and I was so proud of her. Did she get to see the game? Too right she did!

I really appreciated her support, plus that of family and friends.

My brother John didn't go on the coach, he went on the train with about 30 lads from West Derby Comp. I don't know whether Tom Saunders had anything to do with it? He was a teacher there and my first manager at Liverpool Schoolboys before he became a trusted member of that close knit Liverpool FC backroom staff of Bob Paisley &

Co. West Derby had a couple of teachers who were mad football fans.

Walking out at Wembley is something else, a full house, great atmosphere, but all you want to do is get on with the game.

It was a dream start for me and the team. I scored in the fourth minute with a right foot volley (yes my right foot) from the edge of the area that flew into the net and settled me and the England lads down. In the 14th minute Chris Guthrie scored our second and in the second half a cross came in from the right wing. I made a run across the defender to the near post to glance a header into the top corner from 12 yards out.

Not long after that I had a good shot saved, a pity because it would have been the perfect hat trick for me, right foot, left foot and header, but I can't complain. I did score two goals at Wembley in our 3–0 win.

There was an article in The Times by Norman Creek about the game and here are a few extracts:

> *Conditions were perfect, both for the players and the 75,000 spectators. Although Dwyer played a determined captain's part for Wales, he was constantly hustled by Spinner who looked an experienced leader for so young a boy. He was moreover well supported by Guthrie and Goodlass who reminded many of the fathers and schoolmasters present of Duncan Edwards and John Sissons respectively. With so much attacking talent England were able to maintain constant pressure and Hyett in goal for*

Wales was in action every few minutes of the game. He had no chance to save a drive from Goodlass in the fourth minute, though he seemed a little slow in moving to a powerful 20 yard cross shot by Guthrie 10 minutes later.

Clever anticipation by Goodlass enabled him to head England's third goal by gliding a fast centre from Spinner into the top corner of the net and the result was then virtually certain.

Two of my team mates that day were Mick Buckley (Manchester) and Ray Pritchard (Kirkby).

We then went to play in Germany. It was the first time any of the lads had played abroad and it was a daunting task against the highly rated Germans on their home soil.

The game took place in the same stadium as the infamous Nuremberg Rally which was held during the Second World War. This was some stadium for 15 year old lads to play in, a full house and an intimidating atmosphere, but we would be up for the challenge. We lined up on the halfway line, facing the German players and we were confident of winning the game. We were introduced to Uwe Seeler and Willie Schulz, two world class players who three years earlier had played for West Germany against England in the 1966 World Cup Final.

It was a hot day, the introductions were out of the way, and national anthems had been played. It was time to get on with the game. They started well and were putting us under early pressure which got their crowd involved and raised the noise level.

They forced a couple of corners but it came to nothing. We then began to get more possession and forced a couple of good saves from the German keeper. We did well for the rest of the first half and were unlucky to go in at half time 0–0. We started to dominate in the second half and it was no surprise that we took the lead late on.

We caught them on the break and I was involved in the move with Mick Buckley and Paul Smith. We passed the ball from our half and Smithy scored with a good shot across the keeper. You could hear a pin drop, absolute silence around the stadium. We ran after Smithy and started to celebrate and the defenders soon joined the rest of us in a heap on the floor.

The lads' smiles were brilliant to see and when we started to get up, I shouted: "If we win, where are we going tonight, TOWN!"

Everyone just burst out laughing. As we jogged back to the halfway line, the German players looked in shock. They didn't get beat very often but never at home and there wasn't much time left to get an equaliser.

Our defenders did really well for us as the Germans tried everything to get a goal, but the referee blew his whistle and we won 1–0. It was West Germany's first defeat at home and a tremendous performance from the team.

We did go into town, but it was for a meal with all the German players, local dignitaries, managers and both international committees, a great day and one to remember.

It was then Northern Ireland Schoolboys v England Schoolboys at Newtownards. We enjoyed a good trip over to Northern Ireland, but blustery conditions were expected for the next few days. We checked in at reception and went up to our rooms to unpack and get changed for our meal.

I was on the sixth floor and went over to the window to see the view. I looked down and couldn't believe what I was seeing, tanks driving along the streets. What was happening? I realise now it was the start of the 'Troubles'. It was the talk of the group for the rest of the day and we were thinking the game might be postponed.

We got up for breakfast the next day to be told the game was going ahead at Newtownards. We arrived at the ground, went to the dressing rooms and then went to inspect the pitch. It was a compact ground and the crowd started to arrive. By the time it was kick-off time, it was packed to the rafters.

The blustery conditions made it difficult to play good football and to make it even more difficult for us as we lost our keeper Jeyes to injury after five minutes. It was a competitive game, as expected, and ended up 0–0 at half time. Another injury blow in the second half saw Chris Guthrie going off and he was our leading goalscorer.

Northern Ireland took the lead in the 55 minute and then eight minutes later I scored to make it 1–1, the game eventually finishing 2–2.

The people of Northern Ireland made us feel really welcome on our stay there and they still do today whenever I travel back. There are some memories you can never forget, but not for the best reasons!

Another international that stands out for me is when England played Holland at Under 15 level for the first time ever. A good crowd turned up to see a hard fought game at Coventry City's Highfield Road ground. It was a good experience to come up against a team with a different style of play, tactics, team formation and how to keep the ball better.

Chris Guthrie scored the first two with powerful shots, as he normally did. I scored the third, Spinner got the fourth from a clever pass from Mick Buckley and I centred from the right wing for Spinner to head in the fifth in a 5–2 victory.

The Dutch were an emerging football nation at that time and had put a lot emphasis on coaching their young players with skill, technique and the development of ball awareness and passing. It would come to fruition five years later when Holland would contest the 1974 World Cup Final against West Germany where they were unlucky to lose. Ajax and a certain Johan Cruyff would also dominate European football, winning the European Cup three years in succession.

SHANKS AND BOB PAY A VISIT, BUT DAD ONLY DREAMT IN ROYAL BLUE!

THERE were many football clubs showing an interest in securing my signature on association schoolboy forms. Burnley was the first to make contact and their youth system had an excellent reputation. Other clubs came knocking, but the one I was dreaming of, Everton, were notably silent.

Club scouts where still phoning and watching me play for England and Liverpool Schoolboys but a knock on the door this day was a complete shock. It was none other than Bill Shankly and Bob Paisley. My Dad invited them in and showed them into the front room, sorted out the cups of tea and we all sat down to see what they were here for. Shanks started the conversation by saying to my Dad: "We have been watching your son for a while now and like what we see and we would like Ronny to sign for Liverpool Football Club where we will make him into an even better player." On hearing this, my eyes opened wider and my eyebrows were raised, but it was the look on my Dad's face. He was in total shock!

Shankly said: "Have a think about it Mr Goodlass and you too Ronny. It's a big decision." Bob Paisley said: "Yes, take your time, but you will enjoy playing for Liverpool Football Club."

I thought: "Two men of their standing are coming to our house and saying such encouraging words and wanting to sign me." That was great to hear for a 15 year old schoolboy.

My Dad thanked them for coming and for showing such an interest in signing me and said we would chat about it and get back in touch. My Dad walked them to the door and came back into the front room and sat down on the couch.

I said: "What do you think Dad? They want to sign me." Dad got up from the couch and walked to the door, slowly turning to face me. He said: "Son, it's up to you, but if you sign for them, I won't be able to watch a football match ever again."

He walked out of the door and closed it behind him.

OK Dad, I get the message. Thanks for the advice!

We all have our favourite 'Shanks' stories, regardless of whether we are red or blue. Thankfully I wasn't injured that often, so the treatment room for me was to get plasters for my blisters, see when the injured players would be fit, and also to give them some encouragement. The worse thing for most professional footballers is being injured and sometimes the long road back to fitness is a lonely place.

You therefore need someone in the treatment room who goes that extra mile, raises your moral when you are at a low point, lifts your spirits and keeps a cheerful atmosphere. In our case, that someone was physiotherapist Jim McGregor. He was tremendous at his job and the treatment room was always a hive of activity, noise and laughter.

After one game, I felt a slight tightness in my hamstring and the next morning I went in to see him. As I sat on the table, ready to get some treatment, none other than Bill Shankly walked in. He had retired as Liverpool manager on 12th July 1974 and only lived around the corner at 30 Bellefield Avenue.

Shanks said good morning to us both and got on the other table. Jim said: "What can I do for you Bill?" The former Liverpool boss said he had a bit of pain in his shoulder and asked if Jim could take a look at it.

They chatted for a while before Jim put a heat lamp by Bill's shoulder. The conversation then turned to me. How did I play on Saturday? What was the game like? Who were our next opponents and so on? Shanks naturally loved football and listening to him was an education. He was a knowledgeable and passionate football man who wanted to be around football people and talk all things football!

Jim couldn't find anything wrong with Shanks' shoulder, but it didn't matter. The King of the Kop used to come to Bellefield, Monday to Friday for four years. At 11am it would be a cup of tea with Dougie Rose and Sid McGuinness, head and assistant head groundsmen. In the afternoon, Bill would come back to Bellefield and have a sauna and a shower. He was in his element in a football environment and thrived on discussing football and telling his stories.

On another occasion, Shanks came into the physio's room and said: "Look out of the window Jim and what do you see?" Jim walked over, looked out and said: "The sky and the gym."

"What else do you see, Jim?" asked Shanks. Our physio said: "Cars in the car park," to which Shanks asked: "And what's happening out there?"

"Asa Hartford is cleaning his car, replied Jim" as he looked quizzically at Shanks. With his voice now raised, Bill said: "Yes you're right, cleaning his car on a Friday. Get him in Jim, there's a game tomorrow."

Shankly retire as a manager? I don't think so! He might have left his beloved Liverpool FC, but he was still thinking like a top boss and clearly, in his great soccer mind, the little things were just as important as tactics and transfer activity.

Clearly, Bill had become a little embarrassed at spending too much time at Liverpool's nearby Melwood training ground where Bob Paisley was trying to replace a legend and someone the players still called 'Boss'. Bellefield was just a hundred yards from Shankly's front door, and the Blues - for so long the old enemy - clearly offered him the hand of friendship, simply because he was such a remarkable football character, as honest as the day is long.

When Shanks died in September, 1981, the Everton players came to the Bellefield gates to say their own special farewell as Bill's coffin left Bellefield Avenue before slowly making its way past the Everton training headquarters. That says everything about Merseyside where football is a religion, where we have our obvious loyalties and rivalries, but where we know and respect our true football giants.

EVERTON SCOUT HAD A TRICK UP HIS SLEEVE AND IT WAS JOB DONE

THE next day at about 5.30pm there was a knock at the door and I must have been walking past it because for the first time in my life I opened it. "Hello," I said to the man standing there. "Hello Ronny," he replied. I thought: "How does he know me?

"Is your Dad in?" he continued. "My name is Matt McPeak and I'm a scout for Everton Football Club."

I was like Usain Bolt as I raced to find my father and burbled out: "Dad, there's a man at the door and his name is Matt McPeak and he's a scout for Everton and he wants to talk to you."

Dad walked to the door and invited Matt into the front room. "Cup of tea Matt, or would you like anything else to drink?"

"Tea would be fine thanks," he replied. He started talking to me about the English Schools Trophy and the England international games I had played in, telling me how well I had done.

Dad came back in: "There you go Matt, your tea. Do you fancy a biscuit?" He put a plate of biscuits on the coffee table. Matt started to say: "I'm here to persuade Ronny to sign for Everton."

I was thinking to myself: "You don't have to persuade me to sign for Everton, Matt. Where's the pen!"

They carried on talking about how it would work if I signed and what an apprenticeship entailed, from playing, education, jobs around the club, training and going to full time.

They finished talking and shook hands and then Matt got a coin from his trouser pocket, spun it up in the air and, as it was dropping onto the floor, kicked it up in the air and caught it in his top pocket. I thought to myself: "If this is a scout, what are the coaches going to be like?" We all started smiling and walked Matt to the door.

Back in the front room it was clear that I was made up Everton wanted to sign me, but the look on my Dad's face was magical.

Matt came back at the end of the week with the forms

and the Goodlass household was delighted I had signed. Dad and Matt had a drink or two of the hard stuff to celebrate and to finish it off Matt got the coin from his pocket, dropped it and kicked it into his top pocket again. The end to a brilliant day!

Having signed for Everton, they wanted me to start with all the other first year apprentices which would prepare us for going full-time ahead of the playing staff coming back for pre-season training. There was a problem though. I had to go and ask the headmaster could it be possible for me to join Everton early, but this meant me missing all my exams.

I had to get his permission or I wouldn't be able to leave school. I went in to see him and he wasn't happy at this request. He was concerned that I would miss my exams and I had put so much hard work in throughout the year. He asked me what my parents thought about the situation and I explained their view was similar to his, but they had left the decision up to me.

"What do you want to do?" he said. I took a deep breath and said: "I want to leave sir." He replied: "Well you better leave then, but make sure education is still high on your agenda."

We shook hands, he wished me luck and that was the end of my schooldays and the start of my working life.

With everything agreed and with all the appropriate documents signed, I could now officially leave John Hamilton School after five years and it was with mixed emotions. Great friendships were made and I learned a lot. There were some brilliant times and not so brilliant times, but I really can't complain.

I captained every school football team I played for and the school helped and supported me every step of the way. It's something I really appreciated.

I said my farewells to all my mates and teachers (those I liked) and I would now start a new chapter in my life by joining Everton as a full time apprentice.

I remember my first day as if it was it was yesterday, walking along Sandforth Road and tying to find the entrance to the Bellefield which wasn't easy because it was situated between a row of semi detached houses. Eventually I went through the narrow gates of the training ground and suddenly it was like Popeye's tent! A huge area was in front of me.

The house of head groundsman Dougie Rose was on the right. I then passed two sheds with all the equipment in before reaching the 'B' team pitch. To my left was a large 5-a-side pitch we used to call 'Wembley' and then the 60 yard indoor gym. Adjoining it was the building that held the dressing rooms, physiotherapy room, weight room, showers and deep plunge baths which were hot and cold, plus kitchen and eating area, offices and recreation rooms. Then there was the boot and drying rooms and it wasn't finished there. We had the 'A' team pitch behind the building with a 5-a-side pitch at either end! It was an enormous area behind such a tiny entrance.

The Brazilian National Football Association was so impressed with the set up and facilities at Bellefield that they used it as their training base for the 1966 World Cup.

The main security at Bellefield was Dougie Rose's dog called Yogi. He was a lovely black labrador and he amazed me down the years that he could identify all the players, coaching staff and all the Bellefield staff that worked there. But if anyone unauthorised got inside the gate, like autograph hunters or delivery men, he instinctively knew and would chase them out!

It is a big step up from schoolboy football to join a top professional club like Everton and go full time. Starting to learn your trade as an apprentice, in a somewhat harsher and unforgiving environment and at times, it can be a cut throat business. It is everyone's goal to become a professional footballer and to ultimately play for the first team. Many different strengths are needed to achieve this, including – ability, dedication, character, commitment and to make the necessary sacrifices to become a professional footballer. I have seen players with good ability but lacking in the other areas to make progress in the professional game.

I would often think about my childhood days and Everton FC dreams. At the age of ten, I used to climb up the lamppost outside Bellefield by the Walker playing fields and watch my idols training. Little did I know that five years later I would be joining them on the inside at Everton's famous training ground.

I was naturally a little bit apprehensive walking across the Bellefield car park when I first signed, but excited at the same time. It was like leaving junior school for the seniors, you don't quite know what is going to happen next.

Some of the staff were by the reception door to meet and greet and Harry Cooke, who was the chief scout, was there to welcome the first year apprentices to the club. Alan Wilson and John 'Tigs' Smith, second year apprentices who I knew from the Liverpool Schoolboys set-up, came to say hello.

The intake of 1969 consisted of me, Mick Buckley, Stan Osbourne, Ian Bacon, Ray Pritchard and Peter Whitwood. I knew Ian from Liverpool Boys and Buck and Pritch from England Schoolboys, and I knew Stan from Lancashire Boys trials and playing against him. Peter wasn't known to me. He joined from Essex Boys.

We all went up to the Players' Lounge where the introductions and welcome to the club would take place. It had padded seating, a table-tennis table and a TV in a cabinet with a lock on. We later found out that you had to ask for the key if you wanted the telly on. When you wanted to play table tennis, you had to go and ask Jean who was the secretary at Bellefield and a lovely lady. She would then provide a table tennis ball. Oh how times have changed!

Harry Cook and Stewart Imlach, who would be my first coach at the club in the 'B' team, introduced themselves and welcomed us to the club and went through what was required and expected from us as Everton players. The hard work started that day. Stewart had played in the FA

Cup winning team of Nottingham Forest when they beat Blackburn Rovers. It was the Final that Dave Whelan, who played for Blackburn Rovers and who would later own Wigan Athletic, broke his leg.

Over the next few days we are told what jobs we had been delegated to do. Now this was very varied, including looking after the young professionals, reserves or first team training kits and boots. Every player had to have a full training kit on his peg, a towel, his boots and trainers ready for training next morning. If not, watch out!

There was a drying room for the towels and wet kit. Every professional had four training kits and at the end of the week, a van would come to take them to be washed at Goodison. We had to put all the kit in the van and check it when it came back on the Monday.

We had to keep the room clean also and at the end of training, brush the floors and then mop them. The Youth Coach would then come in to see if the rooms were done properly. Only then could we go home.

I was given the job of looking after the First Team room!

The apprentices were then given their training kit, boots and trainers. When they gave you your first Everton kit with your number on it, you finally felt you were really part of the club and it made you feel good: one tracksuit, two shirts, two shorts and two pairs of socks; one pair of studded boots, one pair of rubbers and a pair of trainers. They were yours and you had to look after them.

A key job of mine was to sort out any damaged first team boots. It could be that the side of the boot had split and it needed stitching, damage to the toe cap, the boot coming away from the sole of the boot, or studs when they needed changing. When we couldn't get the studs out, I would walk from Bellefield down to the cobblers in Green Lane. Alan Ball, Joe Royle, Howard Kendall, you name them, I took their boots to the cobbler and he used to do a great job on them. Because of the state of some of them, I always wondered how he did it.

Think of players today with the sponsorship deals they have, as many boots as they require and some players only wearing them a couple of times before changing to another pair. How times have changed.

Nearing the end of the pre-season there was always a 5-side-competition held at Bellefield and all the playing staff would be involved. The teams consisted of two first team players, two reserve team players and one apprentice.

The pitches were marked out, it was then that the teams were announced and I wondered whose team I would be in and which two senior players I would be alongside. I needn't have worried. It was Alan Ball and Johnny Morrissey and I couldn't have wished for any better.

Bally was my idol, he was world class in every way and always wanted to win. Like me, Johnny was a winger, a tremendous crosser of a ball, could score goals and could kick full backs for fun.

What a great experience it was for a 15 year old lad with two great players encouraging me. I studied their skill, technique and will to win.

The cup for the winning team wasn't that big, but the main thing is winning it – and my team did!

LABBY, WESTY AND THE CRAZY WORLD OF BELLEFIELD

THE second year lads told me about joining the players union, the PFA – Professional Footballers Association. The union representatives would come around once a month to collect your subs – 50p. Now that doesn't sound a lot of money now but at a time when the apprentices were earning £7, £8 and £10 a week, it was a fair amount. If you didn't pay your subs one month, it got added to the next month, but you would need a very good excuse as to why you couldn't pay it.

Who were the union representatives for our club? Yes, you've guessed it, Brian Labone and Gordon West. Labby was the Sheriff and Westy his Deputy! The first time they came into our dressing room, all the apprentices had to be there and we were all sat around the benches. Then we heard footsteps coming along the corridor and the door opening. In walked Labby and Westy.

Now, when you are sitting down and are 15 years old, these two look like Man Mountains which they were. I don't know how they got through the door. They both said good morning and then Labby proceeded to tell us about the players union and how important it was to be part of it.

They started to collect the subs off the second year apprentices and each had a book of their own which would be marked with the date to show you had paid that month's subs. Then they would start to collect the subs off the first years.

Westy had the list of names and he read out the first name – Ronny Cutglass! OMG I thought, here we go. "Ronny Cutglass? Is he here?" repeated Westy. I said: "Yes, but it's Ronny Goodlass, Gordon."

Westy replied: "It's near enough and its Mr West to you. When you have played 50 games for Everton you can call me Gordon."

I gave them my 50p and they gave me my players' union book. As they walked out of the door, Westy said: "See you next month," and still had that stern look on his face. Then Labby gave me a smile and a wink and then they were gone, until next month.

Stewart Imlach reminded us that the club had rules and regulations and we would have to adhere to them and he explained a couple. One was that if you were late for training or a game you would be fined. Ken McNaught told me recently that the only time in his whole football career that he was fined was for being late.

He had been fined more than a quarter of his wages at that time – £2.

I have lost count of the times that I would run up Sandforth Road and across the Bellefield car park, hoping that the signing in book was still on the table and the blue pen was still there. The staff would take the pen away and replace it with a red one to sign in so they knew we were late.

Signing in Red, it's a penalty! Penalty for the Reds! That sounds about right!

"Court cases" were a regular occurrence at Bellefield to dish out punishment to the apprentices, to keep some of them in check, and a character builder, to develop camaraderie, but it was never nice to be involved because of some of the punishments that were dished out.

However, it always amused the whole of the playing staff and you could be brought before the 'Court' for some trivial things and made-up stories. These could include things like signing autographs at the gate or being slow doing your jobs which prevented all the apprentices going home.

The punishments would vary considerably. One might

be singing a song of the court's choice in front of everyone, but a couple were not so pleasant. Fiery Jack ointment would be put on your meat and two veg, or you might be thrown in the cold plunge with your kit on just before training. This meant you didn't have time to get dry or change your kit.

Our work was not only confined to the dressing rooms. There were many jobs to do around Bellefield. We had to paint the 'A' and 'B' team goalposts, the many sets of 5-a-side goals, and put the nets on. We would paint two large portable site screens, that were used for shooting practice and passing drills.

Tons and tons of soil would be delivered and dumped on the car park by the 'B' team pitch and the apprentices had to put the soil through giant sieves that were set up to remove the stones and other rubbish that might be in there.

We then had to fill up the wheelbarrows and wheel them over to the 'A' and 'B' team pitches for Dougie Rose and Sid McGuiness, the groundsmen, to scatter the soil onto the pitches. Best top soil bar none.

There was a rota system between the apprentices who would take turns of using the spade, pushing the wheelbarrow or filling the wheelbarrow. If the coaches thought the wheelbarrow wasn't full enough, they would tell you to put more soil in or top it up themselves. You ended up pushing a wheelbarrow that looked like a pyramid and felt as heavy as one.

We were more like building labourers than apprentice

footballers but I can certainly appreciate how hard labourers do work. Could you imagine the Academy players of today doing this work? Errr… NO!

With all the playing staff now back in for pre-season training, the car park was full of the first team's highly fashionable cars. Jimmy Husband was in his gleaming E-Type Jaguar, and he looked the part with his sun glasses on. On the first day, everyone from the playing side of the club was congregated between the Gym and the 'A' team pitch. Manager Harry Catterick walked out in his brand new 'tracky', his training shoes just out of the box. Obviously the cameras were there!

The coaching staff – Wilf Dixon, Arthur Proudler, Tom Casey and Stewart Imlach – prepared to start work with 50 players! We started to walk around Bellefield, chatting in a relaxed atmosphere. After a few stretches we walked again, then more stretches, walked again… we did this for nearly two hours. The first week we never saw a football and then, on the following Monday, the apprentices were told by Stewart Imlach to pump the footballs up at the right pressure because they would be needed for training today. I thought: "Is this right Stewart?" I was like a kid in a sweet shop.

As the training became more intense, we were getting fitter and stronger as the start of the season approached.

The last week of training we were ensconced in Pontins, Southport from early morning, have our lunch break and then training again until late afternoon.

Training would consist of running along the beach,

games, running up and down sand dunes (one was particularly high) and then jogging around to the woods at the back of the dunes to do sprints and endurance work.

The coaches marked out a running circuit through the woods that the players would run around. It was an area where the public walked their dogs and kids played. There were more holes in that ground than a dartboard. The runs were timed and the races very competitive, but was the health and safety of the players considered? Nah, just get on with it, which we did, but how there wasn't more injuries I just don't know. Maybe we were made of sterner stuff then, more than nowadays?

The 5-a-side games between the apprentices were really competitive, a mixture of first and second years. You all wanted to play in the highest team you could, 'B', 'A', reserves or first team. One game I remember was on the beach and it was the first years against the second years. We had some good players in our team, Mick Buckley, Ray Pritchard, Ian Bacon, Stan Osbourne – and me. They had Alan Wilson, Tigs Smith and Peter Scott.

There was always a forfeit to pay by the losing team which could mean press ups or shuttle runs. It was a good game, we were winning and there wasn't long to play. We got a free-kick in their half and a lad called Davey Graham wouldn't get the customary yardage away from the ball. I said to Stan, take it, hit it as hard as you can and he will either move, it will deflect into the goal or it will go for a corner. Stan ran up, hit it hard and it went right into Davey's face. He fell to the floor pole-axed, but he's a

Bootle lad made of stern stuff and got up shaking his head and rubbing his face.

We had to take the free-kick again. I stood over the ball with Stan and jokingly said: "I bet you can't do that again." We both started laughing. Davey was in the same position and Stan took his run up, hit it hard and BANG, right in Davey's kipper again. All hell broke loose, Davey ran at Stan, and they were like two Rams clashing. Everyone ran over to separate them and calm them down. Not long after, Stewart blew his whistle to end the game. I would see a few fights during my time at Everton, but that's the competitive side of football and I'm glad to say, we won the match.

It was the last day at Pontins and it was always a hard physical week when you were really put through your paces and tested to the full. Everyone of the playing staff were involved together as one large group, from jogging along the beach, doing a warm up, and playing different types of games. It all combined to create a great atmosphere. This was the build up though to the hardest part of the week, a stamina-building run up and down the sand dunes. This was really energy sapping and your run was timed and players set off at 20 second intervals.

Every time we did this run, without fail, it seemed like record temperatures hit the Southport area. Add in no drinking water, soft sand and tired legs and it was no surprise that, at the end of the week, no one looked forward to this run.

Markers were put out to show you which way to run

and the coaches were dotted around the dunes, resembling lookouts for the Foreign Legion as they made sure you went the right way with words of encouragement like: "Hurry up, or you'll miss the fuckin' coach back to Bellefield."

As different players slowed up and others quickened, there was a build up of runners. Players would be falling and sliding back down the dune although it was every man for himself. The soft sand was now really taking its toll. When you neared the finish, Norman Borrowdale, the physiotherapist, would be standing there with stopwatch and pen ready to take your time. You had to cross where Norman was standing. If you stopped 20 or 30 yards away and started to walk, he would wait until you crossed the line to take your time. You were delighted and relieved when you finally finished.

With a very hard physical week over, it was now back to Bellefield to fine tune everybody for the start of the season.

My first pre-season at Everton was coming to an end and the start of the new campaign was only days away. From day one of pre-season, everything the coaching staff did was geared towards making you physically and mentally prepared for the year ahead. The training, stamina work and friendly games put you in the best possible condition so that when the referee blows his whistle to start that first game, you're ready. But will you start a game?

Will you be selected? There are too many players for everyone to get a match and some real quality at the club to choose from. It would be a real set back not to be selected after putting so much hard work into the training all summer.

We had known the fixture list for a number of weeks and our first game was – Liverpool at home! I certainly didn't want to miss this one and it would be my first 'derby' game. From the first day you sign schoolboy forms you dream about pulling on that royal blue shirt.

The Friday before, the Saturday fixtures, team sheets go up on the notice board for the first team squad, reserves, 'A' and 'B' teams. Groups of players would gather around to see which team they were in and with the corridor being very narrow, it was packed. The 'B' team was the last to go up, so the wait seemed even longer.

Stewart Imlach came down from the office and pinned the sheet on the notice board, turned and walked back up to the office, not saying a word.

There was only first and second year apprentices left and we made our way over to have a look. It was like exam day, checking if you had passed.

You look up to see if your name is there and it is, but you start to count down to see if your name is in the team, 9, 10, and 11 GOODLASS. I'm in… YES!

Our jobs still needed to be done before the following day's game and we couldn't leave until they were completed, but it wasn't such a chore now, we were thinking about the game the next day. Stewart came down and spoke briefly to say what time we had to report, adding: "Don't be late!"

I turned up a couple of hours before kick-off and was

looking forward to the game and we had a good side which included first year apprentices Mick Buckley, Ray Pritchard, and Ian Bacon. We also had Alan Wilson and Tigs Smith.

As we jogged out, there was a really good crowd with many of my family and friends attending. It was a physical and competitive game as I expected and not much time on the ball, but I enjoyed it and it was great to experience my first 'derby' with a 2–0 win, Alan Wilson scoring the two goals.

We played Liverpool again four days later at Liverpool's Melwood training ground. It was first time for me at their place, strange because it reminded me of Bill Shankly's bid to sign me. A good crowd turned up including many family and friends again.

Liverpool wanted revenge for their defeat at Bellefield on the previous Saturday and we wanted to get the double over them. What a good start to the season that would be. It was a good game with both teams not giving an inch and both teams wanting to win, but it ended 1 – 1 which was about right.

In my next game I was promoted to the 'A' team, my debut for them, and it was against Burnley at home. They had a very good youth policy then and were the first club to show an interest in signing me when I played for Liverpool schoolboys. It was a good game and result for me because I scored my first two goals for the club and we ran out 5–1 winners. During your first year at the club, they try to test you at a higher level to see how you do, but then return you to the 'B' team.

With me being full time now and still developing, they had to nurture me, both physically and mentally and they didn't want me or any other of the first year apprentices to pick up any short or long term injuries.

When I say injuries, I don't just mean hamstrings or groin strains. In the 'A' team, you would come up against a number of reserve players from a lot of other clubs, but also reserve teams such as Crewe, Rochdale and Southport.

These contained seasoned professionals and you had to grow up quickly or you wouldn't survive. It was an era when you could tackle, fairly and not so fairly. A yellow card was very rarely shown. Let's just say that referees were far more lenient in those days. My next game was against Man United away, at United's famous Cliff training ground. Again, this would be a real test for us, but once again I was looking forward to it. We drew 1–1 against a strong United team.

When it reached December, I was enjoying my football and the coaches said I was playing well and called me up to the Youth Team squad to play at Blackburn. I was 16 years old and the rest were 17 and 18, so it was a good experience for me. We played Blackburn Youth away and went into a 3–0 lead, but let this slip and it ended up 3–3.

Manager Harry Catterick was at the game and the replay would be at Goodison the following Wednesday when I would make my Youth team debut. We played really well and won 5–0, with me setting up a goal for both

Mick Lyons and Alan Wilson.

Something happened in the next round against Man Utd that every player and every spectator at the game will never forget and it wasn't the result

We won the toss and chose to kick off. I stood by the ball and played it forward for Bryn Jones to chip the ball to the edge of Man United's penalty area, over their centre-half and full-back but not far enough for the goalkeeper to collect. Meanwhile, Dave Johnson was running from the right wing to get on the end of Bryn's chip and Johno could motor.

As the ball was going over the defenders' heads and in front of the goalkeeper, Johno connected with it to score. It is the fastest goal ever scored at Goodison in a competitive game, officially timed at five seconds. Matt Busby who was at the game, said: "It is the quickest strike I have ever seen in a game."

It was good to be involved in this moment in Everton's history, even though my initial pass to Bryn only went three yards!

SHOCK DAY WHEN PEDIGREE CHUM WAS ON THE BELLEFIELD MENU

IN my first season at the club I made 18 appearances for the 'B' team scoring eight goals, and in the 'A' team I made 10 apps and scored 7 goals. I also played in two Lancashire Senior Cup matches, which included one against Man United.

This game was played at Goodison on Tuesday 29th September 1970 and United had a number of well-known first team players on show. Goodison is a bit special under floodlights and they were quality opposition. This was a big game for me and only six weeks since I made my 'B' team debut.

It was a tight affair and 30 minutes into the game I got the ball deep in our half and started to run forward. I dribbled past one United player and when I reached the halfway line I was tackled and we both fell to the ground. It was just by the dug-outs, but I got up first and went to get the ball.

The United player was sitting on the ground with the ball stuck between his legs and I took a step back and shaped up to kick the ball. As my boot was only inches away from the ball I stopped and the player jumped up in front of me. By now there was another United player standing by me and I said: "If I had kicked that ball, you would be talking like Alan Ball now!"

The two United players started laughing and one with a Scottish accent said: "You are right there son." It was Paddy Crerand and the one with the ball between his legs was Nobby Stiles!

Nobby was a great friend of Bally. Paddy and Nobby were both in the team that two years earlier had won the European Cup at Wembley, beating Benfica 4–1 after extra-time.

They didn't win this Lancashire Senior Cup game though. We beat them 1–0 with Alex Stepney in goal for them, another who also played in the Final against Benfica.

What a great time it was to be at Everton Football Club. My first season was a success and I was playing full time, but still doing my jobs and learning my trade while playing against the best clubs in the country.

Oh, and did I mention what a great season the Blues had in winning the old First Division title? What a great team that was, one of, if not the best in our club's history. They played a brand of football that took your breath away with the 'Holy Trinity' of Ball, Harvey and Kendall, three great players who played as one. Bally said: "We could find each other in the dark" – and he was right.

Labby said, tongue-in-cheek: "It's the only team that won the First Division with only three players!" If opposing teams wanted to play football, Everton would outplay them, if they wanted a battle, they would out battle them… the perfect team, easy on the eye and winners.

Great credit must go to Harry Catterick for putting together a side of this quality, balance, character and a formation that was way ahead of its time, 4-3-3 before Barcelona ever thought of it.

When you wanted to play table tennis at Bellefield we had to go and ask Jean, the secretary, for the ball. The games were always competitive and we all wanted to win. We used to play against each other, but we also played a game called 'Around the Clock' that involved all the apprentices. You had seven apprentices at each end of the table and the first player had to knock the ball over the net and run to the other end. His opponent had to hit the other player's ball back and run to the opposite end and so on. If you hit the net or knocked the ball too long or wide, you lost a life. You had two lives. This day everyone was in a good mood and winding each other up, claiming they were going to win. You could take a chance and spin the ball or do a drop shot to make it more difficult for the next player to return.

A few players had been knocked out and then we started again. This time it was going well, featuring the longest rally we had encountered and no one wanted to make a mistake and get knocked out. Every time a player touched the ball, the lads would shout 'Yeah' to put off whoever was playing the ball next. It kept going and going.

I realised I had to do something to break the deadlock, so I took a chance. The next time the ball came to me I was near the net and so I did a drop shot. The next player was yards away from the end of the table and he had to react quickly and return the ball before it bounced again. That apprentice was Dave Graham who was very competitive and wanted to stay in the competition.

As he sprinted to get the ball, he slipped and his neck caught the edge of the table and he fell to the floor, gasping for breath. Now this was amusing for all the players who were watching this, but obviously not for Dave. The really funny part was that he tried to stop himself from falling by trying to grab the end of the table and missed, but the table made contact with the watch he was wearing and it shattered into a number of pieces. We now had Dave prostrate on the floor, gasping for breath his watch shattered and 13 apprentices laughing their heads off. I'm glad to say Dave made a full recovery.

The legendary Bellefield 'court cases' would come

along every couple of weeks and every apprentice had to go through this initiation. As was usually the case, Westy was the 'judge' with first team players acting as 'jury'. The evidence for the defendants, the apprentices, was always rebuked and the prosecution were like Rumpole of the Bailey. They never lost a case!

One day before training started, Alan Wilson approached me and said he had seen George Telfer smoking by Lime Street station and wondered what we should do. Errrr… court case! It was George's turn.

We went to Judge Westy, and he said: "The court will be in session immediately after training."

George didn't have a clue what was going on and what was in store for him. Twenty minutes after training we are all gathered in the reserves dressing room and Westy was sitting on the table, shouting out to bring in the 'defendant'.

George walked in wearing a trilby hat, a white Mac covering his birthday suit, and with a cigarette in his mouth. Everybody just started laughing as Westy read out the charges: "George Telfer, you were seen walking past Lime Street station smoking. Is that true?"

George said: "When?" to which Westy replied: "It doesn't matter when, and I'm asking the questions! Were you smoking?"

George had that condemned look on his face. "Yes," he answered. A loud 'OOOOOHHH' went around the dressing room.

Westy had a chat with a couple of the jury and put a pair of shorts on his head to give the verdict. He pronounced:

"Guilty as charged."

'Telf' went white. His sentence was that he had to smoke a cigarette while singing a song. We were giving him suggestions like the classic hit "Smoke Gets In Your Eyes," or possibly a Smokey Robinson Tamla Motown song. George duly obliged and the lads joined in.

The hard-worked apprentices had little time to relax or chat before we went out for training, but we would still talk about the pranks and silly things we might have done. A few of us started to tell our tales and then it was Jimmy Burns' turn. We all shouted: "Go on then Jimmy, what have you done?" He replied: "I ate some dog food!"

The silence was broken as someone declared: "You have done what?"

"I ate some dog food," confirmed Jimmy, to which the obvious reply was: "WHY?" He said: "It looked nice," to which I asked: "How much did you eat and what did it taste like?" He said: "A few forkfuls and it tasted ok."

A court case was called, Jimmy was found guilty, and his sentence was that he had to eat some dog food in front of all the lads. With Everton being a class club, we bought him some Pedigree Chum. Well, our motto is 'Only the best is good enough' and Jimmy, to his credit, managed a few mouthfuls.

Well done Jimmy, your wet and shiny nose looked great after that!

Our pre-season training test always took place on the largest sand dunes along Ainsdale beach. It was daunting to say the least. You started in groups of four at the bottom and raced up to touch the board at the top. It was an information board, advising of the regulations on the beach. You had to run up and down the dune six times consecutively while being timed.

It was a lung buster and one of the apprentices on the last run down the dune fell. He was knackered, his legs had gone, and he slid down face first, swallowing half of Ainsdale beach as he went. Arriving at the bottom, he moaned: "I want to die."

He looked as though he had!

In the apprentices contracts the club had to provide alternative education and training opportunities for us and most decided on going to college. This would mean attending Childwall Hall County College on Mondays.

There were numerous courses to consider and we were called in to see the Principal to discuss which courses were suitable and if they were available. I met the other Everton apprentices at the college on the first day of term and discussed the courses to go on. There was a Hairdressing and Beauty option that had a lot of young ladies involved, or we could opt for the likes of English and Maths.

One of my great mates was Mick Buckley. Our friendship started at England Schoolboys and it continued on until the day he passed away. They used to call us the twins because we liked the same things, enjoyed each other's company, and were always having a laugh. We had a chat on which courses we should choose and finally decided on two.

It was my turn to see the Principal and I got a warm

welcome. For the next 15 minutes he talked to me about the college and said he hoped my time would be a pleasant one.

I recommend to anyone, get the best education you can and take it seriously.

It really is your future.

All I wanted to be was a professional footballer and education was put on the back burner.

The Principal asked which courses I wanted to take and I said: "Photography and Cookery."

He nearly fell off his chair and had a really surprised look on his face before he composed himself and said: "That's excellent because there are not too many boys on those courses."

Half smiling I said: "Isn't there?" My testosterone levels were now rising and I went out and nodded to Buck who was registering on the same courses.

I hope you are not thinking that Buck and I took that route because there were a lot of young ladies on them. Surely not! I just wanted to be the next David Bailey or Keith Floyd!

FIRST SENIOR TEST AND I'M ON THE PITCH WITH TEN 1970 GIANTS

EVERYONE was on a high following our 1970 Championship triumph and we were all looking forward to the start of pre-season.

Equally, with England playing in the Mexico World Cup that summer, we were all rooting for the Everton lads who were involved. Could we win football's greatest prize for the second time? I actually felt we had a better team and squad than the one that made history in 1966. We were well represented by Brian Labone, Alan Ball, Tommy

Wright and Keith Newton. The World Cup would be held from the 31st May to 21st June 1970.

Two England games stand out for me, the group match against Brazil with Pele & Co, and West Germany who we played in the 1966 World Cup Final at Wembley

Both games were played in searing heat, but the quality of the players on show was so exceptional, you wouldn't know. The Brazil game delivered a very disappointing result and we lost to a Jairzinho goal, but there were two astounding moments of skill that I remember to this day.

The first involved Jairzinho, a quick, skilful and powerful forward who – when attacking with the ball – was so hard to stop. He was running at full pace and Bobby Moore was backing off, but as the Brazilian got to the penalty area, Bobby timed his tackle to perfection. He won the ball cleanly and casually took it up the field.

The second great moment was when Carlos Alberto received the ball deep in his own half. With the outside of his right foot, he passed it inside Terry Cooper for Jairzinho to take one touch and go past our defender. From the by-line, Jairzinho crossed for Pele to make a downward header which looked every inch a goal. The ball appeared to have gone beyond Gordon Banks when our world class keeper made a miraculous save and pushed it over the bar. This was the best save I've ever seen and it seems to get better every time I watch it, coming against what I believe to be the best team ever to grace the beautiful game.

The second game was against West Germany in the quarter-final and there was controversy before a ball was even kicked when Gordon Banks suffered food poisoning and Peter Bonetti came in to replace him. England went into a 2–0 lead with goals from Alan Mullery and Martin Peters. Our very own Keith Newton was the provider for both with a defence splitting pass and a cross from the right wing.

A two goal advantage after 49 minutes should have been enough, only for Bonetti to give the Germans a lifeline with a poor attempt to keep out a Franz Beckenbauer shot which went under his body.

The second goal was again helped with poor positioning from Bonetti as Uwe Seeler scored with a backwards header. The third goal was also poorly defended, providing exactly the result we didn't want, England 2 West Germany 3 after extra time. It left the players and fans with so many ifs, buts and maybes.

If only Gordon Banks had been fit to play!

We now hoped Labby, Bally, Tommy and Keith wouldn't show a reaction to playing in an energy sapping tournament when they returned for the start of the new season.

Reporting back earlier than the senior professional playing staff was the norm for all the apprentices. We started three weeks before them to get Bellefield in tip top order. We had to do our usual jobs of painting, digging and sifting the soil, amongst many tasks.

It was the time of year when there was another intake of first year apprentices and they would be coming to us in a week's time.

A couple of the lads who were joining us, Jimmy Burns

(Kirkby Boys) and George Telfer (Huyton Boys) had been building up a good reputation on the local schoolboy scene. Jimmy was captain of Kirkby Boys and a midfield player and George a centre-forward with a good goal scoring record.

The first team squad was now back at Bellefield and being put through their paces.

One morning we were behind the top of the 'A' team pitch, sifting the soil and picking stones off the ground to prepare for the turf to be laid. The first team was training behind the bottom of the 'A' team pitch with Wilf Dixon barking out the orders.

It was then that new boy Jimmy Burns wandered out and started to look around before coming over to us as we carried on working. He said: "What are you doing?" As a wind up, I replied: "We are sifting the soil and picking out any stones. You can do this if you want to or go down and watch the first team train."

Jimmy looked at me for a couple of seconds and said: "I think I'll go down there and watch the first team."

"Ok, see you later," I said. "We will get back to work."

Jimmy turned and strolled over to watch the first team. All the apprentices started to smile.

About ten minutes later the coaches, Tom Casey and Stuart Imlach, came out and spotted him. As they approached we could hear them shouting: "What do you think you are you doing?" to which Jimmy responded: "Watching the First Team train. I don't want to pick up the stones."

"Oh don't you!'" bawled Tom Casey. "Get your arse up there and start picking up the stones." Jimmy walked away and joined us very sheepishly. Welcome to Bellefield, Jimmy!

Everyone had now reported back for pre-season training with the England lads getting a slightly longer rest following their World Cup exploits. With the summer break now over, it was time to get back to some hard work to build up our fitness levels.

This included, gym work, shuttle runs, circuit training, a hurdles circuit through sand, and 3,000 metre runs. As well as this other testing runs were: 2 x 110 yards; 2 x 220 yards; 2 x 330 yards and 2 x 440 yards. These were run consecutively and timed.

We would finish one and then jog back to the start to go again and we had to be inside the time we were given by the coaching staff. If you didn't make the time, you had to go again.

After doing all of that for three weeks, you still had the dreaded week in Southport to look forward to and those lovely sand dunes!

The pre-season was going well for me, fitness and playing wise. Mostly the games we played were against local sides and everyone's main priority was to stay injury free, get match fit and be ready for the start of the season.

More ball work and friendly matches were now being played and we all wanted to play in as many games as we could. The fixtures had been announced for all the teams for a number of weeks and the first 'A' team game, if selected, would be against Liverpool at Melwood on the 15th August.

With our quartet of England players now back in full training – Brian Labone, Alan Ball, Tommy Wright and Keith Newton – would there be a negative reaction to their World Cup exploits? As reigning League Champions, we would be at the top of everyone's list to beat. The first test would be against Chelsea on 8th August 1970 in the Charity Shield.

This would be the first time it was held at the FA Cup winners ground and not that of the League Champions. This was because our new Goodison Park Main Stand still wasn't finished and so a Stamford Bridge challenge loomed.

Before that the club staged the traditional Blues v Amber public practice match, which took place on Wednesday 5th August 1970. It was the first team versus reserves and a chance for the supporters to come along and watch established senior players and the younger ones who were trying to break into the first team set up. This game went back many, many years and down the decades it had involved all the greats of our club, but sadly this would be the last time it was staged.

As the game drew near the two squads were about to be announced and I wondered if I might get a call up for the reserves. It was the start of my second year as an apprentice and it would have been a pleasant surprise if I was.

The two squads finally went up on the notice board and

I did get a surprise, but it wasn't a call up for the reserves. I was named in the first team squad!

I trained with them that morning and then had to report to Goodison for the evening kick-off. When I went into the senior dressing room, most of the players were already in there. Westy looked over at me and said: "Are you sure you are in the right dressing room?" I just nodded to him and said "yes" before sitting down where my shirt was. I was one of the two subs, the other being Tigs Smith.

As I looked around the dressing room, I began to think how many great players there were. Only 15 months earlier I had been watching my idols from the Gwladys Street End and dreaming of being in this very room, pulling on a Royal Blue shirt with the first team.

The side that started the game was the one that had finished the season so strongly to deservedly win the First Division title, playing attacking and winning football.

The Blues started brightly and Alan Whittle scored the first, carrying on his tremendous goalscoring form he had displayed in the title run-in. The Blues were playing well and none more so than Colin Harvey who was outstanding.

At half-time Harry Catterick said I would be going on for the second half in place of Johnny Morrissey. What an even better surprise that was. Everyone wished me all the best and out we went. It was now ten players who won the First Division Championship and me! I wanted an early touch of the ball, a good pass, a good lay-off or a good cross to get me up to the speed of the game.

I started to get more of the ball and a few dribbles, crosses and shots later, I was really enjoying the action. It was giving me even more confidence when I kept hearing Bally shouting: "Give it to the young 'un!" After 75 minutes, Colin Harvey went off. Tigs Smith came on as sub for him and almost immediately he scored. Colin had scored four, Alan Whittle got two and the final score was 7–1 with Sandy Brown getting the only goal for the reserves.

It was a great experience for me as a 16 year old. I loved it and in my opinion, I was playing in the best team our club has ever seen.

At the end of the game I went in the dressing room and all the lads were saying I did well. Then Westy walked over with a hound dog look on his face and said slowly: "You did ok." Then he smiled and said: "Well done son. "

I thought: "That will do me for starters."

The following Saturday brought on a great first game for me to start off the season – an 'A' team away clash against Liverpool. You always want to win games, but a derby match is something else at any level and the fact that it was at their place made it an even better challenge. It proved a difficult match as always, but what a great start to the season for us as we claimed a 1–0 victory.

For our next game, we had a real character in the line-up by the name of Steve Melledew. We had only recently signed Steve from Rochdale for £25,000 after he scored a hat-trick against us in a pre-season friendly at Spotland.

Steve was a Rochdale lad, but would always talk in Cockney slang, like: "I'm just going up the apple and pears" (stairs) or "I'm just going to use the Dog and Bone" (phone) – delivered in his Rochdale accent! It used to crease the lads up.

He played in the next 'A' team game and scored four while I scored two in an emphatic 7–0 win and I could now look forward to my win bonus, the princely sum of £1.

We only lost one of our first 14 games and then lost just two out of the next 12. I scored in a 3–2 win against Man Utd and I was also on the scoresheet when we beat Liverpool 2–0 at Bellefield. We would finish the year on top of the league.

We played Bolton at home on January 5th and won 5–0. Archie Styles scored four and I got the other one.

From 12th December when we beat Liverpool, we remained unbeaten until the end of the season which was a tremendous achievement. Now we were Lancashire League Division One champions. A personal highlight for me that season was scoring 12 goals while the team only lost three games, scoring 102 goals.

Everton have always had an excellent youth policy. Bringing on your own young players is the life blood of any club and we were second to none. Out of the 1970 Division One league title winning side, a magnificent seven came through our youth ranks as apprentices. You need a manager like Harry Catterick to make that happen, someone with the faith to play the kids, nurture that talent and develop a youth team set-up that will get the best out of the players.

We won the Lancashire League Division One with this list of players – Mick Buckley, Dave Johnson, Archie Styles, Terry Darracott, George Telfer, Gary Jones, Peter Scott, Alan Wilson, John Smith, Mick Lyons – and me.

Every one of us started as apprentices at our club and went on to play in the first team.

The Blues v Amber game put the first team in a good frame of mind to face Chelsea in the Charity Shield on the Saturday at Stamford Bridge. It was a full house and 43,547 were crammed into the ground to see this eagerly awaited encounter. As the teams came out it had been raining for a while and the pitch was damp, but not enough to affect two talented and gifted sides that liked to attack.

Everton started well and the 'Holy Trinity' was getting a grip of midfield. Bally gained possession deep in our half and passed to Colin Harvey who held the ball up for Bally to sprint into space to take the return pass. There was no stand and admire your pass in this midfield. It was all pass and move.

Bally received the ball back and passed it out to Alan Whittle on the left who took on the full-back, cutting inside and striking a shot high into Bonetti's near post from the edge of the area. It was a well worked goal and finish, giving the Toffees a 1–0 half time lead.

We made another bright start to the second half and it was no surprise that we went two up through Howard Kendall. Jimmy Husband worked hard to win the ball back and it ended up at Joe Royle's feet in the penalty area on the left. He took one touch towards the bye line and glanced up before putting an inviting cross to the far post for Howard to head the ball into the net. Howard turned away with a beaming smile on his face to be congratulated by the lads.

Although Ian Hutchinson pulled one back for Chelsea in the 79th minute, there were no more scares and we ran out worthy winners.

FOOTNOTE: Every player in both teams except Paddy Mulligan (Republic of Ireland) was English along with the managers Harry Catterick and Dave Sexton. How times have changed!!

We were drawn to play against favourites Manchester United at Old Trafford in the 1971 FA Youth Cup and this is what Paul O'Brien, the Liverpool Echo's excellent schools reporter, wrote about the game under the header:

YOUNG BLUES FINE DISPLAY

A brilliant goal by outside-left Ronny Good-lass earned Everton a replay at Old Trafford last night when the young Blues held Manchester United to a 1 – 1 draw in the second round of the FA Youth Cup. They thoroughly deserved a second chance, for they displayed more skill and speed than United.

It was Mick Buckley who set up the goal for Goodlass after 37 minutes. He fought his way out of three tackles in a 40 yard run and then laid on a fine pass for Goodlass to score with a tremendous left foot drive.

The replay was played a week later at Goodison on 7th

December 1971:

EVERTON'S SPIRIT TURNS THE TABLES

*Everton, a goal down after nine minutes, showed
that old Royal Blue fighting spirit to completely turn
the tables in the second half of this FA Youth Cup
second round replay at Goodison Park last night.*

*Don Tobin put George Telfer through on goal.
Healy, the United keeper, came out and Telfer
clipped the ball over him to open the scoring.*

*Ian Bacon scored the winner in the 36th minute
with a shot from the edge of the area. The supporters
gave the team a standing ovation as they came off.*

This was a great result for us. We were still on a high
and decided to make a night of it. We went into town, had
a walk around and elected to go to a place none of us had
been before – The Cavern Club.

We approached the door where the bouncers were
standing, but they said: "You can't come in, you're not old
enough."

I had to think quickly, take a chance and hope they
were Evertonians, so I told them we had just beaten Man
United in the Youth Cup and we wanted to finish off a
great night in The Cavern. Luckily for us, they were Blues
and knew the Youth Team had been playing at Goodison.
Our group was told we could go in, but we were told to
take it easy. We were made up and went in the club.

It was packed and we approached the bar for a drink,

orange juice of course, and we got served. It was hot in there and the condensation was dripping down the walls. I went the toilets where I wished I had brought my wellies! They were always flooded and you had to be careful to manoeuvre your way in and out without getting wet. However, The Cavern finale was a tremendous way to end the night and a good experience for me and the lads.

My first game for the Reserves was at Gigg Lane against Bury Reserves. Now it may not have been the most glamorous of grounds to make my debut but getting selected was a big moment for me.

In the same team that day was Brian Labone, Mick Lyons, Alan Whittle and Dai Davies and I was looking forward to playing alongside them. It was a physical match and that was usually the case against lower league opposition, but this is part of the learning curve as you gain more experience. Bury made a lively start and had a few shots at goal that Dai saved.

Things started to settle down and we created a number of chances before going 1-0 up and it stayed that way until just after half time when I crossed for Mick Lyons to score with a header. They pulled a goal back, but with Labby and Lyonsy back in control there were no more attempts at goal by Bury and the game ended in a 2-1 win for us.

A week later we beat Coventry Reserves 1-0, drew with Bolton 1-1 and then played Blackburn Rovers at Ewood Park on the Saturday. Now this turned out to be a bitter sweet game for me. I was delighted to be selected again, but little did I know at the time it would be Brian Labone's last game in an Everton shirt. Also in our team that day was Andy Rankin and Colin Harvey and in their line up was ex-Everton centre-forward Fred Pickering.

Rovers went ahead, ironically through Pickering, and he went on to score another one. The final score was 3–2 to Rovers, Wilson and Darcy scoring for us.

Pickering was a big powerful forward and was a very good striker. Everton broke the British transfer record in March 1964 when Harry Catterick signed him for £85,000.

Evertonians were angered at first, thinking this signing was a threat to Alex Young's place.

This changed immediately when on his debut against Nottingham Forest he scored a hat-trick at Goodison Park. Fred made 115 appearances for the Blues and scored 70 goals, not bad eh?

It was sad that the Rovers game would be Labby's last for the Toffees, but he left a lasting impression on Evertonians and everyone else who met him, both on and off the pitch. He was a great captain, leader and player, but most of all a great man.

Two other games I can remember is the time we played Bolton Reserves at Goodison and played some really good football. We should have scored more goals, but still won the game 3–0. They had a big team but we ran their back four ragged. At centre-half was a certain – Sam Allardyce!

The other was playing Huddersfield Reserves at home when we went three up after ten minutes and scored another three before half-time. I scored two of those. We only got the one in the second half to finish 7–0 winners.

I got my initial call to the first team squad against Tottenham at Goodison and it coincided with the debut of Joe Harper who had signed from Aberdeen for £180,000. What a debut it was for Joe. He hit the bar twice, post twice and laid two on for Howard Kendall – and he missed a penalty with 15 minutes to go. Not a bad debut. The game ended 3–1 with John Hurst adding the third.

We were chasing the Central League Championship, a league in which the standard of football and players involved were excellent. Sides would be filled with many first team players, no resting of senior stars in those days. The total commitment of players in that league was why managers would put out strong teams because they knew everyone would get a proper game to keep them match fit with no one just going through the motions.

It was difficult to get a game in the reserves with a big playing staff and the quality at the club. We played a game at Burnley and they put out a very experienced team with the likes of Ray Hankin, Steve Kindon and my old mate Billy Rodaway in their line-up. We had Keith Newton, who two years earlier played in the World Cup Finals in Mexico and won the league with us, Ken McNaught, Terry Darracott, and Gary Jones. Our sub was Archie Styles who would eventually go to Birmingham as part of the transfer that took Howard Kendall away from Goodison. I'm pleased to say we beat Burnley Reserves 2–1. I will have to remind Billy about that next time I see him.

Another game was at Sheffield Wednesday. In goal for them was ex-England goalkeeper Ron Springett, while in our side was Gordon West, John McLaughlin, Mick Buckley, Ken McNaught, Terry Darracott, Jimmy Husband, John Hurst and... Bernie Wright! Our sub was Mick Lyons

It was a great experience for me to play alongside and against this type of player. I was called up to the first team squad when we played against Tottenham on the 3rd November 1973. I was playing well for the reserves, getting good reports off the coaches and wondered if this would finally be the game in which I would make my debut in.

Tottenham had some household names in their starting line-up, World Cup winner Martin Peters, Pat Jennings, Alan Gilzean, Martin Chivers, and Steve Perryman. Our team was announced, I was substitute and a crowd of 37,872 awaited kick off, but no one was as eager as me.

We were leading 1–0 at half time, but a Perryman goal in the second half made it a 1–1 draw. I was disappointed not to get on the pitch and that we couldn't keep our lead, but it was good to be involved.

My second call-up for the first team was on the 1st May 1971 against Crystal Palace at Selhurst Park. I'd had a good season in the reserves and I was delighted to be told I would be training with the first team and to prepare for an overnight stay.

To train with this team was an education because of the quality that ran right through the side. Their passing, control, touch, vision, pace, and desire to become even better players was an attitude you had to have if you wanted to play at this level.

We were flying down and I was told that the coach would pick us up at Bellefield to take us to Speke Airport in those days before it became John Lennon Airport. There was no problem with the flight to London. We checked into the hotel and told to report for dinner at 7pm, after which there would be a meeting about the following day's game.

The usual banter occurred around the dinner table and it was now time for the meeting. The boss, Harry Catterick, went through the strengths and weaknesses of Palace and what he expected of the team the next day. There was a doubt over Howard Kendall playing because he had a toe injury and would have a fitness test in the morning.

With the meeting finished, the players made their way out of the room, but the boss called me over and said he wanted to chat with me.

He started by saying: "You know Howard has an injured toe. He will have a test in the morning and if he fails it, you will be playing. How do you feel about that?"

After letting it sink in for a couple of seconds I replied: "Great boss." He said: "Off to bed then and get a good night's sleep."

Get a good night's sleep? I don't think so. I could be making my debut the next day. It was up early, breakfast, walk and then into the dining room for the pre-match meal.

They had prepared a board room table so all the players, backroom staff and manager could be seated together.

Our orders were taken which varied from beans on toast, eggs, scrambled, poached or omelette with toast etc. A couple of minutes later I was the first to get a plate put in front of me. It was a prawn cocktail!

Everyone was looking at me and I said: "I didn't order that." In a raised voice the coach said: "You can't have that for a pre-match meal."

I replied: "I know we can't and that is why I didn't order it."

"But you must have," he said. As I looked around the table, Bally Labby, Howard, and Joe were all grinning. They had told the waiter to serve me the prawn cocktail so I would get pulled up by the boss or the backroom staff. Wind-ups are done at any level.

Howard had his fitness test, past it and played and Billy Kenny was substitute. We called him 'Bill Bill'. I watched the game from the bench and it was good to see it from pitch level and hear the instructions being shouted to the players as well as the half time team talk.

It was not the best of games or result from our point of view because we lost 2–0. It was Andy Rankin's last game for Everton before his move to Watford.

We got a quick shower to get to the airport to catch the flight back to Liverpool. I sat next to 'Bill Bill' and seated behind us was Johnny Morrissey and Howard Kendall.

As soon as the plane was in the air they ordered drinks, four miniature bottles of brandy each. The cabin crew brought the drinks back and then I got a tap on my shoulder. It was Howard passing two bottles of brandy for me and 'Bill Bill'. I said: "No, it's alright thanks Howard."

He replied with a smile on his face: "To get in this team, Ronny, you need to drink."

He didn't need to ask me a second time! It was as if every five minutes I would hear "Ronny" and two mini bottles would be passed to me. The chat and drinks were flowing, and the noise of laughs and ice going into the cups.

The cabin crew were doing shuttle runs. By the time we landed at Speke Airport, this short haul flight ended up feeling very long haul.

Me and 'Bill Bill' then went around Scottie Road where he was from to have a few more drinks to end the night. I later got into a cab talking Yugoslavian!

I had a number of call ups to the first team squad during this period and was then made substitute against Tottenham, but I hadn't made my debut yet. There are periods when you are doing really well and you are hoping to get the nod for a start, but the team is playing well and winning games. The manager doesn't want to change the line-up and in those days there was only one substitute. There are seven substitutes a manager can choose from now, so there is a much better chance to impress the boss on a match day and you can almost build a career out of being a sub.

During the 1975 season I was putting in good performances, creating and also scoring 11 goals for the reserves. All you can do is to play your best and, if your chance comes along, take it.

That chance came for me on the 23rd December 1975. I was with the first team and training was as normal. Then we had the bibs handed out and had a 9 v 9 game with a mixture of players. Then we had 11v11 and a few changes of players were made which is not unusual. The training session went well and at the end, when I was walking back to the changing room, boss Billy Bingham called me over.

"How did you find the training?" he asked. "Good boss, I enjoyed it," I replied. "That's good, you are looking sharp and you are playing tonight!"

Did I just hear him right? Did he just say I was about to play against Manchester United?

Yes he did because after getting changed there was a meeting upstairs in the lounge and he named the team. At number 11 was Ronny Goodlass!

We were told what time to report for the game, and I then went home to relax before reporting back for duty, but it seemed a long time to wait.

On the way to the ground along Queens Drive, we started to see the build-up of traffic, blue scarves hanging out of car windows and then, as we reached Priory Road, there were lots of coaches starting to park up.

Suddenly Goodison Park appeared and is there a better site than our stadium bathed under floodlights?

Portable hot dog vans, chippies packed, pubs overflowing and everyone getting ready for the game. We arrived at the players' entrance with lots of supporters there, and I made my way to the dressing room. There, under the number 11 shirt, were my football boots. Yes Ronaldo, you are making your debut lad!

I was going to feel so proud when I walked out onto the Goodison pitch to make my first team debut, something I had dreamed about all my life. But my thoughts were also thinking of my family who had supported me since I was a kid, my Dad, Mum, our John, nans, granddads, uncles, aunties, cousins and friends. I hope they felt proud because I was proud of them!

I wasn't worried about playing against Manchester United at all. My main worry was how to get tickets for all of them.

Players started to get changed and doing stretches while the boss and coaches were going around the players, reminding us about our specific roles. Then, as it got nearer to kick-off, players were doing different things to psyche themselves up. Some were quiet and thinking about the game. Others talked constantly or butted the wall and ceiling which was normal for Lyonsy!

The bell went for the teams to go out and this was it. The lads were wishing each other all the very best.

From the dressing room until you reach the end of the tunnel leading to the pitch, the floor is made of concrete and the noise of the boots with metal studs banging on the floor only adds to the tension.

I started to hear Z Cars and suddenly we were up the steps and out onto the pitch under the glare of the floodlights. We received a great reception from the 41,732 crowd and with Manchester United being second in the league we were expecting a difficult game. They had

Stepney, Buchan, Coppell, Macari, Pearson and Hill in their side.

In our team that day was Mick Lyons, John Hurst, Roger Kenyon, Martin Dobson and Bob Latchford.

No 45 minute warm up in those days, then back into the dressing room and out again. We had just five minutes warm up and then the kick off.

We made a good start and I had a shot early on from 30 yards that Stepney thought was going well over but missed by inches. We could have taken the lead, but Dave Smallman, had a shot saved before Bob Latchford missed from ten yards which was not like him.

United took the lead after a deflected shot from Hill fell to Macari who scored with an overhead kick. After 40 minutes I nearly scored on my debut to get an equaliser and only a great save from Stepney kept the ball out. It rolled along the goal line and hit the post.

We scored when a Mick Bernard free kick found Dobbo. His header reached Bryan Hamilton who headed it across goal for Latch to smash it in. We celebrated, but Hammy didn't know a thing about it. He was knocked out and needed treatment from the physio before carrying on.

Then the unthinkable happened. The floodlights failed! No one knew what was happening so the referee took both teams off. We were back in the dressing room and informed they were trying to fix it. I was sitting there after all these years waiting for my debut. The bleedin' floodlights fail! You couldn't make it up.

I was wondering how good the electrician who was

asked to find a solution. Five minutes went by which seemed ages, then another ten before they came in and said everything was alright and we were going back out again. I was shouting at everyone to hurry up, just in case it fused again!

I nearly laid a winner on for Latch near the end, but the game ended up 1–1 and that put Man United top of the league, but we were unlucky not to win.

BERNIE THE BOLT AND A SHOCK CHRISTMAS PUNCH-UP AT BELLEFIELD

THE MYTH of Bernie Wright still lives on, 46 years after he signed for Everton. We've had some real characters at the club down the years, but not many like Bernie and the fascination with his story never fades.

I will tell you what really happened and WHY… because I was there!

Bernie signed after impressing for Walsall in a fourth round FA Cup tie played at Goodison Park on 5th February 1972. It was a really heavy pitch that cut up badly, but credit to both teams for putting on an exciting tie in very poor conditions. Joe Royle laid on our two goals, the first scored by Dave Johnson with a volley and the second was an Alan Whittle header. Walsall then scored with the last kick of the game and it finished 2–1 to the Blues, a result that took us into the fifth round.

On his first day, Bernie came into the gym with Stuart Imlach where he was introduced to us. We then carried on with our weight circuit. What you immediately noticed about Bernie was that he was an intimidating figure, tall, muscular and with curly red hair. The group was moving from different pieces of equipment. Me and Alan Wilson had 120lbs weights on our shoulders and were doing heel lifts, first me and then Willo. Stuart said to Bernie: "Just do what you can."

We had finished our repetitions and we were going to help Bernie with the weights. He lifted the weight up with his right hand and did ten lifts and then picked it up in his left hand and did ten more. All the lads looked at each other and we couldn't believe what we had just seen. We later found out that Bernie was a body builder!

We quickly came up with a nickname for him. At the time there was a popular quiz show on TV called the Golden Shot that was hosted by Bob Monkhouse. To win the prize you had to fire a crossbow and the person who loaded it went by the name of Bernie. The shout would go up from Monkhouse: "Bernie, the Bolt please."

From that day on he was known affectionately as Bernie the Bolt.

The first time we played in the Reserves together, he wore the number 10 and I wore the number 11, so we were always next to each other in the dressing room. As he started to get changed, he would roll his shirt sleeves up past his biceps and then roll up his shorts to emphasise his thighs and make him look even bigger. He would then put Vaseline on his eyebrows and his knees. He now looked like Neanderthal man and Bernie would definitely scare the crap out of the opposition.

There was always banter between first team and reserves team players and sometimes it was a little bit tribal. After training we were talking about skills and technique and the senior lads were saying Alan Whittle was the most skilful at the club. Bernie was shouting "No Chance" and we were supporting him with the first team doing the same for Whitt.

The gauntlet was thrown down by Whitt who said that he could juggle the ball the length of the pitch three times non-stop without dropping the ball. You had three lives and if it bounced you had to go back and start again. Bernie accepted the challenge and £5 bets were then placed, with the reserves backing Bernie and the first team supporting Whitt. I can tell you that £5 in those days was a very good night out.

Everyone was there to see it and we were telling Bernie to take his time and he would be fine. They lined up and off they went. The pair was not far apart after one length and both had the difficulty of turning and going back up the pitch again. There were loud cheers of encouragement for both players, but it was louder from those who had placed a bet, including me. They had nearly reached the halfway line when Whitt dropped the ball.

A roar went up from the reserves because Whitt had to start again. Bernie kept on going and reached the top and turned for the final length of the pitch. The reserve lads were now thinking what a good Saturday night we are going to have if Bernie completed this, but then, oh no, he dropped the ball and had to start again. A roar went up from the first team with Whitt now in the lead and doing well, but Bernie didn't panic and just took it in his stride.

They passed each other and Whitt was looking good, but unfortunately for him he dropped the ball again and only had one life left. We were shouting out sarcastically: "Unlucky Whitt," and while he looked dejected, we didn't care. Bernie completed the three lengths of the pitch with no more scares and was greeted by deafening roars of delight from the reserves on the embankment by the gym. Well done Bernie, now to pick my winnings up!

Every year the club gave out a Littlewoods Christmas hamper to all the playing staff. They came in big brown boxes with an A or a B written on them in marker pen. The boxes marked 'A' were larger and were for the first team squad and contained things like tins of Salmon, Ye Olde Oak Ham, a large Christmas cake, Whiskey/Port, and Brandy Snaps while in the 'B' Hamper it was Fray Bentos Pie, Corned Beef, Tongue, Sherry, Mince Pies/ Christmas Pudding.

Everyone received a turkey with the first team given

one that weighed 24lbs in weight while the reserves/apprentices received a 14lb bird that obviously didn't take as long to eat!

At this time Bernie was living in digs by Sefton Park and went back to his flat with a very big hamper for one and time to kill. I came in the next day, got into my training gear and was having a laugh with the lads as normal, but the whole atmosphere suddenly changed when the dressing room door burst open and in walked Bernie looking the worse for wear from the night before

He had a bottle of whiskey in his hand and asked me to have a drink with him. I obviously said: "No, we are going out for training shortly, get your training kit on or you will be in big trouble." He held it out to everyone: "Who's having a drink with me?" We were telling him to throw the bottle away, but he was then asking for orange juice to put in the whiskey.

He went into the showers and we heard something smash so we went in to look and he had broken the neck off the bottle. It had a jagged edge on it now and he came back in the dressing room. That is when Westy came in, took the bottle off him and took him to get changed. Bernie respected Westy and he was about the only one he would have listened too. Not long after the call went up: "Let's go for the start of training." We began jogging around Bellefield and the main topic of conversation was Bernie's behaviour.

The usual banter was going on and some of the lads were winding him up as to why he was training with the reserves when he had done so well and should be with the first team. We came around the back of the gym and across the car park to the 'B' team pitch. We are still chatting, when Bernie said: "I'm going to see the boss. I should be with the first team."

We were trying to persuade him to leave it for another day but he was having none of it. Harry Cooke, the Chief Scout, was standing by the door at the front of the building when Bernie said he was going up to see the boss. Harry, knowing something was amiss, made his way up the stairs and Bernie started to walk through the front door. We could see everything that was going on as Harry quickened his pace across the dining room to reach the boss's office.

Bernie wasn't far behind Harry now and he was moving faster also. If it hadn't been so serious you would have thought it was a scene from a Benny Hill Show!

The first team was now out by the A team pitch and knew something had gone on through Westy and one of them shouted: "What's happening Ronny?" I replied: "Bernie wants to realign the boss's teeth."

There was a back staircase by the Catt's office and he used it to avoid the press or to make a short cut to watch training, I think today this saved him from Bernie's wrath. They locked the door behind them so Bernie had to backtrack to the front door.

The Catt and Harry Cooke were now with the first team and Bernie came out to join us. Then one of the lads shouted out to Stewart Imlach, who was with the first team that Bernie should be with them. Stewart just smiled and said: "Oh, come on then Bernie."

Again a voice from the lads said: "Stuart's taking the piss," to which Bernie replied: "Oh he is, is he?"

He then started to walk over to Stewart and nobody expected what was going to happen next. Bernie punched Stewart in the face, causing him to fall flat on his back. By this time Westy was running over and got Bernie in a bear hug to try and calm him down to defuse the situation. A couple of players helped Stewart to get up. He was unsteady on his feet and he had a cut on his nose, but Stewart was made of sterner stuff.

He came from Lossiemouth up in the Highlands of Scotland and he carried on with the coaching. As always happens at a professional football club, altercations happen, but everything must carry on as normal and it did. The training took place as usual as there were football matches to be played at the weekend.

By this time Bernie had gone to the changing room, got changed and left Bellefield. Many people were wary of him by the persona and reputation that went before him, but once you got to know him, believe it or not, he was a quiet and unassuming lad.

Training on Tuesdays was always physically demanding and we would usually get the Wednesday off, so some of us would often go to the West Derby pub in West Derby Village, more commonly known as the 'Barries'. We would describe our time spent there as team building sessions. Well, that was my excuse and I'm sticking to it.

We used to also frequent the 'Barries' after games and on this occasion a group of us – including Bernie, Gary Jones, Alan Wilson and Tigs Smith went in there. It was always busy and had a good atmosphere with music playing and drinks flowing.

A few drinks turned into a few more and we were all having a great time. Bernie usually had a pint in each hand and the rounds of beer were coming thick and fast. I suggested to Willo that we might go to a club in town and he was up for it. Bernie was drinking so fast that we had the barmaid on casters!

He was also getting more boisterous and there were a few more hours of drinking time to go. Tigs had his car with him, but he hadn't drunk any alcohol and was going home. However, he said he would drop us off near the well known city centre Beachcomber Club in Seel Street. We mentioned to Gary about going to a club in town and he said yes, but we were all worried about the state Bernie was in.

He was rocking a bit and it wasn't to the music! If he was like this now, what would he be like in town in a few hours time? It was decided, in the interests of everyone, not to tell him. We were finishing off our drinks when Tigs went for his car which was parked near the pub. Bernie went to the toilet and we thought this was our chance to get off. We left it a minute, then walked out and Tigs was parked about 30 yards away. As we were getting in the car, Tigs said: "Bernie's just come out." It was panic stations.

Me and Willo were already in the car and Jonesy was

next in. Bernie suddenly appeared and tried to grab him, but he only grabbed his coat and ripped it from the bottom of the vent up to the neck. We were just shouting: "Put your foot down Tigs."

The coat was a full length sheepskin. It was Jonesy's pride and joy and cost £400. As you can imagine, he wasn't best pleased. The coat was virtually ripped in two and he looked more like Zorro!

Tigs dropped us by the Beachcomber and, as we were going into the club, we looked down the road and saw Bernie heading our way. We knew the bouncers and explained he had one too many beers and wouldn't be happy that we went to town without him. They suggested we leave it to them.

Bernie knocked on the door, they started chatting and he asked if we were in the club. We were in the bar downstairs and could hear everything. The bouncers said that none of us were in there and they were shutting the door. Back in the bar, we bought them a drink and the mood became relaxed because we thought Bernie had gone home.

All of a sudden, shouting through the letterbox in a booming Brummie accent, was Bernie saying: "I know you are in there and I'm going to fuck you in the morning Willo."

We started giggling, but Willo's face dropped and he said: "Why is he only going to hit me?" That made us start laughing even more. When we went next into training, Bernie had finally calmed down. To keep him sweet, Willo reimbursed his taxi fare!

EVERTON GIANTS WHO WERE OUR VERY OWN LAUREL & HARDY

I MIGHT be slightly biased here, but let me put this out there. Brian Labone and Gordon West, or 'Westy and Labby' as we knew and loved them, were two of the nicest people I ever met in football or throughout my life.

I knew them for a very long time, ever since I joined Everton as a 15 year old. They were the heart beat of the dressing room. They both reached the top of their profession playing for England and Everton, then winning the FA Cup in 1966 and the League in 1969/70 when they were members of that great Everton Championship side.

I was delegated to do the first team room, from sorting out training kits and towels to boots and trainers. I would clean the floors at the end of the day and prepare the training kit for the next morning, so I was in their a lot and as your doing your work, you hear the chat and banter of the players.

Westy was always at the forefront of practical jokes and mickey taking, sometimes at the expense of Sandy Brown. Sandy was a really nice man, a good player and had the reputation as a bit of a hard man.

This day, Westy took a bottle of sauce out of his bag and said to Labby: "This tastes lovely." Labby replied: "Could I try it?" and Westy said "Yes."

Westy tried to take the top of, but it wouldn't move. Labby said: "Give me a try," but it still wouldn't move. Sandy was looking over now and another player tries, but again doesn't succeed in taking the top off. Westy said: "Give Sandy a go, he will do it."

Sandy rose from the bench and accepted the bottle from Westy, taking a good grip. He started trying to turn it for five to ten seconds, but it still wouldn't turn. He stopped and started drying his hands on his towel.

Westy said: "You have loosened it there Sandy. I think I saw it move slightly." Sandy got hold of the bottle, took a deep breath and tried again. He was really going for it now and was over exerting himself, but he wanted that top off.

You could hear him grunting, he was trying so hard.

Then he started to go purple, but he still couldn't budge it. Sandy looked beaten so Westy took the bottle off him and said: "No problem Sandy, the Mrs will be able to do it later when I get home." He put it in his bag and walked out of the dressing room. Sandy never knew that Westy had super glued the top!

In our late teens during the summer break we used to go for a drink with a few of the lads and one was my great friend Alan Wilson. 'Willo' lived by Park Road, so on a Thursday we would have a wander around a few hostelries such as Knob Hill (The Park), Black George's and the Farmers Arms which had the best Guinness around. We used to get a letter off the club during the summer which had the weight they wanted us to report back with when the pre-season date came around. If you came back overweight you would be fined for every pound over the weight you were given.

When we reported back for pre-season, every professional had to get weighed and it was in no order. I walked in with a few of the lads, including Alan Wilson, from the reserve team room and Westy and Labby were already in there. Both had been weighed and they were standing at the side of the weight machine.

There was a queue and I started to chat to them and they asked me how my summer was. I then got weighed and then it was Willo's turn. It was a machine that you moved the weight along until it dropped. They set Willo's weight to what he should report back with and the marker was still up. They then moved it slowly along, but no change.

This carried on, 4lb over, then 8lb, then 10lb. Willo started shouting, saying: "That can't be right, I've trained through the summer, it must be broke."

I was saying: "It must be all that Guinness in the Farmers Arms to blame," and Westy was saying: "You must have had loads of pies and cakes Willo!"

Willo replied: "Honest Westy, I haven't." He was now as white as a sheet and, don't forget, he would be fined a lot of money.

Next minute the bar started moving down. Willo shouted loudly: "Look I told you it was broke."

In fact, Westy had his foot pressed down hard on the scales and he then started to take the pressure off and the weight went down. Everyone in the weight room burst out laughing and even Willo started smiling. What a relief. No fine!

Labby and Westy attended many of the charity Sportspersons Dinners that I arranged for my charity Health Through Sport and it was always a pleasure to see both of them. The guest speaker on this occasion was none other than Peter Osgood, the ex-England and Chelsea centre forward and 'King of the King's Road Chelsea'. He scored a great flying header against Leeds United in the Old Trafford replay and helped them win the FA Cup.

There was a tremendous turnout for the event with over 350 people attending and everyone was looking forward to a good evening. We finished our meal and then it was time for Peter Osgood to come on. Westy and Labby were on the Top Table with Peter and he started to tell his stories, starting with one about Tommy Docherty. I always assign a waitress to the Top Table and tell the guests to just order what they want, but she must have been busy and Westy was calling me to say that he had finished his drink and wanted another one. This distracted Ossie who said: "Are you OK, Westy?"

Gordon had got his drink and said: "Yes, you can carry on now." Ossie then carried on with his stories and jokes. He then started another one when Westy suddenly burst out laughing and said: "That was funny," to which Ossie said: "I haven't finished the story yet," and Westy replied: "No, the one about Tommy Docherty!"

Ossie said: "That was over 20 minutes ago to which Westy said: "Yes, that one was funny." It brought the house down. Ossie perked up and said: "We should be a double act Westy."

"No," said Gordon. "I've got Labby." Everybody roared with laughter, but that little aside said it all about the remarkable relationship between Gordon and Brian.

We will never forget Westy the joker and Labby the straight man with the brains... great footballers and proper Everton legends.

They would always have a word of encouragement for the younger players, but within minutes would start winding you up or sharing a joke. Labby was the Everton captain, on and off the pitch, and he played this role perfectly.

Without a doubt, he lived up to his tag as the 'Last of

the Great Corinthians'. Labby was the first person I asked to become a patron of my Health Through Sport charity and, with a smile on his face, he immediately said he would support me.

I was delighted with his decision. Indeed, these two greatest friends both supported my charity and would never miss any event or dinner I arranged.

My charity named an award after Labby and we fittingly called it the 'Corinthian' award. The original Corinthians team, founded in 1882, were a force to be reckoned with. Although they were an amateur outfit, they regularly overcame the Champions of the countries they visited. Following one such tour an opponent was so impressed by them after a match that he said: "I remember how they walked onto the field, spotless in their shirts and dark shorts. Yet there was about them an air of casual grandeur, a haughtiness that was not haughty, which seemed intangible - and how they played. It was not only their skill that marked the Corinthians out from the rest however. They also exhibited an inherent sense of sportsmanship and fair play."

Labby embodied those Corinthian values. We are therefore proud to present the 'Brian Labone Corinthian Award' to a person who, through their own efforts and example, can be seen as a role model for their community. That totally sums up Brian. Him and Westy were great company and would light up any room they entered.

You would hear Westy before you saw him because he was either laughing or holding court to the company he was in. They both loved and represented the club with pride and did so until both passed away, two great Evertonians who will always be sadly missed.

They have left Everton supporters with great memories and they will always be remembered.

Before we started a training session one day, Westy was in his usual mischievous mood and came into the young professionals changing room to say he needed our help with something in the car park. We went outside and he asked if we could help lift Andy Rankin's car and move it behind the gym. He said: "Don't say anything to him."

You might be wondering how we might lift a car and carry it 40 yards? No chance! Well, Andy's car was a Robin Regal model, similar to the one in 'Only Fools and Horses' but not the van type. The car was made of fibre glass, so it didn't weigh that much and it would be no problem hiding it behind the gym.

Once we had sorted the car out, Westy asked us to be around the car park after training.

With the training finished, Andy came out and walked out to where he had parked his car, but it wasn't there. You could see him looking around, but no joy. He asked the lads if we had we seen his car, but we just shrugged our shoulders and moved our heads from side to side.

Andy said: "I think it has been robbed." I did my best not to laugh because there were Capris, Ford Granadas and Jimmy Husband's E-Type Jag in the car park, but his Robin Regal had been stolen!

He went inside to tell the staff and report it missing,

and while he was there we went around the back and put it back in his parking place. The staff told him to go and double check it wasn't there. He walked across the car park and realised his car had mysteriously reappeared and as laughter broke out he knew he had been the victim of a practical joke… instigated once again by the irrepressible Westy.

We had many Christmas parties for the players, but the one that was organised by Westy is the most memorable. All the playing staff had to go including the young professionals and it started in the Majestic public house on Hall Lane. The players would have the back room, with the pub regulars in the front and later the manager would bring out a buffet. The music was blasting, a darts competition was organised, and it was time to have a laugh, relax and have a couple shandies!

We then had to vote for the biggest s!*!* house (coward) at the club and the one with the most votes would have to do a forfeit. The votes were being taken with the lads spread out throughout the pub, but earlier Westy had gone around all the players and told them to vote for Alan Wilson. When the votes were being taken, Willo said to me: "Who do you think it will be?" I replied: "I haven't a clue, Alan" – knowing full well it was him and the only vote he wouldn't get was his own. The votes had been 'counted' and the result was given to Westy to read out. He started by building up the tension, declaring that there was never a time when you wanted to 'win' this vote.

Then he said: "By a landslide, the winner is Alan

Wilson!"

Willo looked aggrieved and wouldn't accept the vote, but Westy said it was a democratic and it was final. Westy then went to his bag and pulled out a toilet seat which Willo had to wear for the rest of the time we were in the pub. Willo took it well and had it around his neck for a few hours before we moved on. The regulars were certainly amused.

The next stop was to the Gladray in Upper Parliament Street. It was the first strip club in Liverpool. Cliff Marshall was one of our players, and Westy had found out that his Aunty Alice was the manager of the Gladray and would sort it.

The upstairs at the club was booked for the lads and we surprised everyone when we all walked in. There were loads of characters in there and we were approached by a lad with a big brown wooden box. He opened it up and it was full of jewellery. Hanging from hooks were watches, bracelets, and necklaces. He would then open little draws that were full of earrings, brooches and rings. It was like Felix the Cat's bag, containing everything you could think of.

I went upstairs to have a few drinks with the lads and carry on the festivities. There was a lady who was connected with the Gladray and she went by the name of Gloria. Some of you may have heard of her or even seen her. Suddenly Gloria appeared upstairs to the sound of wolf whistles from the lads, I wonder what she was doing up there? Ok I think you have guessed that.

The MC introduced Gloria to the audience, the music started and she began her act. It was amazing how quickly she got the attention of the audience and all eyes were on her!

It was at this moment she asked for two first year professionals to come and join her. This was greeted with howls of laughter, clapping and cheers. The first year professionals were sitting in a group and she pointed at two of them to come forward. This was like an initiation ceremony and the blushing lads walked out, not knowing where to look.

Gloria put her two best assets to use and put one of the lad's heads to her chest and shook frantically to the amusement of the watching audience. Then the second lad was put through this also with a similar reaction from the lads.

A couple of hours later we called it a day/night, a fantastic occasion was had by all the lads and well done Westy for putting it together.

JOHN MOORES AND A SURPRISE ROLLS RIDE TO THE 'SHE' CLUB

BEFORE we went out on the Goodison Park pitch we always used to go in the gym underneath the Main Stand by the top of the tunnel that leads to the pitch. It is now the 1878 Restaurant, including the Sponsors Lounge. The team used to go in there to do stretches, other exercises, passing, heading and short sprints before we went out.

I remember warming up as usual before one of the games. I started side footing the ball against the wall when the door opened and a large entourage came walking in.

Straight away I recognised it was John Moores, chairman and major shareholder of our club. He wasn't knighted until 1980.

The chairman was getting introduced to the players as he moved around the gym and then he started to walk over to me so I stopped kicking the ball. One of the coaching staff said: "Mr Chairman, this is…" and before he could say my name Mr Moores said: "I know who this is. Ronny Goodlass, local lad, came through our youth policy and is doing really well. Keep it up."

I was blown away as to how he knew about me. Now if that doesn't give you confidence as a young player, what will? That's why he was the best chairman and major shareholder in our history. He knew everything that was going on at the club from top to bottom and was not afraid to let the manager spend money to make the team better. Nil Satis Nisi Optimum.

Moores didn't shy away from big decisions. He famously sacked Johnny Carey in the back of a taxi and his master stroke was appointing Harry Catterick as our manager from Sheffield Wednesday.

As chairman and major shareholder, he oversaw us winning the League Championship in 1963 and 1970 as well as the FA Cup in 1966.

In 1977 he retired as a director when he was presented with a silver salver by then chairman Mr Bill Scott which was signed by all the directors, staff and playing staff. We were in the players' lounge at Bellefield when Sir John came in for the presentation and you could see his delight at receiving it with all the players present. He was a wonderful man who did everything he could to make Everton Football Club the very best.

Here's a story about Bill Scott who followed him and what a really nice man he was. We had played a reserve game at Newcastle. It's a long way there and back, but myself, Alan Wilson and Tigs Smith decided to go into town for a few drinks after we arrived back at Bellefield.

We were not far away and were chatting to Mr Scott who asked: "Where are you going?" Now we couldn't say for a few drinks and to a club so, with Tigs living off Scotland Road, I said: "We are going to Tigs' house, Mr Scott."

He replied: "Do you want a lift? I'm going to the Adelphi Hotel," to which I had to reply: "Yes, if you could Mr Scott. That would be great."

All the players and staff got off the coach and headed to their cars. We three followed Mr Scott to his Rolls Royce with his chauffeur opening the door to let us get in the back. When we arrived at the Adelphi Hotel Mr Scott said to the driver: "Take these boys to where they want to be dropped off." We thanked him for the lift.

When he headed into the hotel, the chauffeur asked me where we wanted to go and we decided to make the most of this because we were not in a Roller every day. We said: "Just drive around until we've decided." The chauffer was a good fella and he just smiled and said ok.

He drove us around town with the three of us looking out of the window to see if we knew anyone. We had arranged to see a couple of lads in town and stopped outside that salubrious 'She Club' in Victoria Street for starters. There was a queue outside the club, but we knew the bouncers who let us in. When we got out of the Rolls, I turned and said to the chauffeur: "You can have the rest of the night off."

He just doffed his cap and said 'thank you' as we walked in the club laughing. Thanks again Mr Scott, an absolute gentleman.

LEAGUE CUP FINAL DREAM TAKES OFF WITH ALLARDYCE IN THE SHADE

WHEN I look back on the 1976/77 season, two good cup runs and, oh, what might have been!

I played in all nine games during the memorable League Cup run and I look back on a campaign that so nearly brought silverware to Goodison Park.

30 AUGUST 1976. ROUND ONE. EVERTON 3 CAMBRIDGE UNITED 0

Our assistant manager Steve Burtenshaw said to me

before the game: "Just go out, play the way you always do and get some crosses in."

I was marked by Brendon Batson who would go on to become chairman of the Professional Footballers Association. Our opponents also included a young striker by the name of Alan Biley.

We started the game really brightly and attacked them from the start. We scored three first half goals which came from Bob Latchford, Martin Dobson and Andy King. The game was virtually over by half time with the scoreline at 3–0, but it was a good win for us and a professional job well done. I got booked by referee Dave Richardson for not retreating quickly enough at a free kick. I think it's now called taking one for the team!

20 SEPTEMBER 1976. ROUND TWO. STOCKPORT COUNTY 0 EVERTON 1

This Stockport team were doing really well in their division at the time and although we were expected to win, it was a potential banana skin. Edgeley Park is a tight ground and I remember there were Evertonians coming out of the rafters – off the roofs, and on the floodlights!

We were awarded a free-kick early in the first half and I curled it into Bob Latchford to head us into a 1–0 lead. I had a couple of good efforts that the goalkeeper did well to save, but Stockport battled until the end to try and get the equaliser and they never gave up. Latch's header proved to be the difference between the two teams and we progressed to the next round.

26 OCTOBER 1976. ROUND THREE.
EVERTON 3 COVENTRY CITY 0

Each round we progressed through gave us more confidence and we were playing some good football and scoring goals. The Coventry goalkeeper, Jim Blyth, was in inspired form and it could have been even more only for him. Andy King had given us the lead in the 18th minute. We couldn't get that second with Blyth in such good form, but then I scored a goal that was ruled out for offside.

It was a perfectly good effort, but I would say that wouldn't I? I asked Martin Dobson about it and Dobbo said: "Nothing wrong with that, Ronny." He was never wrong, so that was good enough for me.

We eventually got our second through Mick Lyons. Blyth couldn't reach a cross cum shot from Lyonsy.

I was seeing a lot of the ball and was enjoying the game and with 13 minutes left, Kingy got our third, game over and another good win.

1 DECEMBER 1976. ROUND FOUR.
MANCHESTER UNITED 0 EVERTON 3

We were drawn away to Manchester United and everyone had them down as favourites to go through, but we had other ideas and were confident of getting a result at Old Trafford. It is always difficult when you play Manchester United, but even more so when you played them at home.

Their manager was the mercurial Tommy Docherty. In round two they had beaten Tranmere Rovers 5–0 and in round four they battered Newcastle United 7–2, both at Old Trafford. In those days, with it being a cup competition, you were allocated more tickets for your supporters and we took nearly 20,000. Their support that night, as always, was brilliant.

Roger Kenyon took a free kick on the halfway line and played it into the Man Utd area where Greenhoff won a header against Lyonsy, but Dobbo was waiting 25 yards out. He chested it and then hit a tremendous shot along the ground to give Stepney no chance and we had a 1–0 lead.

Dave Jones won the ball off Coppell and made a run towards goal and when the ball broke to Kingy, he hit it first time with his left foot. It took a slight deflection off Patterson and flew into the net to make it 2–0 at half time.

Jonesy again won the ball in a tackle and gave it to Latch. He took it forward and waited for me to support him down the left. I took one touch and glanced up to see if Kingy was making a run to the near post, and he was. I crossed and he side footed it in with his left foot for 3–0.

This was the cue for our supporters to go absolutely off their cake!

We were finishing the game really strong and I hit a left foot drive just over the crossbar. Kingy was unlucky not to get his 'Harry Catterick' with a right foot half volley past the post before I crossed for Latch to potentially make it 4–0, but his shot from six yards was saved by Stepney.

This was still a tremendous result and performance by all the players and staff, but special mention must go to our supporters that night. They certainly played their part, and were undoubtedly our 12th man!

18 JANUARY 1977. SEMI-FINAL, 1ST LEG. EVERTON 1 BOLTON WANDERERS 1

This was a very disappointing night for us and also for a crowd of 54,032 that turned up to Goodison hoping to see us take a lead into the second leg. Bolton were playing very well when they came here and had the likes of Peter Reid, Neil Whatmore and, ironically, Sam Allardyce. We created a number of chances, but didn't take them.

We took the lead after 33 minutes when I curled in a corner for Duncan McKenzie to head home past Jim Mc-Donagh, the Bolton goalkeeper. In the future he would sign for Everton. Once you go 1–0 up you think: "Can we get a second and put the tie to bed, but most importantly you have to keep a clean sheet."

Under Ian Greaves, they were a hardworking team and they could play. With two minutes remaining goalkeeper Dave 'Bambi' Lawson took too many steps before clearing and Neil Whatmore scored from the resulting indirect free-kick. This was a bitter blow to us and the game ended 1–1.

Acting manager Steve Burtenshaw, who stepped up after Billy Bingham was sacked after we beat Stoke City in the FA Cup, said at his post match press conference: "Too many people did not accept the responsibility of wanting the ball. Certain people we rely on to put their foot on the ball just did not do it in the second half."

He wasn't a happy chappy!

Bambi was penalised for the four step rule and it was a bitter disappointment because I thought we could have won by at least two or three goals. So when you get pulled back to 1–1 so late on and you've got to go to Burnden Park, you know it is going to be a hard place to visit in front of a full house.

Steve Burtenshaw was so disappointed – not just with Bambi, but because we should have scored more to finish the game off and when things like that happen, you think it could well cost you a place at Wembley.

Bolton where dancing around at the end thinking they had reached Wembley, but I was thinking: "Hang on, we've got another game to play yet."

15 FEBRUARY 1977. SEMI-FINAL, 2ND LEG. BOLTON WANDERERS 0 EVERTON 1

By the time the second leg came around, Gordon Lee had been appointed Everton manager. With another full house of 50,413 the atmosphere was intimidating, very noisy and electric! These are the games you want to play in.

The tackles were flying in and everyone was trying to win their personal battle against the opposing player. In the 24th minute, I received the ball from a Martin Dobson throw-in on the left and went past Nicholson, got to the bye line and crossed for Bob Latchford to power his header past Jim McDonagh. Bolton's Allardyce could only look on as Latch scored to make it 1 – 0 at half time.

It was still a battle in the second half and then we got a penalty to hopefully finish the game off. Sam Allardyce brought down Duncan McKenzie in the area. He got up to take the pen himself, but put the spot-kick wide of the post and it was game on again. Towards the end, they started to put a bit of pressure on and we had a few nervy moments after Duncan missed the penalty.

Typically of Duncan, he told us afterwards that he wanted to make a game of it. We had a few other things to say to him but you couldn't print it.

We won 1–0 and went through to Wembley 2–1 on aggregate.

It was the first time in the club's history that we had made it to a League Cup Final, a proud moment for every Evertonian and a tremendous night. I keep mentioning the supporters, but I think when you're away from home they are vital. It's always the big results that you seem to remember but I think we were starting to galvanise the club with the supporters. They were fantastic and it's lovely to pay them back in this way for their constant support.

LONGEST CUP FINAL EVER PLAYED, BUT HEARTBREAK FOR OUR SUPERB FANS

WHEN you reach any final you have to try and put it to the back of your mind because we had some important league games to play in the meantime. As the weeks go by, the build up gets more intense and frantic, from the interviews with the local and national press and radio, photo commitments and trying to get the required number of final tickets for the family, friends and the milkman!

Mum hired another 52 seat coach and then the scarves, hats, flags and banners had to be bought or made. It was an exciting period for the players, but also for Evertonians who hadn't been to Wembley since 1968 against West Brom. It took the team coach 30 minutes to get down Wembley Way with so many Evertonians there and it was a sea of blue and white.

12 MARCH 1977. FINAL.
EVERTON 0 ASTON VILLA 0
WEMBLEY. ATTENDANCE – 96,223

It was a massive day for the players, from getting up in the morning, pre match meal, a walk and getting to the stadium. You just want 3pm to come around and the referee to blow his whistle to start the game. The supporters were there in numbers and made their presence felt with constant chanting and flag waving. The Scouse wit was also on show with some funny banners.

We arrived at Wembley and first port of call was the dressing room. We then changed and, team talk completed, it was time to walk up the tunnel and out onto the pitch.

The majority of the Evertonians were congregated at the Tunnel End and as we came out the noise was deafening, great to hear and see. It was an incredibly hot day for March and Brian Moore, the ITV commentator, described it as "a beautiful, crisp, Wembley afternoon, perfectly made for a Cup Final"

The attendance was also 96,223 and I remember sharing a joke with Princess Anne as the teams lined-up. She was wearing a royal blue coat and I said she was wearing the right colour and it was good to see she was an Evertonian. She smiled and didn't condemn me to the Tower!

It was a tense final and produced a stalemate at Wembley where we had a few moments. I forced John Burridge into an early save, Bob Latchford was unlucky with a header and Duncan McKenzie also went close with a chip. With Andy Gray and Brian Little in the Villa team, they were always a threat. It was not the best and most open of games that many people hoped for and we couldn't get that goal we were so desperate to score and the game ended 0–0.

The first time I went to Wembley was when I was 12 years old with my Dad and Granddad for the 1966 FA Cup Final against Sheffield Wednesday. I had tears in my eyes when we went 2–0 down and I looked up at my Granddad and he said: "We'll win this son." He was right, of course, and we did. It was unbelievable as we pulled back to win 3–2 with goals from Mike Trebilcock (2) and Derek Temple with a stunning winner.

To think I had watched Everton play at Wembley twice, including the 1968 FA Cup Final, and now I had just worn the blue shirt at Wembley. Well, it's every kid's dream to do that for your boyhood team and it is something I am very proud of.

16 MARCH 1977. FINAL REPLAY.
EVERTON 1 ASTON VILLA 1
HILLSBOROUGH

After the goalless draw at Wembley, the replay was

played four days later at Sheffield Wednesday's Hillsborough stadium where we had great support again with the attendance at 54,840.

There was certainly more attacking play than in the first game and with both teams trying to get that first goal, it was a more open match. We went behind with 11 minutes to go when a shot from Deehan beat Dave Lawson. Roger Kenyon stopped the ball going in the net, but it got stuck under his legs and as he walked backwards he inadvertently knocked it into his own net.

Roger had been tremendous in this Cup run and was so unlucky for this to happen to him. We had a lot of character throughout the team and we would go right to the end to get this equaliser. Gordon Kew, the referee, was already looking at his watch when we won a throw-in on the right. Duncan McKenzie, Mike Bernard, Jim Pearson and myself were all involved in the move for Latch to ram the ball past Burridge from close range.

We were kicking into the Leppings Lane End in the second half and when the goal went in the supporters went crazy, some getting onto the pitch. I then I looked around and Evertonians were on three sides of the ground. What fans they are. Not long after the goal, the referee blew his whistle for full time with the game deadlocked at 1–1.

We showed a fighting spirit and character to get that late goal and take it to a third game.

13 APRIL 1977 FINAL. SECOND REPLAY.
EVERTON 2 ASTON VILLA 3 (AET)
OLD TRAFFORD

We had to wait four weeks for this game because we were still involved in the FA Cup and had a backlog of league games. This time there would be extra time played and if there still wasn't a winner after 90 minutes, the first penalty shoot-out in the history of an English Final would take place.

There was not a spare seat and the attendance was 54,749. We kicked into the Scoreboard End in the first half and in the second half, the Stretford End, which was a mass of royal blue and white.

It was a bright start from us and in the first minute of the game I collected a pass and took one touch before hitting it from 25 yards. The ball was tipped around the post by Burridge for a corner. We were the better side in the first half and Nicholl was booked for a tackle from behind on Latch about 40 yards from goal on the left side.

From this distance I took all the free kicks and we worked a lot on this one at Bellefield. We would isolate Ken McNaught and Mick Lyons at the far post and Bob Latchford would attack the ball from the opposite side. If either won the header they would go for goal or head it back for Latch to put it in. I gave the signal and floated the ball into the area and Ken headed it across the six yard line and Latch side footed the ball into the net. It worked a treat and we took the lead after 38 minutes.

We went in at half time 1–0 up and we deserved to be.

In the second half we knew Aston Villa would have to come out and have a go and push more players forward and take chances. They had more possession this half, but no goal threat. With ten minutes to go we were still leading 1–0.

It was a real surprise when they equalised and from someone you wouldn't expect to score. Dave Lawson is a good fella and no disrespect to him, but for Chris Nicholl to net from 35 yards with his left foot… well! He'd never done it previously in his career and he never did it again. Bambi got his hand to the ball and should have saved it and pushed it around the post.

Within two minutes they had taken the lead through Little who scored from an angle on the right as Bambi rushed towards him to try and save. The ball went under him.

Two goals in a minute turned the game on its head, but I said we had character and we came back to score within a minute. We won a corner on the right and I curled the ball in. Lyonsy won the header, but Burridge saved it and the ball hit the crossbar and bounced down for Mick to head home on the rebound… 2–2.

That was three goals in four minutes. It was two committed teams giving it their all. There were some tired legs because this was our fourth game in 11 days and now we faced 30 minutes extra time, but both teams were going for the winner.

In the first period of extra time, the ball was played to me in the penalty area. I turned the defender and pulled it back across the six yard box to the waiting Latch. I was waiting for the net to bulge, but he miskicked the ball. It was so unlike Latch, but even the best can miss a chance with lots of tired players out there.

Was it going to go to extra time? No it wasn't. They crossed the ball from the right and Brian Little, on the far post, side-footed it in for 3–2 to Villa. There was no time for us to get back on level terms and it was heart breaking for everyone connected with Everton Football Club, players, staff and the supporters.

I would like to take this opportunity to thank everyone who followed the team throughout the competition. The players really appreciated it and your vocal support was second to none. You were a credit to Everton FC and I'm only sorry we couldn't give you the Cup.

BELIEVE IT OR NOT: This was the longest English Cup Final ever played. It involved three matches at three different venues over a period of five weeks from the 12th of March until the 13th April. The three matches lasted 330 minutes. It was watched by an aggregate attendance of 210,000.

Neil Robinson and Terry Darracott both wore the number 2 shirt in the first half at Old Trafford. For the second half Terry wore the number 3 shirt.

Gordon Lee, the Everton manager, was an ex-Aston Villa player.

Ron Saunders, the Aston Villa manager, was an ex-Everton player.

SENT OFF BEFORE WE KICK A BALL: On the Friday before we played at Wembley, our final training session was at Croydon High School for Girls. The groundsman instructed us to use one of the hockey pitches. We were staying near at the Selsdon Park Hotel and, as we were training, an irate P.E. Teacher, Miss Sheila Plant, stormed across and shouted to our coach Steve Burtenshaw: "Everton off! We are playing a first team hockey match on that pitch this afternoon and you are playing at the wet end of the ground. Please replace the divots before you go."

Steve looked shocked and thought it as a wind up, but it wasn't, she was serious.

We moved to another pitch and I said to the lads: "I wouldn't like to be short with her house keeping money!"

Before training Andy King told me he was having problems with his back. I suggested he go to see Jim McGregor, our physio, and he was withdrawn from taking part in the session.

He was having back spasms and Jim said it was down to nerves and he would be ok to play. Kingy with nerves!

Jim was usually right and on this occasion, he was right again because Kingy played the next day.

ON THE WING WITH LATCH & CO – ONE OF OUR MOST EVENTFUL SEASONS EVER

HERE are some of the games that excited me – and hopefully you – during that eventful 1976/77 season when I was thrilled to be involved and helping to provide the service for Bob Latchford & Co in what had to be one of the most eventful seasons ever.

11 SEPTEMBER 1976.
EVERTON V STOKE CITY

This was a damp cold afternoon at Goodison with lots

of brollies on show in the Gwladys Street end. Stoke had an experienced and seasoned line up that included Peter Shilton, Alan Hudson, Jimmy Greenhoff, Terry Conroy and a certain Mike Pejic. Stoke arrived unbeaten.

It was still raining heavily when, after 24 minutes, Conroy was brought down by Roger Kenyon in the penalty area and the Stoke man stepped up himself to take the penalty. Dai Davies went to his right and Conroy put the ball to his left, but lucky for us he put it a yard wide.

We forced numerous corners with Shilton making good saves from Kingy twice and Roger Kenyon, but it stayed goalless at half time.

After the break, we came out with a much more positive approach and this paid off because we scored three goals in 15 minutes and could have had more. Lyonsy was playing in midfield and in the 62nd minute he played the ball forward for Telf to run on and go around Shilton before he put the ball into the net.

For the second goal, after 67 minutes, Dobbo was scythed down and I played the free-kick to the near post where a Latch header was pushed onto the woodwork by Shilton, Telf scoring on the rebound.

This was the game Lyonsy showed he could pass a ball! The third goal in the 77 minute was one of my favourites when playing for the Blues or watching as a supporter because it sums up Everton Football Club and how we have always liked to play.

This is what Gerald Sinstadt, the Granada football commentator, said about it: "Oh, what a goal! Now that's football and everybody involved can take credit. Lyons a great cross-field pass; Goodlass a magnificent centre; Latchford a superb header… three superlatives for three very good players who combined in a magnificent move."

I couldn't have put that any better, Gerald!

Horace Yates wrote this in the Liverpool Daily Post: "My man of the match is Ronny Goodlass. He is a player right out of Goodison's top drawer, a throwback to the School of Science days. He has ball control of the highest order, beats men with dexterity and floats passes with precision. With courage to match, how can he fail?

2 OCTOBER 1976.
SUNDERLAND V EVERTON

Sunderland manager Bob Stokoe had bought striker Bob Lee from Leicester, keeper Barry Siddall from Bolton, and Alan Foggon from Man Utd, and he also had big Jim Holton on loan from United to strengthen his squad.

Billy Bingham was an ex-Sunderland player and was telling us about the Roker Roar, how they would get behind the team and how it was an intimidating ground.

The old adage when you play away from home is keep the crowd quiet, don't give them anything to cheer – and don't allow them to score! We took the first option and scored after seven minutes which gave us more confidence and silenced the crowd even more.

Having won a corner on the right, I jogged over to take it. We practised a lot taking free-kicks and corners at Bellefield because we had some good headers of the ball like Mick Lyons, Ken McNaught, Roger Kenyon , Martin Dobson and, of course, Bob Latchford. There were different corners to be taken and players would need to know their role. Some would attack the near or far post and someone could stand by the keeper, but the movement was very important with other players asked to block off defenders.

I gave the signal that it would be a far post corner and I tried to curl the ball a yard or two from the post and crossbar. The ball curled past everyone, even Jim Montgomery the keeper, and went straight into the net. It was my first League goal which I was delighted with, but the important thing now was to keep a clean sheet for a win.

Dai Davies made two good saves from Lee and a tremendous point blank save from Hughes. There was a good move between Terry Darracott, Dobbo and me before Montgomery saved my first time volley.

Latch nearly scored with a back heel and Montgomery made a couple more saves. It was a composed performance by the team and a good result. This win put us a point off the top of the League and we kept most of the 34,670 spectators silent while the Roker Roar was down to a whisper.

5 OCTOBER 1976.
EVERTON V MANCHESTER CITY

After the win at Sunderland, we knew two points in this game would put us top of the League above... Manchester City. It was a great incentive for us to win. In the opposing ranks were Corrigan, Doyle, Watson, Kidd, Royle, Hartford and Tueart. Mark Higgins made his Everton debut.

We made a good start by forcing two corners and from one of them we went ahead. I took the corner from the right and Dobbo scored with a good diving header, but we only had the lead for 20 minutes. This time it was a City midfielder, Hartford, who equalised with a strong header.

We went ahead in the 74th minute and there was an unusual start to the goal. Joe Royle, now in opposition, obstructed Lyonsy in the six yard box and the ref awarded an indirect free-kick. Eleven City players stood on the line.

Dobbo touched the ball to Telf whose shot hit the wall. Another shot was blocked before Kingy smashed it into the net for his first league goal of the season and if the score stayed like this we would be top.

However, they scored almost immediately when a Paul Power header went over Dai Davies to make it 2–2. It was an exciting game, but disappointing that we couldn't keep hold of the lead.

23 OCTOBER 1976.
EVERTON V WEST HAM

It was a cold and windswept Goodison with the conditions difficult for all the players, but West Ham liked to play football like ourselves and had some good technical players in Brooking, Bryan 'Pop' Robson, and Alan Curbishley, plus other excellent players like defenders Mervyn Day, Billy Bonds, Frank Lampard Snr and Tommy Taylor.

It was not the best first half, but we took the lead when

Mick Lyons scored after 12 minutes. A much brighter second half saw us put on a much better performance and we played some really good football.

Now Latch scored many goals throughout his football career, but not many outside the area and as spectacular as this one. A long pass from Dobbo sent him on his way, running at pace towards their goal.

Latch was confronted by Tommy Taylor, but he cut inside and went past him with ease before hitting a shot from 25 yards out that went like an Exocet missile into the top corner for a great finish. Latch never scored many from outside the box, but this one was memorable. The look on his face and the way he punched the air highlighted his sheer joy.

Latch was now in the mood for more goals and was brought down as he went past Lampard. Everyone thought it would be a penalty, but while we waited for the referee's decision, Kingy stroked the ball into the net to make it 3–0.

With 15 minutes to go, West Ham got a lucky break to get back in the game when a poor shot deflected off Ken McNaught's back to send Dai Davies the wrong way and it looped over his head to make it 3–1. Then, with a couple of minutes to go, Billy Bonds crossed a ball and put his head in his hands, thinking it was going way over the crossbar, but it dipped and deceived Dai, going in at the far post for 3–2.

The score stayed that way for us to pick up the two points, but the score flattered the visitors.

30 OCTOBER 1976.
TOTTENHAM V EVERTON

It has always been a difficult ground for Everton to go and get a positive result. In October 1958 Tottenham inflicted an infamous 10–4 defeat on us and it is still the largest ever League loss we have suffered in our history. With a score like that, many forget that Jimmy Harris scored a hat-trick for us which was some achievement in a defeat. I tell that to Jimmy every time I see him, a lovely man.

Their team included Jennings, Hoddle, Perryman, Taylor, Young, Pratt, Conn, and McAllister, not a bad side at all.

Spurs capitalised on two mistakes we made, the first when Mick Bernard gave the ball away for Pratt to score on 25 minutes. Then, after 35 minutes, no one picked up McAllister who ran to head in a corner and now we were 2–0 down. Jennings made a really good save from Hammy and then a good one from Latch, but he kept a clean sheet until the 56th minute.

That is when a shot from Telf was blocked with Kingy knocking the rebound in to make it 2–1.

We were now going for the equaliser, but Spurs were playing well. Conn went into the area and was brought down by Dai Davies for a penalty. Osgood stepped up to take it, Keith not Peter, and blasted it past Dai to make it 3–1 for Spurs. They thought the game was over, but we didn't and, as I have said before, we had a tremendous character throughout the team and a never-say-die attitude. We kept going and in the 86th minute we won a free-kick that I took for Latch to flick a header across goal where Ken McNaught headed home to give Jennings no chance it was now 3–2 and this was Ken's first goal of the season.

The fight back was now on. Could we get a third? You bet we could! In the 90th minute Hammy pressurised Pratt to win the ball off him as they were trying to play keep ball and play the clock down with not much time left and he passed to Kingy who moved forward to put a lovely ball in for Latch to get away from the two centre backs. It was now a one on one with the great Pat Jennings.

Latch shaped to shoot, but delayed it slightly as Jennings went to ground. Our big striker then clipped the ball over the keeper to make the score 3–3 and a great comeback. I don't know if Latch got many bruises from their defenders during the game, but he certainly got some off his team mates when we all piled on him by the halfway line to celebrate the goal.

Tremendous attitude was shown by the team to go right to the end even though we were 3–1 down and with only four minutes to go we had earned a deserved point. The train journey home was a bit boisterous to say the least with lots of drinks consumed… mineral water, of course.

20 NOVEMBER 1976.
EVERTON V DERBY COUNTY

They had a squad that contained McFarland, Todd, Newton, Rioch, Gemmill, Hector, George and James with quality and lots of experience at international level.

Billy Bingham had the difficulty of having to pick two from three good centre halves in Roger Kenyon, Ken Mc-Naught and Mick Lyons. He went with the partnership of Roger and Ken.

The versatile Lyonsy had actually joined the club as a centre forward. Billy played him in midfield in this game. They had more possession of the ball with Gemmill and Rioch pushing them forward, but after 18 minutes Kingy hit a shot that deflected off Todd. It beat both 'keeper Boulton and Henry Newton on the line to put us 1–0 up.

They had some half chances, but nothing to really test Dai. Roger Kenyon fouled Hector who then retaliated and there was a bit of a scuffle between the two, both being booked.

I know who my money would have been on if that had carried on! We needed to get a second goal which we got with 14 minutes left.

Charles Burgess from the Liverpool Daily Post and Echo wrote:

> *"Goodlass was to prove so useful with a piece of brilliant wing work. It was his quick footwork and ability to flight accurate crosses that created the goal. Goodlass is a great asset to Everton.*
>
> *"In the second half he had begun to get into the game and sent over one delightful cross after some clever ball control. Then, with 14 minutes to go, the winger beat Peter Daniel, selling him a great dummy that sent the defender slipping. Goodlass got to the by-line and his cross found Bob Latchford on the far post who rose above the*

defence to head home his tenth goal of the season.

"The execution was perfect and it made the trip to Goodison worthwhile. The extra width which Goodlass brings to the Everton attack is noticeable and his presence was sorely missed when injury kept him out of the Leeds defeat."

This was another good win two goals, a clean sheet and maximum points.

26 MARCH 1977.
EVERTON V TOTTENHAM

We came into this game with an unbeaten eight game run playing with confidence and scoring goals. Latch was in good goalscoring form with seven in 10 games so could he add to his tally and help us keep our unbeaten record? In any game you try to attack the opposition, test their goalkeeper and score as early as possible. We did all of these things and couldn't have started much better.

We went straight at Tottenham from the kick-off. Bruce Rioch got the ball and played a good pass to Latch who turned first time and beat the keeper with a super shot for us to take the lead after only 88 seconds. Talk about a good start.

It was Martin Dobson, another midfield player, who created the second after being brought down by two Tottenham players for a penalty after 26 minutes. Kingy scored from the spot and this was his first goal of the year.

We were dominating midfield with loads of possession when Dobbo scored our third after 36 minutes. The Daily

Post's Horace Yates wrote: "This game produced no evidence to discount the theory that Dobson and Goodlass are at their most effective when operating together."

After a corner taken by yours truly, Lyonsy scored with a glancing header at the near post to make it 4–0. It is still the biggest goals differential we have imposed on Tottenham in our long history, a good day all round with four strikes, a clean sheet and also a tremendous team performance.

2ND APRIL 1977.
WEST HAM V EVERTON

Our unbeaten run was still intact, but could we extend it to 10 games? We knew West Ham would be tough at home with Taylor, Bonds and Lampard Snr in defence, Brooking and Devonshire in midfield, and Bryan 'Pop' Robson up front with John Radford.

We didn't start the game as we would have liked and we couldn't seem to keep possession at this stage. Then, in the 10th minute and with our first real sortie into their half we scored a goal that I can still remember as if it was yesterday.

I put Alan Devonshire under pressure in our half as he was about to switch the ball out to Frank Lampard, but he only found Latch who headed the ball up in the air. I ran forward into the space for Latch to head the ball again, this time in front of me. As I controlled it I glanced up to see where Mervyn Day was positioned and he was 10 yards off his line.

As it came down I decided to take the shot on and volleyed the ball over the goalkeeper's head for the opening goal. The lads ran over to congratulate me and I appreciated the sporting way the West Ham supporters reacted (even Chas Baxter).

There was a dubious penalty decision after 26 minutes when Radford seemed to run into Lyonsy, but the referee didn't see it our way and Pop Robson side footed the ball inside the post. Early in the second half Telf got injured and was substituted by Jim Pearson and not long after we went 2–1 ahead.

Hammy won a header in midfield and then got a good lay off back from Latch and played a ball to Jim. Kevin Lock tried to intercept, but missed it and let Jim run wide into the penalty area from where he hit the ball hard and low into the far corner from an angle.

West Ham were pushing for an equaliser which they got in the 84th minute. Jennings crossed from the bye line on the left and Robson scored with a glancing header over Dave Lawson.

It was not the end of the game we wanted, but we were not at our best and if you don't play well, at least get a point which is what we did.

FOOTNOTE: Andy King was injured for the game at West Ham where he was sitting in the main stand, but was made up when I scored my goal. He was doubly happy that day because he had put a nice few quid on Red Rum to win the Grand National and it romped home. You could hear Kingy shouting to us that he'd won the National. Jim

Pearson won the players' sweep. What a great night we had when we got back into town.

As for my goal, thanks to everyone who continue to ask me about it all these years later. Whether you where there or have seen it, I enjoyed scoring it and I hope you enjoy watching it.

16 APRIL 1977.
DERBY COUNTY V EVERTON

Only three days after the massive disappointment of losing the League Cup Final, we had to travel away to Derby County and play on the infamous beach (sorry pitch!). The surface was really sandy soft under foot and the poorest in the league.

Dai Davies came in for the dropped Dave Lawson. We had already beaten them in the League and FA Cup that season so they were all out to get revenge and stop three wins in a season for us.

Derby came out of the traps quickly and clearly knew there would be a few tired legs and minds early on for us. They soon capitalised on this.

Gemmill and Daley looked lively and James, who we didn't see in the other two games against us, seemed up for this one. After 21 minutes he went past Neil Robinson in the penalty area and Robbo tugged his shirt for a penalty for Derby from which Daley scored.

Then, after 29 minutes, it got worse for us and we went 2–0 behind. Gemmill, who was influencing the game, put a good pass through to Daley and he went past Pejjy to drive the ball beyond Dai Davies for their second goal.

This was not a good situation for us to be losing 2–0 after 45 minutes and with Derby in the ascendancy it would take a colossal effort to get back into the game. With the half time team talk done, we went out determined to turn things around.

Within a minute they hit the bar and it was Daley who nearly got his hat-trick, but in the 61st minute the fightback started when I crossed for Latch to guide it into the net for his 23rd goal of the season.

Colin Todd then overplayed with the ball outside the Derby penalty area. Hammy took it from him and then Pejjy aimed a shot inside the far post for his first goal for the club. We had now turned the game on its head and were now going for a third goal and it was Duncan McKenzie who would get it.

Latch chested the ball down for Duncan and from the edge of the area he made no mistake to put us ahead 3–2.

"It was a magnificent performance to come back from 2–0 down," Gordon Lee said. "The last15 games had seen just two defeats and at Derby it had been a great performance and a great result with real character shown by all the lads."

The only downside to the result was Bob Latchford turning his ankle on an atrocious Baseball Ground pitch which made him miss both FA Cup semi-finals against Liverpool.

19 MAY 1977.
EVERTON V SUNDERLAND

Your main aim in any game is to win, but in some cases a point could be good enough and this was the case in this Sunderland clash. To stay up, they needed a point or a win and had to hope that either Bristol City or Coventry City, playing against each other, lost and were therefore relegated to Division 2.

The Coventry game kicked off 15 minutes later than ours due to 'traffic problems' which must have been questionable for those Sunderland supporters who came in their droves to take over the whole of the Stanley Park End.

There was a tremendous atmosphere inside Goodison with a 36,075 crowd and with both sets of supporters playing their part.

This was going to be like a Cup Final to them because of their predicament, but we wanted to get the double over them after winning at Roker Park and we were certainly determined to go about our job professionally. It was an open game and when we were awarded a free kick in the 11th minute, Pejjy floated it into the area where Latch lost defender Waldron to place a firm header beyond Siddall to make it 1–0.

Up until half time Sunderland had more possession of the ball, but never really troubled us with our back four looking strong. They had to come out to get an equaliser and Bolton forced Dai Davies to make a good save, but Sunderland supporters were not only worried about what was happening at Goodison. They also had their minds on the happenings at Highfield Road. The Park End erupted when a score of 3–1 to Coventry went around the Sunderland supporters.

At this time there were only hand held radios to listen to games, but when the score went around the ground it always seemed to be wrong – just like Chinese Whispers. Some with radios in the crowd would also wind the opposing supporters up by giving them the wrong score.

These were the days before everybody had mobile phones and so many supporters had to rely on the few with radios. We put this game beyond doubt in the 92 minute when Bruce Rioch ran onto a Neil Robinson through ball to shoot past Siddall and not long after the whistle blew for full time.

The Sunderland supporters concerns now switched to Highfield Road, but then it was announced over our tannoy system that it was 2–1 to Coventry. This is when the Park End started bouncing with Sunderland supporters celebrating that they were staying up, or so they thought!

The score was actually 2–2 and if it stayed like that it would keep Coventry and Bristol City in Division One. Immediately officials at Highfield Road announced that we had beaten Sunderland 2–0 and then it appeared on the scoreboard. There were 11 minutes remaining and neither team attacked each other as they played out a tame 2–2 draw, a result that relegated Sunderland. They complained to the authorities about the tactics that were used for the last 11 minutes by Coventry and Bristol City, but nothing came of it.

It was a deserved win for us, but as Jimmy Greaves used to say: "It's a funny old game."

24 MAY 1977.
EVERTON V NEWCASTLE UNITED

This was an entertaining last game of the season at Goodison and it was good to finish off with a home win. Gordon Lee put out a young back five with Drew Brand, Neil Robinson and Mark Higgins included in the starting line-up. We wanted to win this one, having lost at St James Park earlier in the season which was a disappointing result.

We got an early boost by taking the lead after only four minutes through Martin Dobson. Duncan McKenzie went past a couple of defenders and crossed for Dobbo to finish in style.

It got even better two minutes later when Latch pressurised Nulty on the ball and laid it on for Duncan to score.

This was a really good start, but Newcastle had their moments. Tommy Craig showed his passing ability and then Alan Kennedy shot wide. What was the name of the next club he played for? Alan Gowling was another that started to cause a few problems.

Bruce Rioch took one of his trademark free-kicks and nearly made it three when he smashed a shot against the crossbar and we were unlucky with another free-kick.

Newcastle had a couple more efforts on target but Drew

Brand wasn't troubled and it ended 2–0.

1976/77 had proved an eventful season in which we finished ninth in the League, reached the League Cup final and also the FA Cup semi-final. I would like to thank the fans who followed us the length and breadth of the country to give their support. It was greatly appreciated.

FA CUP RUN BECOMES FOLKLORE FOR ALL THE WRONG REASONS

OF course, 1976/77 wasn't just famous for our League cup run to Wembley. We also had an amazing campaign in the FA Cup that ended in arguably the most controversial semi-final of all time, but more of that later.

All you want when the draw for the FA Cup third round is made is to get a home tie against decent opposition. We got that when we drew Stoke City at Goodison Park at the start of our 1977 FA Cup run:

8 JANUARY 1977. FA CUP 3RD ROUND.
EVERTON V STOKE CITY

It was a damp January day and the pitch not in the best of condition with a number of areas of sand all over it. Stoke City had a good experienced side that included goalkeeper Peter Shilton, so it wouldn't be easy and they would make it difficult for us to progress to the next round.

They were very competitive so we needed a bit of creativity to open up their defence. Step up Andy King. He was coming away from the Stoke goal when the ball broke to him on the edge of the area and he flicked it perfectly into Mick Lyons' path where it bounced once before Lyonsy volleyed it into the back of the net, giving Shilton no chance from 12 yards.

Only for the Stoke goalkeeper, this game could have ended up six or seven nil. He made fantastic saves from Kingy, Latch and Bruce in the first half alone. Shilton was brilliant and voted man of the match. Our second goal came from the penalty spot after Neil Robinson was brought down, Duncan McKenzie scoring. Duncan played really well in this game with his full repertoire of skills on display and for him not to get Man of the Match shows you how good Shilton was.

29 JANUARY 1977. FA CUP 4TH ROUND.
SWINDON TOWN V EVERTON

They are never easy games to play in when you are drawn against lower league opposition in the FA Cup at their own ground. It was a full house with a very vociferous crowd and it was their chance to cause a shock in the FA Cup.

Nobody at the club wants to be associated with a poor result, but the paramount thing is not the performance, but remaining in the draw for the next round. It was win or draw, but just don't lose!

Steve Burtenshaw was still caretaker manager for this game. After arriving at the ground and then going to the dressing room, we went out to inspect the pitch like we always did. We knew it would be heavy from the rain, but what I saw really surprised me. The groundsmen had put tons of sand on the pitch. They should have told us to bring our buckets and spades.

We would all have to go about it in the right manner and be professional to get the job done. The commitment was there from both teams and with the game played mostly in midfield, there were few chances. Then, in the 24th minute, a clearance found Terry Darracott who lobbed the ball back over the heads of the Swindon centre backs. Duncan McKenzie tried to lift the ball over keeper Allan, but at the second attempt he scored.

The tackles where getting a bit tasty now and the referee booked Swindon's Aizlewood, while we had McNaught and Jones cautioned. Another free-kick was given after 29 minutes just ten yards outside our penalty area and the ball was tapped to McHale whose shot was deflected. It looked as if it was going out for a goal kick, but Syrett reacted quicker than Dave Lawson and the ball trickled inside the post to make it 1–1 at half time.

We came out for the second half and created a couple of chances that Allan did well to save. Kingy took a short corner to me and I crossed for Lyonsy to flick a ball to Latch who put it away from four yards. It was a good start to the half for us, but we knew Swindon would come back at us.

From one of their attacks they played the ball in from the left and Lyonsy got his head to it to clear 30 yards out, but Kenny Stroud – who had been in the same England Schoolboys team as me – ran onto it and smashed an unstoppable shot in off the far post. It was voted one of the goals of the season.

It finished 2–2, an exciting cup tie for the neutral, but now we had to come good in the replay back at Goodison on the Tuesday.

1 FEBRUARY 1977. 4TH ROUND REPLAY. EVERTON V SWINDON TOWN

Gordon Lee was unveiled as the new Everton boss before this FA Cup replay against Swindon, joining us from Newcastle United.

It was a very cold night February evening with the manager suited up which wasn't practical for this weather. He soon had to borrow Martin Dobson's sheepskin coat to save him from getting hypothermia.

Newcastle United, Gordon's previous club, had lost at home 3–1 in the FA Cup on the Saturday against Manchester City.

If we lost tonight, our new boss would have the unhappy

distinction of being the first manager to be knocked out of the FA Cup twice in the same tournament within four days of each tie. He didn't want to have that record and the players certainly wanted to win this tie, with Cardiff at Ninian Park waiting for the winners in the fifth round.

The atmosphere was tremendous and we went at Swindon from the start, trying everything to score with some good football. They defended as a team, rode their luck at times and the keeper played well in a goalless first half.

It was similar in the second period with our constant pressure on the Swindon goal, but we couldn't break the deadlock. With 12 minutes remaining they took the lead with their first real chance against the run of play. A cross from Moss was headed by McLaughlin to Anderson who thumped it on the turn into the net.

It was a blow and we had to score quickly. It was the 83rd minute Ken McNaught placed a free-kick into the area that caused panic in their defence. When they failed to clear, Dobbo pounced in the six yard box to equalise and this goal sparked a mini pitch invasion.

We were still putting the pressure on the Swindon goal as we looked for the second, but couldn't find a way through as their players got behind the ball.

With just a minute to go in normal time and with extra time looming, Dave Jones picked the ball up in our half, went past a couple of players and just kept on running. Swindon were backing off towards their penalty area and as the defence opened up, Jonesy didn't need an invitation to go into the penalty area and beat goalkeeper Allan with a cool finish.

Goodison erupted again, this time signalling a massive pitch invasion. The supporters had played their part on the night and they were tremendous.

Jonesy said: "I thought the Gwladys Street End was going to take me home."

It had been an exciting cup tie to watch with all 38,063 fans, excluding the Swindon supporters, very happy with the result. Next stop Cardiff City.

26 FEBRUARY 1977. FA CUP 5TH ROUND. CARDIFF CITY V EVERTON

We knew before the fourth round replay against Swindon at Goodison Park that the winners would play Cardiff at Ninian Park and it would be a tough game. It was always like a Wales v England international, playing for your country with not an inch to be given. It was a sell-out and a passionate Cardiff crowd were on a high after their side beat Tottenham 1–0 at home in the third round.

It was a heavy muddy pitch yet again for us to play on, but a great atmosphere was created by both sets of supporters. They had dangerous players up front in Grapes, Sayer, and especially Tony Evans who was quick to take players on, was direct and a good finisher.

At the back they had goalkeeper Healey and Dwyer and the latter would play over 500 games for Cardiff. Dwyer was a legend at the club and went by the nickname 'Joe'.

Dwyer was built like a prop forward. He had played

against me before, but as a centre-half when I played for England Schoolboys against Wales Schoolboys. I was on the winning team that day and I hoped it would be the same in this clash.

Cardiff, on the front foot from the first whistle, looked dangerous in attack, creating a couple of chances. After ten minutes they took the lead when a cross from Sayer was met by Evans who volleyed it into the net past Dave Lawson. It was 1–0 at the interval and they had played well in the first half although I went very close to equalising, as did Bryan Hamilton.

There were some tasty tackles going in and I was on the end of some hefty challenges, especially from Dwyer. He must still have had a cob on from when I scored two at Wembley when England Schoolboys beat Wales 3–0.

A ball was played up to me and as I controlled it I thought I was hit by a 12C double decker bus from behind! Oh no, it was Dwyer. I went down and he was spoken to by the referee for the third time, but my back didn't feel too good as I got up. Pejjy, who was standing by me, said: "You ok?" He was a man of few words. "I will have to be mate," I replied and as I walked away, looking like I had just finished a marathon, Pejjy said: "I'll sort him out."

We came out after the break to dominate midfield where we started to get more possession of the ball to create even more chances. In the 51st minute I took a corner and Dobbo headed on for Latch to head past Healey for a deserved equaliser. Game on!

It was still a very competitive clash and suddenly there

was a 50/50 ball between Pejjy and Dwyer. Bang! It was an eight on the Richter scale. Pejjy got up, Dwyer stayed down and it wasn't looking too good for him. He was quickly replaced.

Pejjy walked back to his position and I shouted to him. He looked over and with a straight face I said to him: "I love you!" We both burst out laughing and in the 65th minute we were laughing even more because we went 2–1 ahead.

The ball was headed into their half where centre-back Larmour controlled and tried to play it back to his keeper. He under-hit his pass and Duncan McKenzie immediately took the ball into the penalty area, shaped to go around the keeper, dummied to shoot, but then checked back. By now two other defenders were chasing back with one going to the goal line to protect his net. Goalkeeper Healey was slipping around like a one hour old giraffe, trying to save the shot.

Now Duncan was known for liking the odd cigarette, but he was taking so long to shoot he could have taken a packet of tobacco out of his shorts, rolled a ciggie and lit it up!

He hesitated again to shoot and there were now two defenders and the keeper between Duncan and the goal. As another defender came in to tackle him, he finally hit a left foot shot that wrong footed the defender on the line to score. We could now celebrate our second goal.

Cardiff went for the equaliser and fought until the end, but the team stood firm and we were through to the quarter-finals.

19 MARCH 1977. FA CUP QUARTER-FINAL. EVERTON V DERBY COUNTY

It was a surprise to many Everton supporters when the team was announced that Duncan McKenzie had been dropped by Gordon Lee for Jim Pearson. It was Jim's first game since August and he was determined to take his chance.

It was a bright sunny day with the majority of the 42,409 spectators looking for a Blues win. Charlie George nearly opened the scoring early on for Derby with a shot from 20 yards that Dave Lawson saved at his near post. Kingy had a goal disallowed after 25 minutes for offside and we should have had a penalty for handball against Daniel

Our back four were playing well and they hadn't given Kevin Hector, George, Derek Hales or Leighton James any time or space, while Colin Todd marshalled their defence. A looping header by Kingy and a tremendous shot from Lyonsy couldn't break the deadlock and it was 0–0 at the break.

In the second half we were more positive with Mick Lyons hitting the crossbar with a header. We put even more pressure on Derby and then we scored the first goal which is always important.

In the 57th minute Kingy delivered a left foot pass from midfield to the far post where Lyonsy won a towering header to set up Latch at the near post to score from four yards with his left foot.

In the 79 minute a lovely curled free-kick from the right

side, taken by Terry Darracott, was put into the penalty area where it bounced before Jim Pearson who flung himself at the ball to score with a flying header. It gave Colin Boulton in the Derby goal no chance, making it 2–0.

I nearly made it 3–0 with a shot from 25 yards that went just wide and Roger Kenyon was booked for bringing down James, but no chances for Derby.

It stayed 2–0 and we deservedly went through to the FA Cup semi-final.

BEATEN BY THE REF NOT THE REDS IN A GUT-WRENCHING FA CUP SEMI

23 APRIL 1977. FA CUP SEMI-FINAL.
EVERTON V LIVERPOOL
MAINE ROAD, MANCHESTER.

FOR many, this FA Cup semi-final against our biggest rivals would deliver the most controversial decision in Merseyside 'derby' history with fans still debating to this day "the goal that never was."

It was one of the most contentious decisions ever in an FA Cup game and it was all down to one man, but I will talk about him later!

Ever since the draw had been made it was being talked about both locally and nationally in the papers, on the radio or TV and everyone wanted to be there to see it.

All the players would get an allocation of tickets, but as always this wouldn't be enough for my family and friends.

It was not the best of news in the morning to see that Latch had failed his fitness test on his injured ankle and Andy King also missed out with a sore toe, but it was a good opportunity for Mick Buckley and Duncan McKenzie to come in and impress. Duncan had scored in the 3rd, 4th and 5th rounds of the FA Cup, so we were hoping he would produce the goods again.

The weather in the morning was fine, but one hour before kick-off there was a downpour and because the pitch was so hard the water couldn't drain away. This left large puddles and standing water in both goalmouths which made for a greasy surface all over the playing surface. The groundsmen were still pitch forking right up to the kick off.

The ground was packed and it doubled the previous Maine Road receipts record by paying a total of £140,000.

As both teams walked out of the tunnel there was a crescendo of noise that hit us from the 52,500 crowd that was present with banners and scarves everywhere.

We started on the front foot, pushing forward to force two quick corners. I took the first and when Clemence failed to clear, Dobbo tried an overhead kick that went over the crossbar. From the second corner a Duncan McKenzie header brought a good reflex save from Clemence on the goal line.

Then after ten minutes, Liverpool took the lead with their first real attack. Keegan, out on the left, cut inside and played the ball to McDermott 25 yards out who was central to goal. Mick Buckley tried to block the shot, but McDermott checked and moved the ball to his left before beating Dave Lawson with a low left foot chip.

I know goalkeepers have to narrow the angles when players are about to shoot, but Bambie will question his positioning on this occasion. He was ten yards off his line. A couple of paces back and it would have been an easy save for him, but it was a poor goal for us to give away.

We had displayed tremendous character and team spirit throughout the season when we went a goal down and now we would have to show it again.

Jim Pearson put Emlyn Hughes under pressure on the right near the corner when the defender slipped and then Jim crossed for Dobbo to shoot as he was tackled by Jimmy Case. It went to Duncan whose first touch set him up to beat Clemence with a slight deflection off Neal to make it 1–1.

We were back in the game and playing well. The desire and attitude from both teams couldn't be questioned with players committed and tackles going in all over the pitch. Tommy Smith received a yellow card for fouling me and Mick Buckley got one for fouling Smithy and the score stayed level at half time.

With 17 minutes left, Liverpool replaced Fairclough with Dave Johnson and they scored immediately. A free kick taken by Kennedy was floated in from the left. Dave Lawson came out to catch it, but under a challenge from Keegan he punched the ball up in the air and from 14 yards Case headed the ball over him into the back of the net.

Dave Lawson chased after Thomas the referee claiming a free-kick for a foul by Keegan, but the goal stood. It was a poor punch and another disappointing goal to concede and we would have to come from behind again.

They were on a high now with Dave Lawson making a good save from Johnson, but there was still time left for us to equalise.

We made a substitution with eight minutes left bringing on Bryan Hamilton for Martin Dobson. A long kick up field by Dave Lawson found Duncan who won a good header against Smith. Some good link up play with Jim Pearson sent him wide right to cross to the far post for Bruce Rioch to side foot home, a well worked goal to make it 2–2 in the 83 minute.

Now we were on a high and almost straight from the kick-off we won the ball back. Mick Buckley played it to me on the left wing and I ran at Tommy Smith, went past him and crossed for Duncan to help it on and for Hammy to score off his hip.

Clemence was on his line with McDermott and Jones clearly playing Hammy onside. His arms went up in the air because he had to adjust his body for the flight of the ball, so no chance of hand ball. A perfectly good goal was not given and it should have been 3–2 in our favour, a massive disappointment for players and supporters alike.

The linesman ran back to the halfway line, having seen nothing wrong with the goal. John Motson said in commentary: "What a thrilling semi-final it was."

But for us it was all about what might have been because of the man with the whistle!

THE INNERMOST THOUGHTS OF MY SHOCKED TEAM MATES...

I have discussed the goal for many years with my Everton team mates who played on that day and it is clear they were absolutely stunned and shocked by the Clive Thomas decision:

BRYAN HAMILTON

It was a really good semi-final with two very good sides and Everton were the better team on the day. It was approaching the last moments of the game with the score at 2–2 and heading for a replay when the controversy unfolded.

I remember Ronny going past Tommy Smith and getting into a good crossing position on the left hand side after a good attacking run. I made my way into the box and Ronny's centre was deflected by Duncan McKenzie as it came into the penalty area. This changed the flight path of the ball. I had to adjust my body shape and make the decision on which part of my body should make contact with the ball.

It came off my hip and flew into the bottom left hand

corner of the net. I thought this was the goal that would take Everton to their second Wembley final of the season.

The faces of the Liverpool players and a glance to the linesman told me that they were all of the same opinion.

The referee came from a distance to award a free-kick to Liverpool. When I asked him why, he said: "For an infringement."

This, of course, covers all the laws. As offside was not an issue I can only believe he gave the decision because he THOUGHT I had guided the ball into the net with some part of my hand or arm.

I CAN ONLY STATE THAT THIS WAS NOT THE CASE!

I know the part I played that day and I honestly believe that Everton should have progressed to the final of the FA Cup.

MIKE PEJIC

It was so disappointing knowing it was a perfectly good goal. I chased after Thomas to ask him why he had disallowed the goal and he said it was for offside, only to change his mind later saying that it was for handball.

I went into the dressing room fuming and my first reaction was to kick the door leading into the toilets. How I never broke my toe I will never know.

Thomas came into our dressing room later on and that, for me, was a guilty conscience.

BRUCE RIOCH

One of the biggest games in my time at Everton Football Club was the 1977 FA Cup semi-final at Maine Road against our near neighbours and rivals Liverpool. Both teams entered the match in good form.

Everton had just been to Wembley for the League Cup Final and Liverpool were going well in European competition. We began well and put them under pressure, but McDermott struck with a clever chip over Lawson after ten minutes. Duncan McKenzie brought us level after 34 minutes, only for Jimmy Case to put Liverpool ahead again on 73 minutes. I remember their sub David Johnson missing a sitter to put them 3–1 ahead, but we were a confident team and I tapped in at close range from a McKenzie cross.

We really went for Liverpool after that. Ronny Goodlass ghosted past Tommy Smith on our left and crossed for Duncan to flick on and the ball went into the net off Bryan Hamilton's hip with just six minutes left. It was elation – sheer elation – for us, and then instant deflation.

There had been horror on the faces of the Liverpool players, but no complaints and not one appeal from any of their lads. It was a goal, but then NO! The man in black indicated what he called an infringement. We were shouting: "What type? Where? Who was it?"

Clive Thomas didn't say. The decision cost us the game and even today, 41 years on, it was still a goal.

Only one person thought it wasn't.

BRUCE'S MEMORIES OF RONNY GOODLASS:

He was a jolly, happy mickey taking Scouser, good fun in the dressing room and good for the team. On the pitch Ronny, being a left footer, gave us good balance on the left wing. He worked hard up and down the pitch but was at his best in any 1 v 1 situation around the opposition's 18 yard box. This is the area you would want him to be in as often as possible. I'm trying to remember his goals, but I can't. Sorry Ronny. Lol!

I'm not arguing with my old teammate Bruce. This fella knows what he is talking about. He signed the world class Dennis Bergkamp on June 20th 1995!

DUNCAN MCKENZIE

Everyone knew it was a goal except for Clive Thomas. He said it was "offside" but then kept changing his mind. We played well and came back twice after going behind 1–0 and then 2–1. It was difficult conditions, but we played some good football as crunching tackles came in. Tommy Smith clattered Ronny and got a yellow card then Buck did a thigh high tackle on Smithy. When the 'Anfield Iron' got up growling he said: "Who did that?" Smirking, I said: "Me." He looked at me shouting: "Fuck Off!"

In the tunnel at the end of the game, John Toshack who was out injured asked Thomas:

"What did you see that no one else did?"

Thomas replied: "An incident occurred."

Toshack replied: "Where? In your head?"

That says it all.

KEN McNAUGHT

It was a great game with the players giving everything and a match we should have won. I was on the halfway line when Ronny got the ball and crossed for Hammy to score. As we were celebrating I looked over at the linesman who had kept his flag down and was making his way down the touchline.

Phil Neal took a quick free-kick to get on with the game as soon as possible, knowing there was nothing wrong with the goal.

I asked Clive Thomas after the game why he had disallowed the goal and he said: "For offside but it was handball anyway."

He was wrong on both counts.

AND BACK TO ME...

27 APRIL 1977. FA CUP SEMI-FINAL REPLAY. EVERTON V LIVERPOOL MAINE ROAD MANCHESTER.

It was four days since we put in a tremendous performance in the first semi-final when we gave it our all, but it was so disappointing not to have won the game on the day due to an awful decision made by the referee. We would have been the first club to reach two Wembley finals in a season, but now we had to try and do it all over again.

There was naturally a lot of interest in the game again and the authorities squeezed another 79 spectators in to make the attendance 52,579.

It was a cagey start by both teams which you could expect after the energy sapping game played on Saturday. There was nothing between the two teams, both showing commitment, passion and desire, but controversy would raise its ugly head again in the shape of Clive Thomas.

Keegan headed the ball into the penalty area and Pejjy challenged Dave Johnson for it. Johno backed into him making the slightest of touches, only for Thomas to give a penalty.

Pejjy, Lyonsy and Ken McNaught naturally felt aggrieved and remonstrated with him, but he fronted them as if it was 11.30pm in the Wine Lodge with the threat of yellow cards all around.

By this time Dave Lawson was between the lads and the referee and ushered them away as Neal made no mistake from the spot. This was another crushing blow, but we had to go again.

I played the ball up to Jim Pearson and he put Dobbo in who went around Clemence to score, but was given offside so Liverpool led 1–0 at the interval

On the hour we had our best chance from my corner when Duncan brought a good save from Clemence.

There was always a chance to get an equaliser if it stayed 1–0 and we kept pushing forward but with three minutes to go they hit us with two goals and our dream was over. Case scored from the edge of the area and Kennedy scored at the second attempt to make it 3–0.

IN MY VIEW

Liverpool were a good side and won the European Cup a month later in Rome, but we were also playing well. We had played in the League Cup final and wanted to build on that. We had an FA Cup final appearance snatched away from us by a referee with an ego bigger than Mark Clattenberg and Graham Poll put together!

Hammy scored a perfectly good goal that was not offside or handball. The ball went in off his hip and everyone knows that – even the Liverpudlians.

From the position Clive Thomas was standing, he didn't have a good view for the so-called handball. It was impossible for him to have a clear view and be 100% to give that decision. Being Thomas, he surmised or guessed that it was handball, but only after he changed his mind that it wasn't offside!

Thomas blew for two fouls in the Liverpool penalty area for us and they were only penalised with indirect free-kicks and Clemence pole-axed Lyonsy in the penalty area and was given nothing.

We felt cheated. We were cheated! That day will forever remain one of the most controversial in FA Cup history.

DAVE JONES – A FINAL WORD

I loved the day to day training when I got to work with the likes of you Ronny, Ken McNaught and Mick Buckley who were then classed as the young up and coming stars of Everton FC.

You were already an established reserve team player, but you always had a word with the younger lads to ensure they kept going and believed in themselves.

There are so many good times I had, Ronny, at Everton with that group of players. We were so privileged to be part of a bunch that all came through the Everton youth policy over a short period of time and that was probably the reason we had so much fun.

My wife Ann remembers you and your wife Denise coming to Hong Kong and meeting us in the hotel with your kids as you joined South China FC.

There are so many memories of our time together at Everton. Those were the best days of my playing career. Being a Scouser and playing for the team you supported, I can't think of any greater feeling to have.

Just think Ronny, two Scouse kids fulfilling their dream. What more could we have asked for?

CHALLENGED TO A GAME BY THE JAMES LAST ORCHESTRA!

AFTER our last game the club always took us on a week's break and in the summer of 1977 we went to Marbella where it was good for the squad to unwind, relax, eat nice food and get some sun on our backs.

We met up early in the morning at Bellefield to get the coach to the airport with the banter going on even before we got on the coach. I boarded and, as usual, made my way to the tables at the back with the likes of Kingy, Lyonsy, and Dave Jones.

I remember we had a great bond in the team. We were sitting at the table when Gordon Lee walked down the coach saying: "Good morning," to the staff and the lads as he strolled down the aisle. He got a few yards from our table and said: "Well, F Troop is here!"

That's what he called seven of us because we were such a close knit bunch of lads that all got on well together with laughs and practical jokes never far away.

It was a good flight, we had a few drinks on board and it seemed that in no time we were at the hotel. We went into reception to check-in and get our keys, then Gordon wanted to say a few words. He said: "I will see you here in the reception in a week's time, behave yourselves and don't get arrested. Enjoy yourselves."

Within a few seconds you heard loud bangs as everyone was dropping their bags on the reception floor and heading to the bar which was 20 yards to our left. The barman didn't know what had hit him and bang went his siesta.

The session went on all afternoon before we went to our rooms to get showered and changed for a bite to eat in the restaurant. Then it was a reconnaissance mission into town to see where the best places were to go and sample the local wines, for cultural purposes only of course. It was an enjoyable first day.

The next morning the lads started to come down from their rooms in dribs and drabs for their 'brekkie' and a few were not looking too good. Some even had hangovers… no, everyone had hangovers!

After a nice breakfast with lots of coffee we wandered

outside into the lovely gardens with the pool not too far away and relaxed on the sun lounges to chill. Then, from around the corner and moving very fast, came Lyonsy with a big smile on his face. He announced: "I've sorted out the Head Tennis and a bit further over is the five-a-side pitch." In unison we all shouted: "Mick, fuck off!"

A couple of days later we were having lunch when about 30 people walked into the restaurant and I recognised the man in the front of the group. He was tall, long haired and had a Van Dyke beard. I thought it was one of the Three Musketeers, but instead it was James Last with his orchestra, a very big act at the time and I don't mean because of the orchestra!

I started chatting to him and he was telling me that they were on a world tour. He asked us if we would come to see one of his shows when we could make it. He then he invited us to dinner with his party which we accepted.

When we arrived there were two large banqueting tables that seemed to go on forever. We sat down and the food was served and the drinks started to flow. As the night wore on everyone was enjoying themselves. Then I started singing a few Beatles songs and everyone joined in. Other songs were sung and someone then started to play a guitar, then a trombone, a trumpet, a sax, and in next to no time I thought I was in New Orleans.

Then, with lots of drink still being consumed, they challenged us to a match the next day. We just started laughing, but they were serious. The time for kick-off and where to play was quickly arranged and we went off to get only a few hours kip.

Next morning we dragged ourselves out of our beds and traipsed down to the pitch with dry mouths and very sore heads, only to see it was deserted. We waited ten minutes but no show. It was understandable. Arguably, we had won the previous night's drinking session and now the game… 2–0 to the TOFFEES!

Gordon Lee's time at Everton between 1977 and 1981 was mixed. He arrived as a so-called troubleshooter, having been a go-to boss for clubs in trouble. He had spent 11 years at Aston Villa as a defender; became player-coach at Shrewsbury Town; took Port Vale up to the Third Division in his first managerial challenge as a manager; won promotion to the old Second Division for Blackburn Rovers in 1974/75, and took Newcastle United to the League Cup Final and into Europe.

Not surprisingly, he came to us when we were in a difficult position in the League, although we had reached the semi-final of the League Cup and were making progress in the FA Cup in which we would ultimately reach the semis. Everton only lost two of their remaining 18 League games in the 1976/77 campaign to ease any possible thoughts of relegation.

However, I will leave you to make up your mind with some legendary stories about him, in no particular order

One: Gordon and Steve Burtenshaw, our first team coach, were going up to Newcastle to watch a game and they were meeting at Bellefield. Gordon arrived and got out of his car in his suit with his slippers on then Steve said to him: "What a good idea to drive to Newcastle in comfort with your slippers on." The manager replied: "Oh fuck, I've forgot my shoes."

Two: We stayed a few days in Llandudno for a training break by the sea with its famous pier, promenade and beach. The lads where having something to eat in the dining room when Gordon walked in and pointed to one of the player's plates.

"What is that?" he asked.

"Welsh Rarebit," came the reply.

Gordon pulled a face and said: "It looks like cheese on toast to me!"

Three: Gordon thought he knew every player that had played football in England, but especially in the lower leagues. He thought he was a mine of information. We sometimes used to have a pre-match meal at the Daresbury Park Hotel and on this occasion we were walking into the dining room.

Jim McGregor, our physio, was with Gordon when Jim saw the sign over the door, the Lewis Carroll Suite, a tribute to the legendary 'Alice in Wonderland' author.

Jim said: "Of course, Lewis Carroll."

Gordon replied: "Urgh, don't tell me, Halifax Town."

Four: Jim McGregor was sitting next to Gordon on the coach going down to Ipswich Town. Jim said: "Do you know, Gordon, that Bobby Robson has just signed Arnold Muhren from Twente Enschede?" (The word is pronounced Enshcarday). Gordon replied: "Oh, Bobby has just signed a young lad who was twenty yesterday?"

Five: In team meetings, Gordon was always thorough when it came to assessing teams or individual players of the opposition which is good. He would go through the opposing team's strengths and weaknesses, what tactics we were going to play against them what set pieces he had planned, for and against.

The only thing was, it went on a bit too long at times and when he was running out of words on a certain player, the teams 'tactics or defence/attack or any subject, he would finish with the words – De Dah De Dah De Dah. When he started repeating that word we all knew there wasn't long for the meeting to go on!!

BOB PAISLEY RECOMMENDS ME TO DUTCH COACH AND I'M OFF

AFTER the 1977 summer break it was time to get myself ready for the start of the new campaign that was now five weeks away. I knew I had to be prepared for that lovely pre-season training on Southport beach.

At the end of any season the club publish the retained list and also reveal the names of the players they are making available for transfer. These included Dai Davies, Bryan Hamilton, Dave Smallman while Mick Buckley and Jim Pearson had put in transfer requests.

Any new manager looks at his present squad and then assesses it to see where he thinks improvements can be made, sometimes in all departments of the team. It is a game of opinions and the manager always has his own thoughts!

There were rumours in the newspapers and on the radio about the club signing Peter Shilton, with Mick Lyons, Martin Dobson or Duncan McKenzie included as part of any deal. It is no secret that Duncan wasn't one of Gordon Lee's favourite players so this was more feasible than the first two.

Aston Villa had made a £200,000 bid for Ken Mc-Naught. I chatted with Ken who told me he didn't want to leave and that it was a surprise to him that Everton had let Villa talk to him about a move.

He had been at the club for six years and we came through the Everton youth system together.

He asked Villa for four weeks to think about the transfer and wanted to talk it over with his dad Willie who was an ex-Scottish international. There were no agents in those days.

After a couple of weeks of pre-season training I was called into the office by Gordon Lee to say QPR had been asking about both me and Lyonsy and wanted to know my thoughts. He told me to go away and think about it, but he said he didn't want me to leave the club. I had only just signed a new two year contract in the summer.

I went downstairs to see Lyonsy and get his thoughts about the situation. We said we would adjourn to our office which on this occasion was the Jolly Miller pub on Queens Drive to discuss it with Roger Kenyon and Mick Bernard in tow!

We chatted about the pluses and minuses of a move, but the previous season the team had done well and we wanted to help the club do even better in the coming campaign. Neither of us wanted to move and that was it. I was looking forward to doing my best for Everton, but you don't know what's around the corner for any of the players and that included me.

We went on an 11 day tour to Germany and Holland for pre-season training plus games and then travelled to Morocco to play in a four team tournament. After a few days we were relaxing in the lounge when Ken McNaught came in and said he was moving to Aston Villa. He wasn't doing cartwheels about the move, but he was philosophical about the challenge ahead with a new club. He had agreed terms with Villa and the transfer fee would be £200,000.

I thought it was the wrong move by the club to let him go and believed they should have put him on a long term contract after the season he had enjoyed. Ken was a great mate and still is, but he could have been the captain of our club for many years to come.

He went on to win the European Cup in 1981 with Villa when they beat Bayern Munich 1–0 and scored the winning goal against Barcelona in the Super Cup Final, another 1–0 triumph.

Mick Bernard left for Oldham while Bryan Hamilton

moved to Millwall.

There was a lot of speculation about the interest Gordon Lee had in signing David Harvey from Leeds United, as well as Mickey Walsh and George Wood from Blackpool. Two signings that were concluded before the season started saw winger Dave Thomas and goalkeeper George Wood joining us.

They were two good additions to the team/squad and I particularly asked Gordon Lee about the signing of Dave in my position. I clearly wanted to know where I stood in this decision. He indicated that he could play with two wingers, but said it also strengthened the selections he could make and that was fair enough.

I thought that playing with two wingers would create more chances and take us back to the successful Johnny Morrissey and Jimmy Husband style, not that I'm comparing myself to either.

The first game was at home to newly promoted Nottingham Forest who played attacking football and had a manager who was building up quite a reputation for himself. His name was Brian Clough.

His Forest team had taken the Championship by storm and we knew this would be a real test for us as Wood and Thomas made their debuts with me as substitute.

There wasn't much between the two teams in the first 20 minutes, but Forest then started to take control and after 31 minutes they went into the lead with a Peter Withe header from a near post corner. Worse was to follow eight minutes later when a Mark Higgins headed clearance found John Robertson whose shot flew in off the far post to make it 2–0

Just before half time we got back in the game when Lyonsy headed a ball down for Jim Pearson to hit a good shot to make it 2–1. After an hour I came on for Terry Darracott as we went for an equaliser and ironically I laid on a very good chance for Thomas to equalise, but he put it over the bar from eight yards and shortly after Forest scored their third goal. John Robertson crossed for Martin O'Neill to score in the 77th minute and we lost the game 3–1.

Over the next few years Forest and Brian Clough would make names for themselves in the football world, but this was a disappointing day for us and not the start to the season we wanted.

However, there was no time to dwell on the result because we were playing Arsenal at Highbury on the Wednesday. I was included in a 13-man squad, but would I be selected to play for the team?

Bob Latchford returned after missing the Forest game. I wasn't selected and Higgy was made substitute although a defender as sub away from home was the norm.

It wasn't the best of games with not much created and only for the performance from George Wood it could have been an even heavier defeat, so it was now two games played and two defeats. Some of the players suggested the manager should have played me at Highbury and it goes without saying that I thought the same!

I had made my mind up that I would see Gordon Lee

for clear the air talks and to clarify my situation. As we say locally, I had a cob on. After training I went up to his office and we started chatting. That's when the phone rang and Gordon answered it, speaking for a few minutes before he said: "Who told you that? He is not for sale."

He took the phone from his ear and said to me: "It's someone who wants to talk to you." I took the receiver off him and asked who it was. He said his name was Hans Dorjee, manager of NAC Breda in Holland and that he was looking to sign a left winger for his team. He had been at Liverpool's nearby Melwood training ground and had discussed it with Bob Paisley who had recommended me to him.

Hans asked if I would come over for a week to train and have a look around see what I thought about the town and the club and take it from there. I didn't know anything about NAC the team, but I said: "Why not?"

Over the next week arrangements would be made for me and my future wife Denise to go over there for a week and they said they would send a private plane to take us to Breda which suggested they were very keen to sign me.

Off we went to meet up with two representatives from NAC Breda at Speke Airport, now called John Lennon Airport, of course. We headed for reception where they were waiting and were quickly whisked to where the plane was parked.

We were chatting as we passed a large Boeing passenger jet, and other planes taxiing along the runway as we kept on walking. Then a few 28-seater jets loomed and I kept glancing at the two gentlemen as if to say: "Is this it?" Then a Learjet was 30 yards in front of us and I said to Denise "this is it," but we carried on walking. The planes were getting smaller and smaller until we got to the end of the row. Parked there in front of us was a Cessna four seater which, by the look of it, you could have started it with a large elastic band.

With Denise not having flown before I thought this would put her off for life. What an interesting trip this was going to be. We both climbed into the plane where Denise was both excited and apprehensive, but she was looking out of the window as we flew over the River Mersey on a lovely sunny day. We were about 30 minutes into the flight when we flew over Coventry City's Highfield Road ground. It was looking good in the sunshine when the co-pilot turned to say we would be landing at Luton Airport to get flight clearance to carry on our journey to Holland.

It was not a long delay at Luton before we headed out over the North Sea with a great view of all the shipping and the water below. As we approached the coastline it looked misty and then the weather changed dramatically. It started to rain heavily and then turned into a thunder-storm. The plane was shaking and moving from side to side and you couldn't see anything at all because it was raining so hard. This carried on for about 15 to 20 min-utes with the pilot and co-pilot talking and occasionally turning to give us a little smile.

This was going on a bit too long for my liking so I tapped the co-pilot on his shoulder and asked him if everything was ok. He turned, smiled and said: "No problem, but we can't find the airfield."

Denise and I just looked at each other and thought: "How is this going to end?"

After another five minutes we were flying low and we could see the tops of some trees and then we saw the airfield. This is when the co-pilot turned and said: "Found it."

We looked at one another, grateful we had arrived safely. After landing we could see reporters, photographers and a camera crew waiting by the building. The rain had stopped, they opened the door of the plane and there to greet us was Hans Dorjee, the manager of NAC. We went into the building and Hans asked us what we would like to drink. Being the professional that I am I had a coffee but fancied a brandy! Denise had a lager.

I was interviewed by the waiting press reporters and a local radio and camera crew and was then taken to the NAC Chairman's house where we would be staying for the week. We received a warm welcome from the Chairman and his family they were very hospitable. They also told us they had a prior engagement and would be leaving for a few days, but to make ourselves at home.

I went into training the next day to meet the players, train and then meet the board. It went well and during the subsequent board meeting they said they were playing MSV Duisburg from the Bundesliga in a couple of days and would I play in the game. I should have said no in case I got injured, but I thought facing a good German team was good experience for me and an opportunity to play for NAC and assess how it went.

I played in the game and enjoyed it, experiencing the continental style football of both teams. The NAC crowd seemed appreciative that I laid on two goals and we won 3–2 so, all in all, it was a good night.

In the players' lounge and the boardroom after the game the supporters were asking when I would be signing for NAC. I told them I was thinking it over and no discussions had taken place yet. I spoke to the local newspaper reporter who said I played well with supporters keen for me to sign.

We were off the next day so we made our way back to the house to have an early night so we could look around Breda in the morning and have a meeting with the manager, secretary and financial director.

Arriving back at the house we went to have a night cap. They said they had a games room downstairs so we went to have a look, have a quick drink and then go to bed!

The games room was a fair size with a large bar which I went behind to get a few drinks. We settled for two bottles of cool Grolsch with their distinctive flip tops. I put the music system on and we sat on the bar stools, played some darts and chilled. After playing in the game I had to hydrate myself, that's my excuse anyway, so we had another Grolsch, then another and then another. You know how it is? I turned the music up and put the lighting system on. This made it look like we were in the Continental or Chequers nightclubs in Liverpool.

The Grolsch took some stick and it was late, but a nice way to finish off a good day. It was then early to rise and breakfast before Denise suggested we take the Chairman's dog for a walk in the woods. It was a lovely well groomed Afghan hound. I attached its lead and off we went on a sunny day. As you know, they are large dogs and everything was fine, but no sooner had I handed over the lead to Denise than the dog spotted a rabbit and nearly dragged her through the hedges.

She had to let go of the lead and this is when the dog darted through the hedge and was in the field after the rabbit. I was calling out its name and walking around the footpaths in the fields, but it was nowhere to be seen. Thirty minutes had gone by and we were getting a bit worried about finding the dog. This wouldn't look good when the Chairman came back to his house and I had to tell him that I'd lost his beloved dog.

It then came out of the field with Denise shouting "get hold of him." It had gone from looking like a Crufts Champion to a bedraggled mutt. We were still relieved we had found him and went back to the house to give him a wash and brush.

I met up with NAC officials to discuss my situation at Everton and the possibility of signing, but I also wanted to talk to Gordon Lee because it was going to be a massive and heart breaking decision for me to leave Everton.

I made sure I flew back on a commercial airline and the next day the discussions continued at Goodison between both clubs to decide what the transfer figure would be. I talked to Gordon Lee who said he didn't want me to leave, but the fact that he had decided a fee and let them talk to me was a big question mark.

The fee was £100,000 and I then talked to NAC about my salary, deciding to sign a short 20 month contract, just in case it never worked out in Holland.

A pre-season game against Everton was arranged to be played in the August as part of the deal. It was the start of a new adventure for me, but it didn't make it any easier to leave the club I have loved all my life.

Obviously Denise knew what was happening. We would be getting married in the December, but I had to go home now and tell the rest of the family, including Dad, our John, and my granddad.

I told them I was leaving and they were all visibly upset. My nan walked out into the kitchen and then burst out crying. I had never seen her like this before and that hurt me more than anything. However, it was not long now to prepare for the move because NAC wanted me to play on the Saturday.

We had little time to pack a few cases, but I made sure my boots were a priority. NAC quickly arranged a flight and it was goodbye for now to family and friends.

My debut would be against Go Ahead Eagles in Deventer and I didn't know who or where that was in Holland. Coming from Liverpool, I don't think you could have written the script with the name of their team for my debut: 'Go 'ed Eagles!'

I would be staying in the Hotel De Clock in the Grote

Market in Breda which was in the town centre and it was a family owned business. When I arrived they were all there to greet me and from the first minute they made me feel welcome. They couldn't do enough for me and it was as if I was one of the family.

They were all NAC supporters so took a real interest in the team like most people do in Breda. We played on the Sunday with the manager/players saying it was a difficult place to get a result. I had only played the one game with my team mates against MSV Duisburg so would have to get to know them quickly because this was my formal debut.

Go Ahead Eagles started putting us under pressure from the kick-off so we had to defend well. I threw in a couple of slide tackles which had our left-back Tommy Dekker calling me 'Tiger', but we still had a couple of good chances to take the lead.

In the 40th minute our opponents took the lead which was a blow just before half time and we went in 1–0 down. Hans Dorjee had his team talk, but I had to say something. I had a go at Jan de Jong, the keeper, for punching the ball too much instead of catching it to take the pressure off the defenders. I used a lot of expletives, but effectively I was saying: "Let's get into these. We can beat them." They looked at me as if I was an 'off-my-cake' crazy Englishman.

Hans made two substitutions, taking off Brouwers and Mohorovic and bringing on Neeskens (no not that one) and Damen. Almost immediately there was a response from the team and we equalised after 54 minutes through Henk van der Ent. It was much better now with the team playing with more confidence and pushing more players forward and in the 85th minute Henk scored again to make it 2–1 which was the final score.

We had turned a 1–0 deficit into a 2–1 win with a good battling team performance and a winning start for my NAC career. Our next opponents would be Telstar, my home debut if I was selected to play! My Dad, our John, Uncle Ray and two family friends Peter and Colin would be making the trip over to Breda.

The NAC Stadionaan de Beatrixstraat was a ground with a lot of character. The stadium was tree lined and near the River Mark which is an old Dutch word for canal.

I sorted the tickets out for my visitors to watch the game. Nothing has changed there then!

The warm ups for the games were different than in England. We used to stretch in the dressing room and then went out five minutes before kick-off. Here we went out 40 minutes before kick-off, more like modern day football, so that was forward thinking on their behalf.

I received a tremendous reception from the home crowd, welcoming me to NAC which was appreciated.

It was not the start we would have wanted after going a goal behind again, but this time it was in the 19th minute. We created chances in the first half, but didn't take any of them

Hans made a substitution again, taking off Neeskens for Storm who was a centre-forward.

The score stayed the same before the manager made another substitution in the 63rd minute, replacing the previous week's goalscorer van der Ent with Damen and not long after this we equalised in the 65th minute.

We were awarded a free-kick 25 yards out from the Telstar goal with a few NAC players over the ball discussing how they should take it. I wandered over to put my tuppence worth in. I looked at how the wall was set up and realised it was perfect for a left footer.

I said: "I'll take this" and they moved out of the way. I hit it well and scored on my home debut 1–1. Two minutes later, in the 67th minute, we got another free-kick in a very similar position to my goal. I told Addy Brouwers, the striker, to stand by the wall where I would chip the ball over for him to shoot. He gave me that 'err OK' look. Telstar thought I was going to hit it again, but my chip surprised them and Addy peeled off to volley in a goal that made it 2–1. I knew we couldn't keep giving the opposition a goal start every week in the hope that we would fight back. We were ahead again, but with ten minutes left Telstar equalised to make the final score 2–2.

It was not the result we would have liked before the game, but at least we had battled to get back in the game and earn a point.

THE WORLD OF 'TOTAL FOOTBALL' IS VERY MUCH HOME FROM HOME

I HAD arranged to meet my Dad after the game in the players' lounge and by the time I got there they were having a drink. I introduced them to the president of the club, Mr Tim Meeus, who did a lot for NAC. A few players and club officials asked if we would be joining them for a drink later in Le Cordial, a club by the side of the ground. I said: "Does night follow day?"

We went around to the club and standing by the entrance was Thomas the doorman who was a big fella. He was the one you had to impress to get in. I was introduced to him and received a big welcome. Our Ray, who had a grip like a vice, shook the doorman's hand and gave him one of the many Romeo Y Julieta cigars he always carried with him. By the end of the night it was as if they had known each other for 30 years.

Once inside the club it was bouncing with music blasting and everyone dancing or drinking. Then they put the NAC song on which had everyone singing. It was customary for the patrons to hit the lampshades hanging from the bar and soon the lights were flashing everywhere like a Disco!

Frans Bieings, the NAC Chairman, was also the Skol Chairman, being the club's sponsors, and he came over with a large tray of lager for our group. I introduced Frans to my Dad and he joined us for a few drinks before leaving. Dad said to me: "You are going to enjoy it here son."

On the same evening in Le Cordial, Ben Maas – Chairman NAC Supporters Club came over to introduce himself to me and congratulated me on my goal and my assist with the second. He said I had played well and welcomed me to the club on behalf of the NAC supporters.

Ben joined our group that included my Dad, John, Peter and Colin, as we carried on drinking. The supporters chairman began to explain about NAC and the town of Breda.

At closing time Ben asked if we would like to have another drink in town and we all said yes. I had to go and get my bag from behind the bar that contained my boots, towel and toiletries.

In all the years that I played in Holland I always took my football boots home with me after games to clean them. Old habits die hard, but I knew they would be done correctly and be well looked after.

After saying our farewell to the bar staff we went outside with Ben and walked over to his car which was parked by the Mark river across the road where we found ourselves standing by a lovely Pontiac car. I said: "That's nice, Ben, but there are six of us and I also have my bag. We won't be able to fit in your car and the boot looks small."

Ben said: "No problem." He took my bag off me, walked around to the boot of the car and opened it up. He then took the spare wheel out and bounced it down the bank into the river before calmly putting my bag in the boot and saying: "Come on then, get in, we are wasting drinking time."

We all started laughing packed and packed into the Pontiac with not much room. Ben was a real character and a good friend to me over the years.

Our next home game was against FC Amsterdam and I was hoping for a better start in this game because in the first three we had conceded the first goal. Yes, you've guessed it, after five minutes FC Amsterdam scored and it stayed that way until the 60th minute when right-back Ad Krijnen equalised. We then scored two more in the 76th and 77th minute to put us 3–1 up, but four minutes from time they pulled one back to make it 3–2. It was a tense finish, but we won.

In Holland they have what is called a 'Winterstop' when Eredivisie teams, having played 17 games to the halfway stage in the league, stop playing for roughly six weeks.

We played a couple of games in December before we had the break and the first one was against NEC Nijmegan in Breda so we wanted a win to finish the mid-season break strongly. In the NEC line-up was Guus Hiddink, later to manage Chelsea to an FA Cup win and also manage Holland. He was a very good friend of our manager Hans Dorjee, but both wanted to win this game. Guus was a competitive midfield player and a good passer of the ball who would go on to become a very good manager.

In the 16th minute Ad Krijnen was on the scoresheet for the second consecutive home game with Vreijsen adding the second on 75 minutes. There was no time to relax though because NEC scored two minutes later to make it 2–1, but they couldn't get an equaliser.

The away game before the winter break was against ADO Den Haag at Zuiderparkstadion, always a difficult place to go, but it would be good to get back-to-back wins.

Den Haag had a good youth system and two of their players in the team that day, Martin Jol and Romeo Zondervan, would make names for themselves in England. Martin played for WBA and managed Tottenham and Fulham. Romeo had a good career with Ipswich Town and WBA so Den Haag had some quality on show.

Our team played well that day, especially in the first half, and it was great for me to score the first goal after 31 minutes. We were still pushing forward in the second

Liverpool Schoolboys celebrating a 3–0 first-leg win over Swindon.

A great moment for me scoring my second goal at Wembley for England Schoolboys… with my head!

A proud day – my first session as an apprentice at Bellefield with (from l-r) Mick Buckley, Ray Pritchard, Peter Whitwood, Harry Catterick, Stan Osborne and Ian Bacon.

My first pen pic as a professional at Everton.

Traditional Bellefield team photograph 1976/77 standing alongside my mates Buck and Bruce Rioch.

On our way to Wembley! Bath time after the semi-final win at Bolton.

Going past Colin Todd. We were two down at half-time and went on to win 3-2.

1977 fashion icons! Looks like our dapper accountant Bryan Hamilton already had his Wembley suit!

Pre-season photo call at Everton.

Pre-season 1978 photo session at NAC Breda.

The resultant team photo from the session above.

Talking tactics with the manager who signed me for NAC Breda – Hans Dorjee.

Goodlass in familiar pose at NAC Breda.

Scoring on my home debut for NAC Breda against Telstar.

Crosses make goals! Another assist for me at NAC Breda.

Delighted to score the winning goal (with my right foot!) against Feyenoord for NAC Breda leaving 1974 and 1978 World Cup Final legend Wim Jansen and future team-mate Aad Mansveld in my wake.

From the same game above, going close with a long range free-kick.

Scoring for NAC Breda – with my right foot again!

On the wing for ADO Den Haag.

Arriving at Schiphol airport to be met by
ADO Den Haag manager Pete de Visser.

Meeting up with old pal Dick Advocaat,
ex-Sunderland boss at Goodison.

1979/80 ADO Den Haag team photograph.

Laying on another goal for ADO Den Haag.

Keep getting the crosses in Ron!

My goal and an assist for Fulham against Alan Ball's Blackpool who later were relegated to Division 4.

Signing in at Fulham.

Going past the full-back again trying to create another goal!

A future Everton legend can only watch as my 25-yard volley crashes against the Bury post.

Back at Everton under Joe Royle as Youth Coach. It was a pleasure to coach the likes of Michael Ball, Danny Cadamarteri and Richard Dunne.

I was at the 1966 Portugal game at Goodison when the great Eusebio scored 4! It was a thrill to meet him some years later at our home Europa League match versus Benfica.

Presenting Labby with the Health Through Sport Award. He'd expected to be our first Patron but sadly passed away weeks later. The Last of the Corinthians.

It's always good to meet up with friends and Everton greats at Goodison through my work with Radio Merseyside.

Photographed with a great friend (Tony Kay), an idol (Alex Young) and the man who made my dream come true (Billy Bingham).

Along with Joe Royle I present the first Alan Ball 'Ball of Fire' Award to Stephen, the father of Rhys Jones watched by Jimmy Ball, the son of Alan.

Honoured to receive the Everton Pride award from a good friend and team-mate Bob Latchford.

half and striker Cees Storm scored our second goal. They pulled one back in the 74th minute, but we were heading back to Breda with the points and a good win again.

After a couple of good victories and with the winter break now on us, I headed back to England for one of the biggest days of my life... my wedding day was coming up on the 23rd December, exactly two years to the day since I had made my Everton debut, yes, on the 23rd December!

I flew back to England for the wedding. I was only home for a few days so I didn't have a minute to spare. I was married at Brougham Terrace, a hundred yards from where we used to live in Canton Street and two hundred yards from Mill Road Hospital where I was born. Ben and Ria, friends we made in Breda, flew over to attend with family and friends it was a great day, at least what I can remember of it!

On Boxing Day, Everton played Man Utd at Goodison so I couldn't miss that one could I, even though I had only just wed three days earlier?

My manager from NAC, Hans Dorjee, even came to the game. I told him what the Goodison crowd was like and how good the atmosphere was. We sat in the Main Stand and I was going through the Everton team, explaining to him about each player, how good they were and how we were strong defensively. I also said what we were going to do to United.

By the end of the game we had lost 6–2. Lou Macari scored a header which says it all. It wasn't the best result for the supporters or the lads, but always good to visit

Goodison.

I didn't have much time left, but I did train at Bellefield and caught up with what was happening at the club before going back for the second half of the season with NAC. It was like a mini pre-season to get us match fit again after the break with a few friendlies arranged and then our first Eriedivisie game against PSV Eindhoven in the Philips Stadion, Eindhoven.

It was the first time I played there and it was a fabulous state of the art ground with the facilities second to none. The winters are really cold there, but they have heaters in the stands to keep the supporters warm. It does help though when you're owned by Philips!

You want to play against the best and they were the best with their team full of Netherlands internationals. PSV had pace and power with technical ability throughout the team. Willy van der Kuijlen in midfield could pass the ball anywhere he wanted to.

We were playing well and holding our own when Rene van de Kerkoff, who could catch pigeons, scored in the 41st minute which was a real blow just before half-time. It was similar in the second half. We created a few chances, but in the 70th minute Jan Poortvliet scored from a PSV corner. It was an unlucky 2–0 defeat, but still disappointing.

In five months PSV's two goal scorers, Jan Poortvliet and Rene van de Kerkoff, plus his twin brother Willy, would play for the Netherlands against Argentina in the World Cup Final in Buenos Aires, Argentina.

Our first home game after the winter break was against

HFC Haarlem, managed by Welshman Barry Hughes who was a real character and who managed in Holland for a number of years. The next season Ruud Gullit would make his debut for them.

I've mentioned before about NAC giving a goal start to the opposition, but it was in the 45th minute when we went 1–0 down again. Hans Dorjee wasn't a happy manager, taking off Addy Brouwers and Martien Vreijen and bringing on Gerry Damen and Cees Storm.

We were trying everything to equalise but it stayed 1–0 until the 80th minute when I scored with a shot from the edge of the box to put us level. Now we were going for the winner, but shots and headers were being saved or blocked. Finally, in the 86th minute, a good pass was played in to me and I smashed home the winner. Tremendous character was shown again by the team and I was delighted with my double, so not a bad Saturday night.

Our friends in Breda, Ben and Ria invited me and Denise around in the week to their apartment for dinner which was nice of them and we accepted. When we arrived they poured us some drinks and we chatted as Ben and Ria prepared the meal.

Soup was for starters with lovely homemade bread and then more drinks with the evening getting off to a good start. They were preparing the food Witloff (Chickory) which is lovely, red cabbage, salad, and fries with mayonnaise.

The main meal was put in front of us and it looked delicious. Needless to say, nothing was left on our plates and we really enjoyed it. I said to them: "That was one of the nicest steaks I've ever tasted."

Ben and Ria started giggling and when I asked them what they were laughing at, they replied: "You have just eaten horse meat."

Would I be galloping along the wing in my next game?

The top three teams in Dutch football are Ajax, PSV Eindhoven and Feyenoord. They have all won the European Cup and historically they have always dominated the domestic scene in Holland.

Ajax won three consecutive European Cups in 1971, 72, and 73 with world class players like Johan Cruyff. My first game against Ajax was played in Amsterdam at De Meer Stadion.

They prided themselves on bringing players through from their youth academy to progress into the first team and of playing a certain style of football. They had experienced players like Ruud Geels who was Eriedivisie leading goal scorer in 75, 76, 77, 78 and 81 so he knew where the goal was. They also had world class defender Ruud Krol.

We didn't get off to the best of starts and conceded two quick goals after 12 and 19 minutes through Simon Tahamata, but it got even worse when we let a third in.

Mohorovic pulled a goal back for us to make it 3–1 at half time when Hans Dorjee made two substitutions, taking off Vreijsen and Mohorovic and bringing on Damsma and Brouwers. We did better after that, had more possession and created a few more chances but it remained 3–1.

The Dutch have what they call the 'Carnaval' or 'Vastenavond'. The eve of the festival involves a fasting exercise throughout the Netherlands, but mainly in the Southern regions of which Breda is a part.

No Eriedivisie fixtures are played on that weekend with the celebrations going on for six days. Normal daily life changes with the factories, local businesses and many shops closed with nobody cooking, but using the bars, restaurants, and fast food outlets which are all packed.

There are not many taxis for hire during the festival period because lots of drivers are not working and joining in the fun. We wanted to go to Prinsenbeek, a small district that is about 20 minutes outside Breda where my friend had a bar.

Peter said he would take his car, but it wasn't very big. We went outside to get in but there were seven of us and we wouldn't all fit in with our Ray and John being big strong lads (see how I worded that John!). Denise said she would get in the boot, then looked at me thinking: "You will get in with me won't you?" Sorry Denise, I had to show Peter the way. Then, before I could say anything, my Dad said he would travel in the boot and by then some passers-by were looking over and thinking: "What are they doing?

As we drove away all we could hear was hysterical laughter coming from the boot. We finally arrived in Prinsenbeek and when I got out of the car some NAC supporters recognised me. They came over to chat and you can imagine the look on their faces when I opened the boot and Denise popped out, followed by my Dad! One of the NAC supporters said to me: "Are there any more in there?

What a great day we had one to remember for all of us with my Dad being the worst for wear like most of us. I volunteered to go back in the boot of the car.

With the Carnaval on, this is when I really got to know what authentic Dutch food is all about. I would quickly gain an understanding about their eating habits with many selections of food to choose from including:

Frikandel – a long meat sausage in a roll with curry ketchup, mayonnaise or tomato ketchup. You can add on-ions if preferred and it was one of the first things I tasted when I arrived there. I'd certainly recommend this and it is very popular in Holland.

Bitterballen – a Dutch meat-based snack containing chopped up beef or veal. They are the size of meatballs, but are coated in breadcrumbs and egg mixture then deep fried and served with a ramekin of mustard for dipping. These are usually available in pubs and bars, and for me must be washed down with some sort of beverage or two!

Haring (Herring) – the Dutch like to eat it raw and Lex Schoenmaker, a friend of mine and an ex-Feyenoord player, showed me how to eat one the traditional way. You grab the fish by the tail, tip your head back, put the fish in your mouth and bite upwards. You end up looking like a Disney character holding up a fish skeleton. You then eat some gherkins. Not bad for the first time, but an interest-ing way to eat a herring.

Friet (Chips) – thin chips compared to ours, but they

are always accompanied with mayonnaise or sate sauce. The sate sauce with chicken is something else and at the top of my list.

I hope you have learned something from my quick insight into Dutch cuisine and I have just booked the flights to go back to Holland. I know what's first on the menu for me.

Most people wear fancy dress and live bands play music to cover all tastes throughout the town centre so there is something for everyone.

There is a fantastic atmosphere where everyone enjoys themselves and I would recommend anyone now to go over and sample it. Everyone gets involved from within the community and whole families join in from youngsters to adults.

The next game up for us was one I was really looking forward to because it was against the famous Feyenoord club. They were the first Dutch team to win the European Cup when they beat Celtic 2–1 in the San Siro Stadium, Milan in 1970.

Rotterdam is not far from Breda so there is a big rivalry and I was soon to find out that they had as much of a hooligan problem at that time as we did in England. We had been warming up for about 15 minutes when there was a bit of a commotion on the far side of the field. I looked over and saw concrete slabs being broken up then thrown over the fence. Riot police with dogs were going into the crowd and this was 30 minutes before kick-off.

Calm was restored and all the missiles plus the concrete

was cleared off the pitch as both teams came out to a great atmosphere. We needed to make a good start and we did, attacking Feyenoord with two wingers. NAC had signed Vreijsen from Feyenoord and he put us 1–0 up after 21 minutes with a low strike.

Feyenoord's team was full of Netherland internationals that included Wim Jansen who played in the 74 World Cup Final in West Germany as well as the 78 World Cup Final in Argentina. They were pressing us at the start of the second half and we needed to get that second goal to ease the pressure and this came our way after 55 minutes. The ball was played into their penalty area from the right wing and I hit it on the half volley with my right foot, yes, it wasn't just for standing on! The shot gave Eddy Treijtel, their keeper, no chance and it was a great feeling to score and put us two up.

Our fans were right behind us and we needed their help because Feyenoord were pushing us back and creating a few chances, but our keeper, Jan de Jong, did well.

Then, in the 88th minute, Snoecks scored for them to make it 2–1, but there were only a few minutes to see the game out which we did to get a really good victory and send the NAC supporters home happy.

After the good win against Feyenoord on the Saturday at home, could we repeat the performance and result when we played FC Utrecht four days later also at home?

What we didn't need was to give away another early goal, but we did after just ten minutes when van Veen scored for them.

FC Utrecht were a hard working and well organised team and they were always going to be difficult to break down. We battled hard to get back into the game and finally grabbed the equaliser through Josip Mohorovic with a good finish. Mocoh was a skilful midfield player who could score goals, was a good passer of the ball and a good lad also.

Hans Dorjee made one substitution at half time and their manager Hans Berger made two substitutions so both managers couldn't have been happy with what they had seen in the first half. We stepped it up straight after the break and scored two minutes into the second half through Martien Vreijsen, just the start we wanted. In the 56th minute Martien scored again to make it 3–1. We were dominating this half, but could we get a fourth to make the game safe.

In the 82nd minute we finished it off when I scored to make it 4–1 which made it back to back home wins.

I made my NAC debut in October at Go Ahead Eagles and we beat them 2–1 so could we now get the 'double' over them. I knew they would be trying their best to beat us. We were scoring goals and got off to another good start in the 15th minute when Mohorovic finished off a nice move to score with a low shot into the far corner.

It was perfect for us at the start of the second half when we scored a minute after the resumption. We spoke about scoring the second goal as soon as possible and it's always good when they materialise.

Vreijsen used his pace to beat the keeper in a one on

one to make it 2–0.

We should have finished the game off by taking at least one of the chances we were creating, but in the 86th minute Walbeek scored for Go Ahead to make it 2–1 which led to a nervy finish to the game. However, it proved a good win and we could have scored more, but we deserved the 'double' over Go Ahead Eagles.

We used to have our team meetings after training on the Friday in the players' lounge at the ground. The manager would announce his team selection for the game and how we were going to play. He would then go through the strengths and weaknesses of the opposition. After this we would relax and have a tea/coffee with some sandwiches. I don't like butter so the sandwiches were ruled out for me and they asked if I would I like some steak tartare.

"Yes please," I replied and thought a nice hot steak sandwich was about to be served up with a cup of coffee.

I was talking with the lads when they brought it over to me, raw meat on a roll! I started laughing and said: "OK, you can cook it now," but Hans Dorjee, the manager, smiled and said that is how they had it.

Steak tartare is a meat dish made from raw ground meat (beef or horsemeat). It is served with onions, capers, black pepper, gherkins, shallots, plus other ingredients mixed together.

I tried the tartare and then was pleasantly surprised by the taste so it was something else I had learned about Holland that day.

As my first season at NAC was coming to a close I was

thinking back to when I had first signed for the club. It was a massive decision for me to make the move to leave Everton and take on a new challenge abroad. At the time I was one the first English players to move away from a Division One club like Everton to play in a new country with a different language and culture. It is obviously much more common nowadays, but not back then.

It was all very different, the style of football and tactics, training times and sessions, kick-off times on Friday and Saturday evenings, plus Sunday afternoons or evenings. This was all before SKY Sport.

The supporters were always great with me and this was really appreciated. The players and staff were also very welcoming, but a special mention must go to head coach Hans Dorjee, team manager Tim Meeus, NAC Chairman Frans Bayings, players Theo Dierickx, Addy Brouwers, Jan de Jong and the club secretary Netty Brouwers who was fantastic at her job and made settling in at the club even smoother with no job too small to do.

The last game of the season was against ADO Den Haag which is the reverse fixture from the first game of the campaign which we won 2–1. Could it be another double?

A win would be a good way to finish my first season off with NAC, but in the opposing line-up was Hans Galje, a good keeper who would go on to play for Ajax and the Orange, and also Martin Jol with Romeo Zondervan.

It was an even and open game in the first half, but no goals. In the 60th minute Theo Dierickx scored to his and our delight. Theo was a wholehearted player who gave everything for the team and would play in midfield or at centre-half when required.

Theo went off after 70 minutes, having taken a knock, and he was replaced by Gerrie Damen, a skilful midfielder. Our defence was playing well and we didn't give them many chances during the game, running out 1–0 winners which was a satisfying way to finish the season.

We thanked the supporters for following us home and away and now it was a summer break before the start of pre-season training.

While in Holland, I would come home for a couple of weeks at the end of the season to catch up with the rest of the family and friends. I went into town with Denise for a meal and a few drinks. A popular area in town was Harrington Street which had pubs like the Pen and Wig, Why Not, and the Crocodile which were all in walking distance of each other.

We went into the 'Croc' and walked into the bar at the back then ordered our drinks. I then heard someone say 'Ronny' and as I turned it was a lad called Gary, manager of the Brookhouse pub on Smithdown Road who was the brother-in-law of my ex-Everton team mate and good friend Gary Jones. I hadn't seen any of them for a few years and I asked him how they all were. He said: "Not good, my missus has left me for Gary Jones."

It shocked me and I said: "I'm sorry to hear that."

He replied: "I know, I'm fucking gutted, I loved Jonesy!"

EVERTON TRY TO RE-SIGN ME BUT MY DREAM IS SHATTERED

IT WAS a good first season for me which I had very much enjoyed. The manager said he was pleased and that I had played well and was building a good relationship with the supporters who seemed to take to me from my debut game against Go Ahead Eagles. I had scored five goals and NAC only missed out on a UEFA Cup place by 4 points.

At the end of the season we went back to England for a summer break to see family and friends and catch up with what had been going on while we had been away. I have mentioned before about my great friendship with Mick Buckley since we were team mates together with England Schoolboys so we had arranged to go on a fortnight's holiday with our wives Denise and Joan.

Dad had a friend called Peter Cail who had bars in Lloret de Mar on the Costa Brava coast in Catalonia. Dad had been out there on a couple of occasions. He had enjoyed it and Peter was always inviting us over, so this year we thought why not?

It was good to see Peter and it wasn't just because he knew all the best places to go to eat, drink and which clubs to visit. We had a great fortnight there with sun, sea, lots of laughs nice food/drinks and it was tremendous to see Buck really having a good time.

When we got back to Holland all the talk was about the 1978 FIFA World Cup which was staged in Argentina from 1st June to the 25th June.

England had failed to qualify for the second World Cup in succession, losing out to Italy. Having played against most of the players starring for the Netherlands team out in Argentina and because I was now living in Holland, they were my chosen team to support and they played some tremendous football. They reached the final where they played hosts Argentina and almost won when Rob Rensenbrink had a great chance in stoppage time to clinch it, but his shot came back off the post. The game went into extra time in which Argentina ran out 3–1 winners.

Pre-season training in Holland started in July with the

first League game at the end of August. We would go to a training camp for a week which was not unusual, but I would have to get used to the different regime on the continent. We would be woken up at 7.30am to go for a run through the woods at 8am and then back for a bit of breakfast. It was then more fitness training, in for lunch and then out again in the afternoon to do some work with the ball on skills and technique.

I was looking forward to one of our pre-season games that had been arranged as part of the deal that took me to NAC Breda and it was against Everton at Goodison on Saturday 5th August 1978.

It was good to come back and play at Goodison, but strange going into the visitors' dressing room. I received a tremendous reception from the crowd which was appreciated and although we lost the game 4–2 it was good preparation for the start of the season. However, what was going to take place over the next few days would leave a bad impression on me.

Gordon Lee said he wanted me to come back and sign for Everton and asked where my thoughts might be on this. My thoughts! I was thinking I had just won the lottery.

I was delighted and told Denise and I was looking forward to getting it sorted. I thought that the clubs would discuss it and negotiate with no problems. How wrong I was. I spoke with Lee and he said the fee NAC wanted was too high. I was transferred for £100,000 in October and now NAC wanted £250,000. I spoke with NAC and they said I had done very well, they didn't want me to leave and this was the sum they wanted.

I then talked to Jim Greenwood, the Everton secretary and later chief executive. Gordon Lee was there and they said that NAC would have to lower the fee for it to go ahead. The discussions went on for a few days with me stuck in the middle trying to resolve the matter between the two clubs. I had enjoyed my time at NAC, but this was my beloved Everton wanting to sign me back and from my standpoint it was an absolute no brainer.

Everton said they would keep an eye on the situation with me as the weeks went by, but NAC wouldn't budge and I felt really disappointed that the move back to Everton never materialised.

I had played in losing League Cup Finals and FA Cup semi- finals, but this was the biggest disappointment in my football career!

After the heartbreak of the move back to Everton breaking down it was back to the 1978 Eredivisie for me. The Netherlands reached the World Cup final in Argentina, but were runners-up again as they were in 1974 in Germany. For such a small country compared to England, Germany or France they have produced so many quality players and to reach two consecutive World Cup finals was exceptional. The country was still on a high after such an achievement and supporters of every Dutch club were looking forward to the start of the new season.

In our first few games we were conceding too many late goals which made us draw games and drop more points against FC Utrecht, MVV Maastricht, and NEC

Nijmegen.

There are many coincidences that happened during my playing career, but here's another one. In goal for FC Utrecht in the first game was Hans van Breukelen who played at Nottingham Forest for two years, but then moved to PSV Eindhoven where he won six League titles, three domestic Cups and then, in 1988, the big one - the European Cup. Playing for NEC Nijmegen in midfield in the third game was Guus Hiddink, who was the manager of PSV Eindhoven when they won the European Cup in 1988. Who was the assistant manager at PSV that year... none other than my manager Hans Dorjee.

I should have gone into the bookies and put some money on those three to win the 1988 European Cup. What a treble that would have been.

Our next home game was one we needed to win, not draw, and our next opponents were ADO Den Haag. Manager Dorjee told us to have a go at them early on, put them under pressure and try to get an early goal. The early goal came, but it was for ADO, a header from Jos Jonker after only four minutes to make it 0–1 and another goal start for the visiting team. This woke us up and we started to play some good attacking football, deservedly equalising in the 26th minute through a Vreijsen penalty with the score 1–1 at half time. We should have been leading after creating a number of chances and they made two half time substitutions to stop us dominating the game and taking the lead.

Six minutes into the second half we went ahead through

striker Cees Storm and now the next goal would be vital to who won the game. I'm pleased to say that when it came, in the 67th minute, I scored it. Every goal you score makes you feel good, but this one was a bit special for me for a number of reasons, starting with the build-up and then the execution.

With the penalty area crowded, the ball was pulled back to me 14 yards out. Defenders were on the line and goalkeeper Hans Galje came out to make the target look smaller. I stopped the ball and shaped to hit it, but decided to chip him.

It could have gone over the bar, the defenders might have headed clear off the line or the keeper could have saved it. I don't think anyone in the ground, including the players, expected the lob so it was clearly important I got it right.

I clipped the ball over the keeper with the defenders staring as the ball dropped inches underneath the crossbar. It seemed to be in the air for an age, but went in perfectly and slid down the back of the net. Everyone was delighted with the goal and the crowd were great, cheering me back to the halfway line which was tremendous.

The game finished 3–1 and as I was walking off the pitch the fans were shouting: "Mooi goal Goodlass, Mooi."

I got back to the dressing room and everyone was made up with the win and kept saying to me "Mooi goal Ronny." I got showered and then the physio had to look at a bad cut I had on my ankle to see if it needed stitches. He wanted to put a dressing on it and so I went to the treatment room and got on the table. There were a couple of ex-NAC players in there discussing the game. I knew one of them and he said to me: "Mooi goal Ronny."

I finally asked what 'Mooi' meant and just hoped it didn't mean SH**?

He said: "It means 'Beautiful, a beautiful goal'. That sounded good to me and it is now my favourite word in the Dutch language.

After all, it is the Beautiful Game!

The next few weeks were not the best for us results wise with injuries not helping. We were giving away too many late goals from winning positions and drawing far too many and this was costing us points.

We had drawn games at home to HFC Haarlem, Vitesse and Roda JC Kerkrade and in between these games we lost to a late Rene van de Kerkof goal against PSV. We were winning at Feyenoord 1–0, but lost to an 82 minute effort from Petursson which was his second goal. We had a good win at VVV Venlo who had a certain Dick Advocaat, a future Netherland manager, playing in midfield. However, w we would need a few more because the pressure was on manager Hans Dorjee.

The last game before the winter break was against FC Volendam at Veronicastadion and we needed a victory. Volendam is a popular tourist attraction in Holland. It's a lovely and quaint fishing village where the fish is fresh and the restaurants superb. I know because I've eaten there, but they take their football very seriously and we knew we would have to be up for a battle.

It was a sunny day and they made a good start, but few scares for us. We then had more possession of the ball and started to create a couple of chances ourselves, but in the 25th minute they scored two goals in 60 seconds through Kramer. Obviously we didn't expect that and disappointingly went in 2–0 down.

We needed a goal quickly to get back into the game, but Volendam broke away for Kramer to score his third and give them a 3–0 win.

It would have been a poor result for us at any stage of the season, but we wanted a confidence booster at the halfway and it just didn't happen. This put even more pressure on manager Hans Dorjee.

We came back in January to start building up the training for the second half of the season and rumours were rife of the board replacing the manager. It was a heavy couple of weeks training to get us match fit after the break with a few friendlies arranged against local teams. We had been back training for a few weeks when Hans was called to a board meeting.

Now this can only go two ways. Either the board can give the manager a vote of confidence and allow him to carry on with their full support and backing, or they sack him.

On the 21st January 1979 the NAC board decided to sack Hans Dorjee. It's never nice when anyone loses their job and Hans had brought me to NAC. He was a good manager and person, but boards have to make big choices for the good of the club and they believed a change at the top was needed.

The next day it was announced that Jo Jansen would be taking over, but there was a bit of a problem. IA Akranes of Iceland wanted Jo as manager and he had travelled over to meet with club officials and look around the area training facilities and stadium. When Jo signed for NAC as manager IA Akranes were not amused.

Jo had been at NAC for a number of years, running the youth set up as co-ordinator. He then became a coach before being promoted to Assistant Coach and the board clearly thought it was time for him to have a chance with the first team. He was a good fella, always had a smile on his face and was very enthusiastic about his job. He was well liked at NAC and it was good to see him getting a chance to manage at a high level. He knew NAC and I wished him all the best.

It was a really cold winter with lots of games postponed and our first game after the winter break would be on the 3rd March. Our last game had been on the 17th December, a long gap with no League action.

We played the Dutch Military team at NAC with the pitch covered in six inches of snow. There is no way you would play a game with the pitch in that condition nowadays. It was actually the worst pitch I've ever played on, but we needed to play games. We had two other friendlies against local teams WHS and played against Peursum in Oosterhout.

The first game in charge for Jo would be at home to PEC Zwolle. They were a hard working team and were difficult to play against, marshalled superbly at the back by Rinus Israel who Celtic supporters will remember although not with much fondness because he had scored the first goal for Feyenoord when beating Celtic 2–0 in their European Cup win in 1970.

We were playing well and unlucky to go behind after 17 minutes, but we carried on creating opportunities. Their keeper made some good saves and their defenders were blocking our shots and headers.

They were leading 1–0, but at half time their manager made two substitutions so he was clearly worried with what he had seen in the first 45 minutes. Five minutes after half time we finally scored and it was a well taken goal from Ton Sprangers. Ton was a young player who came through the youth system at NAC so it was a great moment for him.

It was similar to the first half, but we couldn't get that second goal and it ended 1–1.

Jo Jansen's first game inspired a good performance, but we just couldn't get the win and his next game would be even more difficult because it was Ajax away.

Any time you played Ajax it was tough, but at home they were very strong and Jo was positive with his team selection and pre-match team talk. Ton van Eenennaam was selected to play in goal and was another product of the NAC youth system. Jo Jansen knew him very well from his time coaching the youth teams and Ton was a good trainer and a bubbly character.

Ajax had great passing ability and we would have to

pressure them into mistakes. When we had the ball, we had to keep it and make it difficult for them. As it turned out, we were compact and didn't give them any time or space to play to their tempo .It was a good performance and we came away with a goalless draw. It was NAC's first point won at Ajax for 15 years.

The next two games ended 0–0. Jo had the team organised and we were keeping clean sheets, but we needed to start scoring goals again and taking our chances. That was four draws in a row so could Jo Jansen get his first win as a manager in the next game at home to Sparta Rotterdam

We played some good football and were unlucky not to get more than just the penalty by Vreijsen that gave us a 1–0 lead, but in the second half we started to really get on top and it was a Ton Sprangers double in the 47th and 67th minute gave us a 3–0 lead before Marijt scored after 78 minutes to give Sparta a lifeline back into the game.

In the 86th minute a player called Louis van Gaal (I wonder what he did when he retired from playing football?) scored to make it look more respectable for them, but we played really well and we were glad to get the first win for the new manager.

Jo Jansen had done well since being appointed as manager. He brought his enthusiasm to training sessions an organisation to the team that made us hard to beat and we went 11 games undefeated which shows a consistency in the team performance levels.

In this run we went away to ADO Den Haag drew 1–1, beat FC Twente 3–1 at home after conceding a goal after only two minutes. We played this game on the Saturday night, 14th April, and with the very bad winter and due to postponements we had to play Twente at their place on Monday 16th April where we drew 1–1. Then we had another good 3–1 win at home against Go Ahead Eagles.

The team that ended our 11 game unbeaten run was AZ Alkmaar. We were leading 2–1, but lost 3–2 to an 80th minute goal by Kees Kist, his second of the game. They were a good side full of Dutch internationals like Metgod, Hovenkamp, Spelbos and Jan Peters who scored the two goals for Holland at Wembley in 1977 to give them a 2–0 win and the first over England in their history.

We got back to winning ways with a 2–0 win over VVV Venlo. It was straightforward and we didn't look in any trouble

On our substitutes' bench that day was a young player called Ton Lokoff. He didn't get on in that game, but would have a good career with NAC, PSV Eindhoven, Feyenoord and NAC again. He would also become Head Coach at NAC and another player who came through their youth system.

We played Feyenoord on the 2nd June drew 0–0, but we still had to play Roda JC in Kerkrade on Monday, 5th June. The pre-season for next season was only weeks away.

This season was the longest I had ever experienced or knew about and there hasn't been a longer one since!

Once the season was over I had to decide what I was going to do. I was out of contract and had to make a decision on my future. I had enjoyed my time at NAC and wanted to hear what they had to say. Jo Jansen made it clear he wanted me to stay and to sign a long term contract. I liked Jo. He was honest and I respected the way he went about things from the training to how he wanted NAC to play. He came to my house on a number of occasions to try and persuade me NAC was the place to play. There were tentative discussions with the NAC board, but nothing concrete.

I was disappointed the way the NAC board were going about things. It's not rocket science to set up a meeting make an offer on your salary and the length of the contract and then take it from there.

I don't know whether it was because the sacked Hans Dorjee had signed me or linked with the breakdown of my move back to Everton. I did tell them at the time in no uncertain terms how I felt about the way they had handled that situation. I used a lot of expletives when trying to express my disappointment and did have a right 'cob on'. My granddad worked on the Liverpool Docks all his life, but he would have blushed hearing me going on my rant.

The papers and radio were asking me what was happening, but I couldn't tell them anything because I didn't know myself. There were rumours going around that I might be leaving and a few clubs made an enquiry. One of them was ADO Den Haag.

If NAC had given them permission to talk to me then I would have agreed to talk to them, but that says a lot about NAC's attitude in trying to make me sign a new contract.

We talked over the phone about ADO Den Haag's interest and arranged a meeting to discuss it further.

So had I made an impact during my new career in Holland and could I take it to the next level? Sometimes it's not what you think yourself, but how others see you. Here are some thoughts from people I played against and from local newspapers reports on those games:

27TH FEBRUARY 1978.
NEWSPAPER DE STEM AFTER THE GAME
AGAINST AZ ALKMAAR

"The Englishman tormented Peter Arntz. The defender didn't know how to defend against the wizardry of Goodlass who passed him every time as if the defender wasn't there."

This comment pleased me because the Netherland squad was getting announced on the following Monday for the 1978 World Cup in Argentina with Peter Arntz the favourite to get the full back position. The Netherlands Head Coach was at the NAC v AZ Alkmaar game. Peter Arntz subsequently never got selected for the squad to go to Argentina.

23 MARCH 1979
KEES RIJVERS, PSV EINDHOVEN MANAGER

"Jan Poortvliet couldn't keep up with Goodlass. I had to put another defender on to mark him."

This was encouraging from an opposing manager, especially because Poortvliet had played in the 1978 World Cup Final against Argentina.

NEWSPAPER DE STEM AFTER THE 2–2 DRAW AGAINST TELSTAR ON MY HOME DEBUT FOR NAC

"The former Everton player has a lot of tricks and can do some unexpected things. On Saturday evening Ronny Goodlass decided to open his box of tricks. The people in the stands loved it and the crowd cheered him on all the time."

ADDY BROUWERS, NAC PLAYER TALKING TO THE NEWSPAPER PZC

NAC didn't have a left winger. After buying Ronny Goodlass we have the most prolific winger in the Netherlands.

NEWSPAPER PZC AFTER THE 2–0 VICTORY OVER FEYENOORD

Ronny Goodlass, the left winger, had a hard day at work. He was fouled six times. He had to be stopped the hard way.

Comments like this certainly lifted my spirits at this time and I was particularly proud to receive some thoughts recently from former Den Haag manager Piet de Visser, the man who gave me my second club challenge in Holland. It is always intriguing to understand what coaches see in you as a player and here was a guy who would later be given a crucial scouting role by Chelsea's Roman Abramovich.

PIET DE VISSER

"*I was searching a long time for a good left winger in Holland, but could not find him. Then I got a tip to have a look at Ronny Goodlass in England. I did and from the first moment I was impressed by his very good skills, his speed and dribbling qualities, and his excellent left foot when crossing and shooting. I was very happy that we could sign him and from the beginning he played all the games in the first team and proved a very good left winger.*

"*I also liked the fact that he was a nice boy, not only with talent, but also a great passion for football. I remember that he played very well in the big games.*

"*I also recall the game for the Dutch Cup when we played home against the best team in Holland, PSV, and we won 3–1 with two excellent assists from Ronny who also scored an important goal.*

"*Later that season when we played at home against the big team, AJAX, we won 1–0 with the match winner scored by Ronny. In this game he also showed his great dribbling skills and you could compare him with the best AJAX could offer.*

"*I only worked with Ronny for one year because at the end of the season I left Den Haag and so did he. I had another three teams in Holland as manager – Roda, AZ and Willem II and after my heart problems I had to quit as a manager/coach.*

"*From then on I became a scout, first for PSV and later Mr. Abramovich asked me to be his personal scout. I have now worked for him and Chelsea for the last 15 years.*"

HOW A YOUNG RUUD GULLIT PROVES HE IS WORLD CLASS

MY first game for FC Den Haag was against Vitesse in Arnhem and you always want to start brightly and get a good result as soon as possible with your new club. However, we went a goal behind after ten minutes which was not a good start. Piet de Visser, the manager, made two substitutions, but although we played better in the second half and had a few near misses to equalise, we lost the game 1–0. It was disappointing, but all you can do is move onto the next game and win it.

The next match was at home to FC Haarlem on Wednesday 22nd August, 1979. They were run by Welshman Barry Hughes who had managed in Holland for a number of years.

Now Barry was a real extrovert character and would make his presence felt from the sidelines. He would go on to manage nine different clubs in Holland.

He needed to get his Dutch diploma for coaching and German coach George Kessler, who became a very successful manager across Europe with a number of clubs, ran the course Barry was on. Barry said George made his time hell, disagreeing about everything he said and failing him that first year. He passed him the second time he took it, but Barry said that if the opportunity ever came around to get his own back, he would.

Barry was clearly a man of his word. When his Haarlem team played Kessler's he decided that every time his team scored, he would take out a Party blower and blow it in George's direction. Lucky for Barry his team won 3–2 and the crowd loved it. What a way to get someone back publicly, but with humour.

Our club signed a few players during the summer and one of them was Andre Wetzel, a right sided midfielder who I remembered playing for FC Amsterdam. He got us off to a good start by scoring after 11 minutes. We were playing some good attacking football and we needed to get a second goal while we were on top.

We did this in the 38th minute when I picked the ball up on the halfway line. I went passed a couple of players before Henk van Leeuwen, our centre forward, showed on the edge of their penalty area. I played a one-two with him and it was a good set up for me to hit first time from outside the area. I struck the ball well and it arrowed low into the far corner to make it 2–0. I had scored again on my home debut for my new club.

Haarlem never gave up and they had a player in their team who looked a class act and he would end up to be one of the best players in world football – Ruud Gullit.

They scored in the 90th minute through Hendricks, but we were worthy winners.

I was delighted to score, but even more pleased with the win.

Only four days after this we played at home against AZ Alkmaar, managed by… George Kessler! That's when I thought to myself, should I bring a Party blower?

They were a good team that consistently pushed for those European places and they would be a test for us in this game, eventually finishing the season as runners up to Ajax.

It was a good match with each team trying to attack, but both keepers played well and at half time it was goalless.

Piet de Visser told us to keep attacking and the goal would come and he was right. After 56 minutes Henk van Leeuwen finished off a good move to put us 1–0 up. We now defended well as a team and it finished with a lone goal victory for us. It was a good team performance with an excellent result.

Our next game was against Feyenoord at Zuiderparkstadion, our home ground, and there was a great rivalry between the two clubs and their supporters. The Hague is less than 17 miles from Rotterdam. It was our 'derby' game.

We had a few ex-Feyenoord players in our team, including Aad Mansveld and Lex Schoenmaker. Aad was a great defender who organised the defence superbly, but had good skill/technique and was also a good passer of the ball who could come out of defence into midfield to start attacks. He had a great attitude to training and on match days he raised the standard he wanted from others.

Lex was a tall midfield player, good in the air and very comfortable with the ball. He knew when to make late runs into the penalty area and could score goals.

This was shown when Lex scored in the second minute when he lost his marker to get us off to a good start. It was a decent game, but we conceded a Petursson goal after 34 minutes to make it 1–1. Into the second half Lex scored again with a composed finish in the 65th minute to put us 2–1 in front. Feyenoord immediately made two substitutions and after 77th minutes they were awarded a dubious penalty which allowed Peturssson to score and it finished 2–2. This was a disappointing result for us after putting in a good performance and leading twice, but not getting the win.

Our next away game was at Roda JC in Kerkrade, a difficult place to go, but when opponent Dick Nanninga was on his game he was almost unplayable. He is the tall centre forward who scored the equaliser against Argentina in the 1978 World Cup final, a great header of the ball. He was aggressive, strong and could hold the ball up. I would have liked to see him play in England, and in this game he scored a hat trick that helped them to beat us and gain the points.

It was still early in the season and the team was taking shape with the midfield containing Dick Advocatt, Jos Jonker and Lex Schoenmaker, a talented hard-working and balanced midfield.

We had a poor performance at Roda JC and were then at home to FC Twente. We had some good characters in the team so we needed to show it in this game when we again conceded early on after 18 minutes. We kept going and from one of my corners, Simon van Vliet came up from the back to score. Five minutes after the first goal we were awarded a penalty in the 78th minute and Lex slotted it into the corner for a 2–1 win. It was not a good return for FC Twente players Martin Jol or Romeo Zondervan, both 'Hagenees' with the score finishing 2–1 for us with tremendous character shown by the team.

When you move to a new club you have to get to know the ways of the manager, what your role is in the side, the formation, and how the manager wants the team to play. Other players who signed for the club, like Dick Advocaat, Andre Wetzel and Jos Jonker, also had to settle in.

Manager Piet de Visser selected all of them to play in our midfield in the next game against NEC Nijmegen at home in the hope that we could get back to back wins.

Aad Mansveld was quite rightly regarded as a legend

at ADO Den Haag because he gave everything he could in every game and was a tremendous character to have in the dressing room or out on the field. Only for an injury he would have been in the Netherlands squad for the 1974 World Cup finals in Germany and made six appearances.

His position was sweeper, but he could have played in midfield and scored even more goals than he did as a defender. He used to take some free kicks, but he was always dangerous at corner kicks. I took one in the 38th minute when he scored.

Then Henk van Leeuwen came on as substitute to score when he shot past the keeper to seal a good 2–0 win for us. All week, Aad then told the forwards in training how easy it is to score goals!

One of my favourite grounds was the Philips Stadion in Eindhoven with PSV one of the teams I loved to play against. They were a club full of Netherlands internationals and you wanted to play against the best teams with the best players. PSV were certainly up there with the best.

They had players like keeper Jan van Beveren. Willy and Rene van der Kerkhof, along with Jan Poortvliet, played in the 1978 World Cup Final. Willy van der Kuijlen played for PSV in 528 league matches and scored 308 goals, a tremendous achievement for a midfield player. They inspired PSV to win the 1978 UEFA Cup.

You don't want to concede an early goal that will make it even more difficult to get a result, but we did after 18 minutes when Postuma put PSV 1–0 up. Just after half time they made a substitution when Erwin Koeman came on. This was the uncle of the future Everton manager Ronald Koeman and his assistant brother Erwin.

We started the second half well, put pressure on the PSV defence and created good chances. Aad Mansveld came up with the goods again with the equaliser and his second goal in two games.

The defence played well for the rest of the game with Hans Galje making a couple of good saves. Then Aad Mansveld took a yellow card for the team, but we deserved the 1–1 draw. Along with the rest of the forwards, I could now prepare myself on the team coach for Aad to tell us how easy it is to score goals as we travelled back to Den Haag.

It wasn't just the electric heaters in the Tribunes (Stands) at the Philips Stadion that kept the supporters warm from the harsh Dutch winters, but a hard earned point against a very good team.

For the next three games the performances were all good, but we couldn't see the games out to win and had to settle for three draws against MVV Maastrict at home 1–1, Willem ll in Tilburg 0–0, and then 2–2 with Sparta in Rotterdam after van Tiggelen gave them the lead after three minutes. We equalised through Jos Jonker after 15 minutes and then we took the lead when Henk van Leeuwen scored on 55 minutes. We were ahead for only two minutes and it was so disappointing when Lengkeek put the ball past Hans Galje to level at 2–2. This was now four draws in a row.

In the Sparta team that day was Trevor Whymark who

made his name at Ipswich Town. On the substitute bench was Danny Blind who would captain Ajax to win every major European Trophy and the World Club Championship. He is also the father of Daley Blind, the Netherlands and ex-Manchester United player.

I would like to give a special mention to Aad Mansveld. During these games he was playing really well as normal, but he had now scored four goals in the last six games and this from his sweeper position – an absolute goal machine Aad!

The last game before the winter break would be a bit different for me because it was against my ex-club NAC and it would be the first time I had faced them since my move. I had enjoyed my time at NAC and most of the squad were still there. I would be playing against former team mates, but you have to be professional and I wanted to win this game just as much as they did.

There wasn't much difference between the teams in the first half with very few chances, but in the second period we really got on top with more possession and started to create a lot more chances. We scored in the 53rd minute with a calm finish from Lex Schoenmaker and kept pushing for a second goal and finally scored two in two minutes to finish things off. It was Harry Melis on the scoresheet in the 65th minute with a low shot before Lex Schoenmaker quickly showed his skill and technique with a great goal.

I had made a run down the left wing and cut the ball back from near the bye line. Lex seemed to have run in too early and the ball was going behind, but from about

14 yards out he swivelled in mid-air, raised his left leg about four feet off the ground and volleyed the ball with the outside of his left foot. It flashed into the net to give the keeper no chance and what a way to secure the game with such a sensational effort. It finished 3–0 and this was a good win to take us into the winter break.

This gave me a couple of weeks of free time to relax with the family over Christmas and enjoy The Hague even more. It is a fabulous place with lots to see and do. One of the eight districts is called Scheveningen and it is the most popular seaside resort in Holland with a long sandy beach, and lovely restaurants. With fresh fish from the North Sea, it has something for everyone, young and old. I would highly recommend a visit to The Hague and Scheveningen where I'm sure you will really enjoy your time there.

Right that's my bit done for the local tourist board. Our first league game after the break was on Saturday 12th January at home against Vitesse. Could we start the second half of the season like we had finished the first with a win?

It was a comfortable game for us with Harry Melis scoring a brace in the 19th and 46th minute to help us take the points and keep another clean sheet in a 2–0 win.

Our next game was at Haarlem where the team talk went something like this: "We are playing well, scoring goals, keeping clean sheets and winning games. Let's see if we can get an early goal and keep it going!"

I had scored on my home debut against Haarlem and

this was a good chance to get the double over them. Sometimes you achieve the start you want with an early first goal and we got it through Lex Schoenmaker. Lex silenced their crowd with less than a minute on the referee's watch, but we needed to concentrate and not let them back in the game.

It was all going well until the 25th minute when a certain Ruud Gullit scored. You could see from an early age he had the skill/technique to become a world class player. He was 6ft 3in tall, tremendous in the air, very quick, agile, two footed, could score and create goals and could play in a number of positions. What a player.

The good thing is he never scored again, but neither did we and the game ended 1–1 a fair result in the end.

It had been a decent game against Haarlem away, but could we now get a win against FC Utrecht at Zuiderpark? They made a bright start to the game and took the lead on 17 minutes from a de Kruyk shot. This would make it an even more difficult game and it proved that way as we went in at half time 1–0 down.

They got players behind the ball and had something to hold onto and it wasn't until the 70th minute when we equalised through defender Simon van Vliet. He chipped in now and again with a goal, but not usually two in one game, However, in the 79th minute he came up with his second from a corner to put us 2–1 up.

It was a good fight back with character shown yet again to give us confidence for our 'derby' against Feyenoord at the De Kuip in Rotterdam. In the future this stadium would hold great memories for all Evertonians!

It was always a good atmosphere when we played Feyenoord, but the De Kuip was a special place where Holland played a lot of football internationals and it held over 60,000 spectators. It was a state of the art stadium in the day and the teams came out from under the ground like modern day gladiators.

They had a team full of Dutch internationals, including Wim Jansen who played in both World Cup Finals for Holland in 1974 and 1978. He also played in the Feyenoord team that defeated Celtic 2–1 in the 1970 European Cup Final in Milan.

It was a typical derby with tackles flying in and with a few chances created for each team. We seemed to be heading for a goalless first half, but Feyenoord got a controversial penalty in the 43rd minute and Petursson scored from the spot.

We hit right back after half time in the 54th minute through Harry Melis which pleased him a lot because we had signed him from Feyenoord in the summer.

For the next ten minutes we pushed for the second goal and nearly scored on a couple of occasions, but we were punished when we were hit on the break after 66 minutes when Budding made it 2–1. We battled right to the end, but couldn't get the second goal. It was a good performance, but a disappointing result.

We now faced the reverse fixture from the first half of the season and so the next up was Roda JC and we owed them one, having lost the first fixture to a Dick Nanninga hat-trick and he was playing again that day.

Jan Jongbloed, the Roda JC keeper, was the original sweeper goalkeeper and he wouldn't look out of place in any modern day football team with Pep Guardiola at the front of the queue to sign him. He was like a midfield player, was a real character, and wore the number 8 on the back of his jersey in both the 1974 and 1978 World Cup Finals.

In midfield they also had Theo de Jong who won 15 caps for the Orange so that was good quality through the spine of their team and a difficult side to beat.

Our manager Piet de Visser picked an attacking line up with six forward thinking players on from the start and we dominated from start to finish. Jongbloed was brought into the game early on when he made some good saves to keep it goalless and it was a committed performance from both teams with three yellow cards shown.

We were playing at a high tempo with quick passing and movement and we went ahead in the 31st minute when I hit a sweet volley past Jongbloed.

Roda then made two substitutions in the second half to try and change the game, but it made no difference because Dick Advocaat scored to make it 2– 0 with a good finish. It had been a good attacking team performance with everyone playing their part.

Dick was another 'Hagenees' that came up through the youth ranks. He was an English type of player who was known as 'The Little General' and he always gave 100%, liked to tackle but was a good passer of the ball. He was also very vociferous and always wanted to get involved in the action. He liked the English style of football and was always asking me about it. I think he would have loved to have played in this country. He was also an intelligent player and it was no surprise to me that he would go into football coaching and then into management. Dick has had a long and distinguished managerial career and got Netherlands to the quarter-finals of the World Cup, finally losing to the eventual winners Brazil 3–2.

When Dick was the manager at PSV Eindhoven in 1995 he invited me over to watch them train and I was looking forward to seeing the different methods of fitness work, the skills/technique sessions, and the tactics used for games. I went for a week and really enjoyed the hospitality shown by Dick, his back room staff and the players. Ronald Waterreus, who played for PSV for ten years, would give me a lift and drop me back off at my hotel. He was a really nice lad.

After watching the morning training session we would have lunch and then the players would go back out for the afternoon work.

Two of the younger players in the squad really stood out for me with their skill/technique, passing, crossing and shooting ability. I was chatting to Dick when I mentioned these lads. I didn't know them by name, but said that if they stayed clear of injuries, one would have a very good career and the other a truly exceptional one.

One of the players came off before the other and Dick told him I used to be a team mate of his at Den Haag where I played as a winger. His reply was: "I also play as a winger." I introduced myself as Ronny and he replied: "My name is Boudewijn."

It was Boudewijn Zenden, who would go on to play for PSV, Barcelona, Liverpool and Chelsea and become a Dutch international.

The other player was still out having some shooting practise I carried on watching his finishing. It was un-believable. The ball was crossed in from wide areas for headers and volleys. He would smash them in from all angles. The ball was played into him for one on ones with the goalkeeper. His skill at pace to go around him with mesmerising moves like step-overs and feints was amaz-ing. His dribbling at speed was his trade mark which he made look so easy and his body swerve would have players going in all directions.

Almost every time he would score, but he always hit the target. Like Boudewijn, this player was 18 years old and with the training finished he went in and got changed.

I said to Dick: "He's a bit special" and he said: "Oh yes, you are going to hear a lot more of him."

We were having a coffee in the clubhouse when the lad came over with a big smile on his face. Dick introduced us and I said to him: "That was a great training session. I would like to wish you every success for this season and for the rest of your career."

He thanked me and I asked Dick to take a photo of us together. Now there were no mobile phones in our day so you would take the film to Max Spielman to get developed. When the prints came back we all thought we were famous photographer David Bailey!

Dick took the photo of the two of us, we shook hands and off he went. When I got back to Liverpool I went to get the film developed. I gave the lady the camera to remove the film and to my horror she said it was empty. Loads of photos I thought had been taken were not there, but what disappointed me most was that there would not be a photo of myself with… Ronaldo. He was known as 'O Fenomeno' or 'The Phenomenon' and one of the greatest footballers of all time in his prime. He gained 98 caps for Brazil (62 goals), was FIFA World Player of the Year three times, won the prestigious Ballon d'Or twice, claimed two FIFA World Cups and secured countless other titles and awards. What an absolutely fantastic career.

By the way I never went back to Max Spielman again!

Next game up was against PEC Zwolle with the experienced captain Rinus Israel playing at centre back. It was another good team performance with Aad Mansveld scoring after 25 minutes. His goals return for a defender that season was very impressive.

We didn't give PEC any chances in the second half and Harry Melis put us 2–0 up in the 63rd minute. It stayed that way to give us the points. This put us in a good frame of mind to go into our next game against PSV Eindhoven.

They were a really good team with van Beveren, Poortvliet, Brandts, Willy and Rene van de Kerkhof and a certain Erwin Koeman, no not him his uncle.

There were always goals when we played PSV. These

clashes were always action packed with the first goal always important. We didn't get off to a good start and you don't want to give PSV an early goal, but we did after nine minutes when Paul Postuma slotted home to give them a 1–0 lead. We needed to hit back immediately and succeeded two minutes later, scoring courtesy of another defender, Simon van Vliet. He was in good form and swept the ball home from inside the penalty for 1–1. What did I say about goals in these games!

We were really pressing PSV, creating chances and looking dangerous, but a real blow came when Willy van de Kerkhof scored in the 45th minute and we went in 1–2 down. The score wasn't a fair reflection on the first half action, but we had to go out after the break to give it a go and we certainly did.

We could have equalised on a few occasions, but Jan van Beveren was in good form in goal and he was saving everything until the 75th minute when I scored. The ball came into the area where I struck it first time and caught it well, my shot flying past van Beveren to make it 2–2, but it was what we deserved and now both teams were going for the winner.

With us pushing for the third goal we had to be careful of being hit on the break and ten minutes from time this is what happened when Postuma scored his second and PSV's third to give them a 3–2 lead. We pushed for the equaliser until the final whistle, but couldn't get it and it was disappointing not to get at least a point from the game.

Another of our close rivals from Rotterdam was Sparta,

a decent team featuring Louis van Gaal and Danny Blind who would both would go on to manage Ajax and secure Eredivisie titles.

Andre Wetzel got us off to a good start with a goal after only four minutes which settled us down and put them under pressure from the start. We had a few regular first teamers out, but Piet de Visser selected some of the younger players and they did well. Den Haag has a history of youth development through to the first team and so the tradition was carrying on.

One goal can be enough in some games, but when Ruud Geels is in the opposition you usually need to get a second goal and that came along after 58 minutes through Lex Schoenmaker. Sparta made two substitutions, but it didn't change the course of the game and it ended 2–0.

DUTCH MILES AHEAD IN TERMS OF BIG MATCH PREPARATION

PLAYING on the continent is a totally different experience than playing in England and I don't just mean the atmosphere, but the build up and the tactics teams play.

Every club has a brass band playing hours before kick-off to get the crowd in the mood. It's a long standing tradition in Dutch football before games, but you get used to it after a while.

In England we used to do stretching exercises in the dressing room 30 minutes before kick-off. Then the bell would go off and the team would go out together at 2.55pm or five minutes before an evening start. We would jog around, more stretches, then sprints and kick off.

On the continent the players would have massages from the physio/masseuse before every game and everyone had their ankles strapped up for protection and support. The squad would then go out 50 minutes before kick-off for a session of various exercises, sprints and then ball work, plus short and long passes. Then the strikers would finish off with shooting practise while the defenders worked on their heading.

The goalkeeping coach would work with the keeper separately before joining us for the shooting practise. In England I would put crosses in for our goalkeeper minutes before we kicked off. The goalkeeping coach in Holland would do all of this in his warm-up routine with the keeper.

Don't forget this was in Holland over 30 years ago. They were far more advanced in training methods and pre-match preparation than we were at this time, but now all English clubs do this pre-match routine.

We only had four games left in the season and travelled to play against a third team from Rotterdam which was SBV Excelsior. They were established in 1905 and had a good working relationship with Feyenoord. They would get loans and transfer of players and Excelsior were also having a good season.

The manager picked the same team that beat Sparta 2–0, but we went behind to a Tijl goal after only seven minutes. The character in the team came through again and we equalised through Lex Schoemaker in the 59th minute to earn a point.

The next game was against Ajax and it was always one of our biggest of the season. The match, on a Saturday evening under floodlights and in front of our fanatical supporters, was something special.

Ajax, steeped in history, had players like keeper Piet Schrijvers, Frank Arnesen, Soren Lerby, and world class defender Ruud Krol. They were also top of the league.

We knew they liked to keep plenty of possession and had a number of players that could score goals, but we also had good attacking players and we needed to impose ourselves on them and play to our strengths.

Aad Mansveld missed the game, but the team worked really hard to deny Ajax time and space. When we had the ball we kept it well and started to get on top and create chances. We had the better of the half, but it ended 0–0 with all to play for in the second half.

They made their second substitution after 63 minutes, taking Bonsink off and bringing on Tschen La Ling, another 'Hagenees' who had come through the Den Haag youth ranks, playing 172 games for Ajax and winning 14 caps for the Netherlands.

Our midfield was playing well, showing a real commitment, and energy in starting attacks. With quick passing, we were going for a winner.

We won the ball in midfield and then it was played to me on the left. Ruud Krol came out to tackle me. I was going to cross left footed, but I checked onto my right and then checked again with Krol trying to stop the cross. Again, I checked onto my right foot, but this time I curled a low shot wide of the post, hoping it would curl enough to beat Piet Schrivers in goal. As soon as it left my foot I followed the flight of the ball and it went inside the far post to give Den Haag a 1–0 lead with seven minutes to go and with the crowd going wild.

It was most important now to keep a clean sheet and deny Ajax any chances to equalise. It was important to play in their half and keep possession. The crowd played their part and they roared us on to victory. It's always tremendous to beat Ajax and I was delighted to play my part by scoring the winner.

With only two weeks of the season to go I was having chats with manager Piet de Visser about signing a longer contract with Den Haag. I was interested in what he wanted for the following season and wondered about new signings. I had got on well with Piet from the start and he was one of the reasons I signed for Den Haag. He was honest, a very good coach, enthusiastic and funny when he needed to be, but he would tell players when it was going wrong for them and the team.

A few teams from England had made enquiries about me possibly coming home, but once the season was over I could sit down and get it sorted.

We were playing NAC in our last away game of the campaign, but there was something more on my mind than the game at NAC.

My wife Denise was pregnant and was due to have the

baby at any time! When we first found out she was pregnant I suggested she could give birth in Holland where he or she would have dual nationality with the Dutch, very good at football and various sports. As the months went by it was brought up now and again, but Denise was given a date in early May.

She decided to have the baby in Liverpool and flew home in April.

It's not like modern day football where players can miss a game to be at the bedside of their wife and see the birth of their child. We were playing NAC on Sunday 4th May and I phoned on the Thursday to be told there was still no news.

There were no mobile phones then and we just had landlines. On the Friday I heard nothing; Saturday, nothing; Sunday morning and still nothing. I went to Zuiderparkstadion to get the coach with the rest of the team to Breda for the game in the afternoon.

The coach arrived at the ground with jeers from the home supporters which was expected, and then even more jeers when I got off the coach because I was going back to my ex-club.

NAC were desperate for the win and two points because they were near the bottom of the league.

One supporter shouted "F... Off To England!" Now I only heard the word 'England.'

I thought: "That's nice; they must know Denise is pregnant and they want me to go back to England to be with her and see the birth of the baby? Errr... NO!

When I played in Holland for NAC Breda and ADO Den Haag, I used to fly home during the winter break, end of the season or pre-season. The winter stop is when teams stop playing any fixtures because it is halfway through the season and they have a break over Christmas and the New Year. The fixtures usually resume in the third week in January.

When I moved to NAC, it was arranged to play Everton in a pre-season friendly. I went with a mate to have a haircut before I came back. At this time in Holland, it was the start of the fashion for the Curly Cut. My mate suggested we should get one and I said: "Why not!"

With my Curly Cut now done, I played in the game against Everton and this is when Andy King and Bob Latchford saw me and decided to get their own Curly Cut done. Tranmere had a game at Marine and I went there with my brother John to watch the game. At this time Westy was a player at Tranmere Rovers after coming out of retirement.

We went through the gates and went to stand behind the goal near the back, out of the way. The teams came out and there was now a good crowd inside. Then about five minutes before kick-off, someone behind me started laughing and said: "Fuckin' hell, it's Shirley Temple." I knew by the voice that it was… Westy!

He must have laughed until kick off. As he went over to look after the Tranmere team, he glanced at my Curly Cut and said: "I might get one of those, see you later."

FULHAM NEXT WHERE SUPERMAC SHOCKS EVERYONE WITH HIS 'PLAN'

HAVING decided that I was going to leave ADO Den Haag to play again in England, the club contacted the Football Association to circulate my name telling clubs that I was available for transfer.

ADO Den Haag was a very good club with passionate supporters and a good group of players, plus a very good manager in Piet de Visser, but he was also leaving.

I received a phone call from Bobby Campbell that he was interested in signing me for Fulham and asking if I would travel to London for discussions.

I went down with a friend of mine, Vic Waugh, who had played in the same Liverpool Schoolboys team as me. There were no football agents in our day. I was met by Bobby at Euston Station and from the outset I got on well with him.

He was Scouser with a good sense of humour and he knew his football. He had also coached at Arsenal and QPR. They were putting me in a hotel, but Bobby said they would also book a room for Vic. He added that if the talks didn't go well, we could have a good weekend down in London on Fulham. A big smile came across Vic's face!

We drove back to Craven Cottage with Bobby and he was selling Fulham to me all the way. We met a few of the staff and a man called Gerry who was on the play-ers' entrance on match days and knew everything about the club, a lovely man. I went up to the manager's office with Bobby and he introduced me to the office staff which included Dave Barnard who would eventually move to Chelsea and be a very successful secretary there for many years.

I began discussions with Bobby and also the secretary, talking about terms and length of contract. Bobby was very enthusiastic about me signing for the club. I agreed terms and we shook hands on it.

Bobby then called Vic back into the office and said I'd agreed to sign which he was delighted to hear. Bobby then said that some reserve team players were training and he wanted me to join them to get me up to match fitness as soon as possible.

I told him I hadn't brought my boots, but Bobby said they would sort out a pair for me from the boot room with some training kit.

This is when Vic asked Bobby could he join in the training session and proceeded to give his playing career CV. Bobby looked at me, then turned to Vic and said: "No, I don't want to see the headlines tomorrow reading: 'Goodlass signs for Fulham', but his mate has a heart attack."

I went to get changed with the training kit now hanging up and a pair of boots on the bench. The reserve players were already out warming up. I looked at the boots and they were so out of shape it was unbelievable, but there was no one there to change them so I took a chance.

It was a struggle to get them on, never mind running around in them.

We trained for an hour with the session based on crossing and shooting. I enjoyed the training, but not wearing those boots. I went back to the changing room and took them off. It was like a Disney cartoon in which my crunched up toes sprang back into shape and straight again! Sheer relief, but I still had sore feet.

I found out the boots belonged to first teamer Les Strong who must have been bandy or pigeon toed!

Fulham were on a poor run of form and I made my debut against Exeter City at home. In our line-up that day were a number of players with top flight experience such as Roger Brown, Kevin Lock and John Beck. Others who would go on to have good football careers were Gerry

Peyton, Tony Gale, Sean O'Driscoll and Gordon Davies.

We never took our chances that day. Exeter only had a couple of shots in the second half, but they scored from one of them and we lost the game 0–1.

Another home defeat against Burnley 0–2 was putting the pressure on Bobby Campbell, but again Burnley proved more clinical than we were. Their team featured Eric Potts, Brian Laws, Billy Hamilton and a good friend of mine and ex-Everton team mate Martin Dobson who was playing centre-half.

We then had to play at Plymouth on the Tuesday night and went a goal down when Sims scored after only three minutes, but John Beck equalised after 43 minutes, only for Argyle to take the lead again through Bason after 45 minutes. We couldn't get the second goal to earn a point. It was a decent performance, but another loss and when you are on a poor run things don't go your way.

The team were playing well against Millwall at the Cottage and we had deservedly taken the lead through a good Gordon Davies goal, but when we were on top we couldn't get that second which we needed. The second half was similar with us attacking and creating chances, but Millwall scored through McKenna to earn a point and it was disappointing not to have won.

Making his debut in this game for us was Dave Clement, ex-QPR and England who was a great professional a good footballer and a cracking lad. His son Paul has gone on to earn a great reputation as a coach and manager.

It was a big disappointment for me to see Bobby Campbell go after the away game at Newport. As the weeks and months went by, I started to see what new boss Malcolm Macdonald was really like and I didn't like what I saw. He wasn't my type of manager.

His first two games in charge were at the Cottage where we drew 1–1 against Chesterfield before a 0–0 draw against Plymouth Argyle. We then played away against a Carlisle side that included Peter Beardsley and was managed by Bob Stokoe. We drew again, but this time it was 2–2.

The first defeat was when we went two goals down away to Colchester United. We pulled it back to 2–2, but lost to a late goal. Their keeper that day was a certain Mike Walker who would later manage Everton, in name only though!

We were becoming the draw specialists, sharing the points in 1–1 clash with Rotherham who had Ronnie Moore up front.

We were drawn to play Reading at Elm Park in the FA Cup first round and they were a good side that included Neil Webb, Martin Hicks, Lawrie Sanchez, Stuart Beavon and Kerry Dixon. This was at the time Fulham Rugby League FC was founded with a lot of ex-Widnes players such as big Jim Mills. If he said it was a Thursday, it was Thursday. Reg Bowden, who played scrum half, was also a terrific player and both teams would go to watch each other to show their support. I was a regular when they played at the Cottage and the Rugby League lads were watching us against Reading.

It was a good crowd and a great atmosphere with tremendous support from the Fulham supporters. We were warming up in front of the goal where all the Fulham supporters were congregated. I then jogged along by the main stand that was packed with Fulham fans and you couldn't miss the rugby lads who were standing up clapping.

The pitch was heavy with periods of rain, but it was a typical FA Cup tie with crunching tackles and real commitment from both teams. Chances were being created, but it was 0–0 at half time. We came out in the second half and played well and finally scored through Gordon Davies after 59 minutes. However, the lead only lasted 14 minutes when Earles equalised after 73 minutes which was a blow.

There was good character in our team and in the 80th minute we broke up one of their attacks then hit them at pace on the break. The ball was played out to me on the left, I went passed Joslyn and I looked up to see Tony Mahoney make a good run to the near post. I crossed and Tony finished off in style.

We celebrated with the Fulham supporters behind the goal and as I jogged back I looked up towards the rugby lads who were pumping the air with clenched fists and big smiles on their faces. It had been a really good team performance and an excellent team goal, fit to win any FA Cup tie. We then drew Brentford at home in the second round.

Back in the league we played Barnsley at Oakwell. The last time I had played there was for Liverpool Schoolboys in the semi-final of the English Schools Trophy when I scored and we won. Could it happen again?

We came out of the traps and scored after only six minutes through Gary Peters, a right-back and a real wholehearted player. Then I scored my first goal for the club when I shot home after 22 minutes to put us into a two goal lead and it was looking good. However, Barnsley scored two minutes later to get them back into the game and it was 2–1 for us at half time.

The game had begun in windy cold conditions, but when we came out in the second half it was blowing a gale and started snowing with Barnsley having all the elements in their favour.

For the whole second half it was backs to the wall with Barnsley throwing everything at us. We held them at bay until the 77th minute when Ian Banks scored. By now it was still blowing a gale, but accompanied by a snowstorm. What do you expect at the end of November in Barnsley?

They wanted to get a win, but we were determined not to give it to them. The ball got played to me on the halfway line by the dugouts and I got scythed down. All hell broke loose with players from both teams steaming into each other. We had a few lads who could handle themselves with Roger Brown, Gary Peters, Steve Hatter (Galey was too good looking to get involved) and they had Trevor Aylott, Bobby Downes, Mick McCarthy and their manager... Norman Hunter! The former Leeds legend raced onto the pitch to get stuck in. Where was our manager? He was sitting in the dug-out.

When you say we battled to the end, it is very apt. We did and what a display it was, a point certainly well earned. It is performances like this that show the character and attitude of players which was first class. Back in the dressing room after the game the lads were pleased that we dug in and stuck together. Then Ernie Clay, a proud Yorkshireman and chairman of Fulham, came in and said how delighted he was with the performance. He then looked at me and said: "That's why we bought you. That was a top flight player's finish for the goal, brilliant." The players were great, but as for the manager… no comment again.

It's a long way back from Barnsley to Fulham and it takes a while when you are on a coach, but this trip seemed to go quicker than usual. One of the directors of Fulham at the time who was travelling with us came over to introduce himself. He sat next to me for the rest of the journey. It was Alan Price who was in the Animals when they had hits with 'The House of the Rising Sun" and 'Don't Let Me Be Misunderstood'. He was a very successful musician, singer-songwriter and musical arranger, a talented man. It was good to hear how he got started in the music business, going on tour and writing songs. He was from Washington, County Durham, so it was two Northern lads getting on famously together.

When I arrived at Fulham in 1980, I moved to a little known area called Molesey. Little did I realise that I would be joining what was affectionately known as 'The Molesey Fun Bus'!'

This was a car pool that was shared by Ray Lewington

and two of Fulham FC's mickey-takers in Les Strong and Tony Gale. I will hand over here to Ray:

RAY LEWINGTON: *The Molesey Fun Bus spared no one, but saved its best for people who lived outside London. Ronny, with his strong Liverpudlian accent, was fair game for Les and Tony on the journey in and home. I have seen lesser people fold under the constant abuse Les and Tony could dish out, but Ronny not only stood his ground – he gave some back also. Being the quite one of the four, I sat back for most of the hour long journey into training, giggling to myself. Once you could stand up to Les and Tony you were 'in' at Fulham and Ronny quickly settled in at the Cottage.*

Sadly I had very little playing time with Ronny as I had knee trouble during a lot of the time he was at Fulham. Ronny gave the side much needed balance with his crossing ability, but it will be the journeys into the Cottage that I will always remember in 'The Molesey Fun Bus''

Thanks for that great memory, Ray. Fulham trained daily at the Bank of England Sports ground in Roehampton which had been the training headquarters for the England football team during the triumphant 1966 World Cup. Your early days at a new club are all important. I struck up a good relationship with lads like Ray, Les and Tony. The latter was one of the brightest young talents in the game and was also our young club captain. Tony Gale had joined the club as an eleven year old and stayed at Craven Cottage until he was 24 before spending ten years at West Ham, so a real London boy. Of course, he won a

Premier League Champions medal with Kenny Dalglish at Blackburn Rovers and is a Sky TV pundit these days, but this was all for the future.

Our lack of consistency brought on a change at the top and Malcolm Macdonald was suddenly appointed to replace Bobby Campbell who had signed me. This is never a good thing for a fairly new player. Macdonald had just arrived as manager, having played for Fulham earlier in his career. Of course, he had made his name as a top class centre-forward at Newcastle and Arsenal and won 14 England caps. The fans called him SuperMac and let's just say he could be full of himself at times.

My first few days under his new regime are best summed up by our skipper at that time, or rather a man who quickly became my ex-skipper. I will let him explain below…

TONY GALE: *"I remember Ronny arriving at the club. He was a talented player and we got him straight from his successful spell in Holland. Bobby Campbell had bought him, but he would only make 22 appearances for the club as Macdonald came in with his own ideas. Ronny wasn't the only one to suffer at this point.*

"Malcolm immediately clamped down on what I would call the more talented players. Ronny was one of those. He had played at a high level at Everton and had then continued his career in Dutch football.

"I had been made captain at 18 by Bobby Campbell and was proud of the role. Malcolm immediately decided to take it off me, determined to assert his authority in those early days. Now he might have been a great player, but he was a novice manager.

"*He began calling the better players into his office one by one to tell us the five things we lacked, hardly a confidence booster. My so-called deficiencies, according to Malcolm, were that I wasn't quick and couldn't head the ball. Strange that when you look at the rest of my career. He rattled off some other negatives.*

"*I was a chirpy 20 year old and had been skipper for two years. I felt as if he had destroyed me and it didn't end there. He dropped me at Charlton and then called Ronny and the others into his office to highlight the five things they were not good at!*

"*Malcolm was a character, but he had lost his profile as an ex-England international. Of course, five years earlier, in 1975, he had famously scored five goals in a European Championship qualifier against Cyprus at Wembley, the most goals scored in one game by an England player. The famous newspaper headline was 'SuperMac 5 Cyprus 0'.*

"*Now he was our manager and he was offering my captain's role to my great friend Les Strong. He told Les that Bobby Campbell had given me the job at too tender an age. Les told him that he couldn't take the role because of our friendship and the fact that he knew my family well and particularly my mum.*

"*Les and I used to travel into training together and we were very close. Les told Malcolm that if he took the captain's role, he could never look me in the face again.*

"*Malcolm said: 'You'll get £50 a week more'. Les said: 'Ok, I'll take it!'*

That's football. It was Les's testimonial year and we were all supportive of that. He had a testimonial event looming and he asked Malcolm if he had anything from his playing days that could be auctioned. Malcolm immediately said that he had the boots that scored the five famous goals against Cyprus and that he would sign them with a gold pen so Les could auction them.

"We all attended the function. Ronny was there as well. The price kept going up and reached £1,000 which was a lot of money then. This geezer bought them and handed over the cash on the spot. Les was well pleased.

"On the following Saturday we were driving to the game and the guy who bought the boots was walking down the street near the ground. He shouted to us: 'Tony, Strongy… those boots I bought that Malcolm Macdonald wore to score his five goals against Cyprus… I've just watched a video of the match and he got all five… WITH HIS HEAD!'

"We all laughed and Les was able to keep his £1,000.

"Ronny will remember Les Strong well because he bought his house when he was in London. It was a new city and I felt for Ronny because he must have felt a bit out of it, but he was a football talent, a good old fashioned winger that hugged the touchline and was great when it came to one-on-ones. He never gave the ball away cheaply and then, like me, he was also being told the five things he wasn't good at.

"I always enjoy catching up with Ronny whenever we meet these days in our new roles as pundits. He's never short of an opinion on Radio Merseyside so he's certainly not Ronny Chatless! I know how much he thinks of Everton, a club that is close to his heart. I always think of Everton in the same way as I think of West Ham, another People's Club… terrific!"

Our next home game was against another Yorkshire team, Huddersfield Town, a club with a goalkeeper I knew very well from my Everton days – Andy Rankin. He was brave, athletic a good shot stopper and would have played more games for Everton only for the ability and consistency of Gordon West. It was an entertaining match that finished 2–2, but only because of two fantastic saves from Andy to earn Huddersfield a point.

It was going to be a busy festive period for us but before that we had a home FA Cup second round 'derby' game against Brentford. These were always very committed clashes, but with the added spice of the FA Cup. With Ron 'Chopper' Harris and Terry Hurlock in the Brentford team, this game would be no different. A lot of noise came from the fans as we emerged at the Cottage with both sets of supporters playing their part to create a good atmosphere.

It was a hectic start with no time or space to play for either team, but we did get the important first goal after 17 minutes. It proved a good game, but no more goals and we advanced to the third round.

We played at Reading on the 20th December and drew 1–1, but then had two games on the 26th and 27th December against Sheffield United at home and Charlton away, then an FA Cup third round tie at Bury.

The Sheffield United game took place on Boxing Day, a good name for the way it was played, a rough, tough battle against players like John Ryan, Stewart Houston and a player who would leave his mark on me, centre-half John MacPhail.

From the first whistle it was a battle of attrition with not an inch given. Then we were awarded a penalty which Kevin Lock calmly put it away in the 37th minute and we had this lead at half time. The second half was the same with crunching tackles going on all over the pitch. In the 61st minute I received the ball 35 yards out and dribbled past one defender to get into the penalty area. Then I went past the full back, but had to slide the ball across the six yard box from the bye line. By this time MacPhail had come across to get his covering tackle in. I was on the ground and he must have thought he was going back into his house and was wiping his feet on his welcome mat, but it was studs on both of my thighs and left knee. The only good thing is that Gordon Davies tapped it in from four yards to put us 2–0 up. The physio came on and took one of MacPhail's boots out of my thigh and gave it back to him. The physio could see the stud marks on both thighs and I had a dead leg plus a sore bleeding left knee, but besides that I felt great!

I had to come off, being replaced by Gary Peters. Bob Hatton got a late goal for Sheffield United but we won the game 2–1. The disappointing thing for me was that we were playing Charlton the next day and I had to miss the game through injury, but hopefully I would be fit for the FA Cup third round tie at Bury on the Saturday.

I had treatment through the week and then passed a fitness test and was selected to play. It was a difficult game against fired-up opponents. We played well, but Bury had an outstanding young keeper by the name of Neville Southall. Hilton scored for Bury after 75 minutes, but Tony Mahoney equalised for us in the 79th minute to make it 1–1 and earn us a replay. This was at Craven Cottage on the Tuesday. I remember the game for two reasons.

ONE. I couldn't have hit a volley from 25 yards much better and Neville Southall in goal could only watch as it smashed off the post and came back out of the penalty area.

TWO. Neville showed that night that he could become a top class keeper. He was absolutely outstanding and his performance alone earned Bury another replay.

Jim Iley, the Bury manager wanted to toss a coin for the choice of ground, but the FA said that a neutral venue should be selected and the second replay would be at West Bromwich Albion. Both clubs were not happy with this decision.

We played Millwall away on the Saturday and then played Bury on the Monday night at the Hawthorns on a freezing cold evening after it had snowed all day. We thought it might get called off with snow covering the whole pitch and with ice in certain parts, but the game went ahead. It wouldn't have been played today. The pavements were iced up all around the ground and for health and safety reasons alone it should have been post-poned. The tie wasn't a classic by any means, but the players deserve credit in awful conditions. It looked like it was heading for another replay but in the 89th minute Gordon Davies clipped the ball over Neville and into the back of the net to put us through 1–0 and into round four.

You would hear a lot more about Neville Southall in three years time!

I was playing well, but got dropped and went to see the manager. I knew that he still saw me as a Bobby Campbell signing. This story sums up the predicament I was in with this manager. Macdonald didn't even include me in the squad for the Blackpool game at Bloomfield Road so I trained on the Friday morning and then went home.

Just as I walked into the house Denise answered the phone to tell me it was the Fulham secretary. He said that Ray Lewington had been rushed to hospital and wouldn't be fit to play at Blackpool the following day and that the manager wanted me to link up with the team.

Lew had an operation on his knee, but he had caught an infection following the surgery. It was so serious we later found out that he nearly lost his leg.

I wanted the secretary to pass two words on to the manager, quite simply 'Fuck Off', but I was determined to be professional about it and didn't want to let my team mates or the supporters down.

I had to get from East Molesey to Euston where a train ticket was being left for me to pick up that would get me to Blackpool. I eventually arrived at the team hotel, checked in and made my way to the dining room. It was empty, but they had prepared a meal for me and I sat in a cubicle and waited be served. It was then that Malcolm Macdonald appeared and slid into the seat alongside me. "Are you ok?" he asked. "I certainly am." I replied. "What about you?"

He started to say: "We need to be…" and then I interrupted him. I said: "I will be professional like I always am or I wouldn't be sitting here now. It would have been easy for my wife to have said that she couldn't get in touch with me, but I'm not like that. Now I want to eat my meal!"

Macdonald said 'ok' and left. After eating I phoned my Dad to say I was in the squad, but didn't know if I was playing. He said he would be there with my brother John.

I played against Blackpool the next day with the great Alan Ball in opposition as player/manager. Willie Morgan, Terry Pashley and Colin Morris were in their line-up. I remember it was a bright sunny day with Blackpool desperate for the points, but we made a good start, keeping the ball and making them work hard to get the ball while restricting chances.

Then, in the 24th minute, I crossed for Tony Mahoney to score with a neat finish to make it 1–0. We had good possession and had Blackpool chasing the ball for the rest of the half.

The second half was similar to the first. We kept possession a lot better than they did and this was frustrating Bally more and more as the half progressed. He was screaming at his players to get tighter and keep the ball when they won it back. He always worked hard, but he was trying to do everything and was getting angrier when his players couldn't do what he was asking of them.

If we could secure a second goal the game would be over and this is what happened in the 88th minute. The move started deep in our half with good passing up to their penalty area. I was then set up to smash it past Hesford in the Blackpool goal to make it 2–0

The final whistle went not long after I had scored and I had a quick chat with Bally, but he looked dejected and although I was delighted about my goal and the win, I felt for him.

There was a good atmosphere when I got into our dressing room. It's always difficult to win away from home and the lads were coming over and saying well done and that I had played well.

I wasn't expecting anything from the manager... and he didn't disappoint!

I got changed and went into the bar where I had arranged to meet my Dad and our John. When I walked in I looked over and they were standing at the bar with Bally and Bally Snr. What a great sight that was. I went over and we talked about the game. Bally said I had been a thorn in their side all afternoon. We had a few drinks and a lot of laughs and it was a very enjoyable time. My only regret was that I never had a photo taken with my former Everton hero, his dad and my Dad, but this was again before mobile phone days.

I was made up for Dad and John to meet Bally and his father because you couldn't wish to meet two nicer people. We had to go and I wished Bally all the best for the rest of the season. My weekend was finishing far better than it had started.

I trained well all week before the next game at home to Portsmouth, a big club with a tremendous following.

This was a game I wanted to play in. After training we had a meeting in the dressing room at the Cottage where the manager started saying how well we had played at Blackpool and what a good win it was. He proceeded to announce the team to play Portsmouth the next day. Now I played number 11 and it would take a bit to get there, but obviously I was hoping to hear my name called out.

Macdonald got to number 11 and my name didn't come out of his mouth. All the team looked at me with Galey shaking his head from side to side. I was not even mentioned as substitute.

It wasn't only me shocked, but the whole team. I would have had more respect for the manager if he had pulled me to one side after training and told me then. As I've highlighted, his man management skills were not the best. I wasn't happy and I went to see his secretary to ask for a meeting. In the manager's office at Fulham, a glass door leads to the secretary's room and Ernie Clay, our chairman, was in there. He waved to acknowledge he had seen me.

I started chatting to Macdonald, saying: "Thought I did well last week, laid on a goal and scored one in a game that was away. You played me, tomorrow we are at home and I'm not even substitute."

Now as we were talking I could see Ernie Clay walking up and down past the door and looking in and smiling. My voice was getting louder the longer the conversation continued.

Macdonald replied: "You are not playing tomorrow

because you didn't try a leg last week!"

I stood up quickly and called him a "lying fucking tosser." I felt like jumping over the desk and was fuming because he had accused me of not trying. That's when Ernie Clay quickly came in and got in front of me, saying "Now now lads."

When I walked out I knew there was no future for me at Fulham while he was manager!

Everything at the club was right, well almost right. I liked the players and the tremendous staff behind the scenes. The club's passionate supporters were great to me while I was at the club which I appreciated. I got on with the chairman Ernie Clay who used to wind up the players. Whenever I went back to Liverpool he would wink at me and say: "Don't forget to get me half a dozen Liver Bird eggs." I would reply: "I won't forget Mr Chairman." The lads used to look at me as if to say: "What are these Liver Bird eggs like?"

I've said enough about Macdonald. All that you want to do is play football and that's what I still intended to do.

Macdonald apart, we had some great people at the club, a good dressing room and great camaraderie between the players. Derek Wright was a young physio at Fulham when I was there, but has been Head Physiotherapist at Newcastle United for over 30 years, a great lad.

I appreciated the backing from the Fulham supporters from the first minute I joined until I left and any time I go back to the Cottage I always get a great welcome.

I was therefore delighted that Fulham beat Aston Villa

1–0 in the 2017/18 Championship promotion play-off final at Wembley with a Tom Cairney goal. I'm so pleased to see them back in the Premier League where they belong and I am looking forward to seeing Dave Wicks and the lads. Wicksy has been a family friend for many years and a passionate Fulham supporter who I always meet at the Cottage. Wicksy, see you at Goodison soon.

THE NIGHT I BECAME LEAD SINGER WITH THE DRIFTERS

A COUPLE of months before I left Fulham FC I received a phone call from Cees Storm, a former team mate of mine at NAC Breda, asking my thoughts on a possible move to Hong Kong to play for a new team called Morning Star. They had just been promoted from the second division and were looking for new players to strengthen the team.

I was thinking about moving from Fulham to another club, but to Hong Kong? It never crossed my mind. Cees was already out there playing and went on to talk about the weather, food, life style, fashion, Stanley Market, cameras, swimming in the South China Sea and a recruitment drive by other teams to make the standard of football even better. He said it was going to be an exciting time to play there.

Football was and still is a very popular sport in Hong Kong and also Asia, but the game is a precarious profession over there with wheeling and dealing going on all over the place. This was something that worried me from the outset.

I was very excited about the move, but Denise was not so keen. We had two young boys at the time and she worried about how they would settle to life in Hong Kong. We discussed the positives and negatives before deciding to make the move.

It was a long flight and the plane only stopped at Abu Dhabi to refuel with everyone having to stay onboard, not the best of situations when you have two young children. However, they took it all in their stride.

We were flying into Kai Tak airport in Hong Kong which pilots say is one of the most dangerous to land. Planes would fly in very low over the shanty houses and with the runway not being the longest, the plane had to pull up rather sharply or it would end up in the South China Sea. Nothing to worry about then!

After collecting our cases we came into the terminal to be greeted by Cees, club representatives and about 50 reporters and camera crews.

We were escorted to a room for all the interviews which lasted about an hour, but after a long flight all we wanted to do was get to the hotel. After a couple of weeks we moved into an apartment in Kowloon which was not the largest I had ever seen and not the best for four people to live in, but land in Hong Kong is at a premium and they have to build upwards so we gave it a go.

This was not England, of course, where you take things for granted like private training facilities. We trained on local parks or amateur football pitches. Each team was allowed four foreign players and most in the league were British, Dutch or German. Timekeeping with the local players was not the best, but you had to be professional about it yourself.

Sometimes, when training was taking place, there were thousands of cockroaches on the field and the local players would kick the footballs towards them to make them fly away. Of course, they were used to doing this. I should add that these cockroaches were so large some of them had landing lights!

We trained for a few weeks when we were entered into a pre-season 8-a-side competition at one of the stadiums with all the league teams participating.

There were already rumours about financial difficulties at the club with sponsors holding back the money due for the players' wages.

I had to put these rumours to one side and get on with playing in the tournament. It was a full stadium with a noisy atmosphere and the team was playing well, securing some impressive results with good attacking football. We reached the quarter-final where I came up against Chris Galvin, ex-Leeds United, who would become a good friend. He was the brother of Tony Galvin, ex-Spurs.

It was a really good game and we went a goal behind, but I equalised when I broke clear from the halfway line with only the keeper to beat. I had time to think of what should I do, go round him, side foot it, blast it or chip him? The keeper started to come out to narrow the angle and with the goal looking smaller I shaped up to blast the ball, but chose to chip him and it sailed into the net.

This went down really well with the crowd and I was pleased to get a great ovation back to the halfway line, but we lost to a late goal. Still, it was a great experience and I was looking forward to the start of the new season.

I went into training the next day and the players were arranging a meeting to discuss the finances of the club. We needed to decide what our next step would be regarding our wages with payment due in a few days.

Reporters were arriving at the ground with questions about the finances and with the owners nowhere to be seen and no statement forthcoming from the club.

It was a worrying time for me. I was married with two young boys to look after and I needed some clarification as to what the situation really was.

The next day a statement from the owners was published to say they couldn't pay the wages and they might struggle to fulfil the fixtures. As a precaution I phoned Gordon Taylor at the Professional Footballers Association

(PFA) to explain what was going on. He was a great help and asked to be kept informed. He reassured me that they would be there to help in any way they could which I appreciated.

They do some fantastic work and I am proud to say that I am still a member of the PFA to this day. A few days went by, but there was still the uncertainty surrounding the club, but eventually the announcement came that it was folding and this was a major talking point on the TV, radio and in the press.

I then received a phone call from Peter Lam, the manager of South China and the biggest and most successful club in the history of Hong Kong football. He asked me if we could set up a meeting as soon as possible because he was interested in signing me for South China.

We met up at the stadium where he showed me around the club, and told me the history. I was pleased to sign.

The next day I was taken to see an apartment by Victoria Park which is on Hong Kong Island. The size was totally different from the previous apartment. You could have played a 5-a-side game in this one and it was overlooking the harbour and the South China Sea. Our apartment was on the eighth storey with the floor below a playground which had equipment such as swings, slides, and roundabouts, but there was also equipment for the kids to play on!

The training facilities where much improved from what I had been used to since arriving there. We trained at a smaller stadium owned by South China which had individual rooms for players to relax.

The training was either early morning or late afternoon because of the heat and humidity problems. It also went from one type of extreme weather condition to another. The monsoon season brought downpours and strong winds like I'd never experienced in England. Large oil tankers would get swept out to sea and with a great view from my apartment, I began to realise just how powerful Mother Nature is.

There were always big crowds watching the South China games. They were the best supported club with a great atmosphere generated by the supporters.

There was a big push at that time to take their standard of football to another level by signing overseas players from the major leagues in Europe.

The Hong Kong Football Association was desperate to qualify for a World Cup tournament with money no object, but this brought its own problems with many clubs having financial difficulties.

The nationality represented most was the Netherlands with names such as Dick Nanninga, Jan Peters, Wim Suubier, and Rene van de Kerkoff, all top international players.

In my South China team we had a Scouser (me), a Dutchman, a German and a Glasgow Rangers player called Billy Semple who also ran a bar in town. It was inevitable we would become mates!

Billy had played football in Hong Kong for a number of years and it was good to have him playing in left midfield and we talked a lot about league football there. A team called Eastern brought over an English manager with some players. The boss was Bobby Moore while the players were none other than my hero Alan Ball, and Graham Paddon (ex-West Ham and Norwich).

Another team called See Bee paid a fortune to bring out George Best, a real coup for them and the Hong Kong FA because of the publicity it inspired.

I could watch most of the league games if I didn't have prior commitments because the Hong Kong Stadium was where South China played all their league games and who wouldn't want to watch Bally and Besty playing football?

Hong Kong was a vibrant bustling city that was open 24/7. If you had money you could spend it in casinos, nightclubs or bars.

We used to head back to Billy Semple, my team mate's bar, which was called 'Rumours'. A bar on Smithdown Road would go by the same name the following year. I wonder who owned that bar?

Billy's place was where ex-pats met as well as players, and was a typical British pub with good beer and a great atmosphere. Everyone felt welcome.

On one occasion I was in there when Bally came in with Bobby Moore and they sat with me at the bar for a drink. The next minute George Best walked in, came over and joined us.

I got the round in and asked what they wanted to drink. As the barman was sorting out the order, I glanced along the bar and in our round was Besty, Mooro, Bally and… me!!

I'm with two World Cup Winners and one of the best players to ever put a pair of football boots on. Does it get much better than that?

My only regret is that I never had a photo taken with them. Hong Kong was a hot bed for cameras, but no mobile phones.

Another time, after I'd played in a game, I was given a few days off and went to a couple of bars before heading back to 'Rumours' with a few of the players. As the drinks flowed, a karaoke session started and we were enjoying ourselves. Billy suggested I might give a song.

I got up and started to sing the classic Drifters hit 'Up on the Roof'.

When this old world starts getting me down.
And people are just too much for me to face.
I climb way up to the top of the stairs...

Then the bar door opened and who should walk in but... The Drifters group who were on a world tour. They joined me onstage as I finished off the song.

Not many can say they had The Drifters as their karaoke backing singers and what nice fellas they were, clearly up for a laugh.

A lot of teams from around the world came to play in Hong Kong and not just at the beginning or end of the season. Sides from countries like Holland, France, Germany and Brazil would have mid-season breaks from league games and then they would play a few friendlies before their respective leagues started up again.

It was good to play against these quality teams, players and world class football clubs.

Bayern Munich came over to test my team South China. The Germans were a top club with top draw players and I had always admired Paul Brietner, one of the greatest German players of all time. He was a Bayern Munich legend who scored a penalty in the 1974 World Cup win against Holland, but he also scored in the final of the 1982 World Cup final. He is one of only four players to score in two different World Cup final games.

Brietner is in a very exclusive club with the other three players being – Pele, Vava and Zinedine Zidane. I wouldn't mind being in that club!

At the end of the game we did the customary handshakes between the players and for the first and only time ever I asked an opponent to swap shirts with me? Paul said yes and would bring the shirt after he got changed.

I met him outside the dressing rooms where he came over and gave me his full Bayern Munich kit and his boots. Now whether he wanted my shirt or not he was getting it anyway! He thanked me and I thanked him for his kind gesture and put his stuff in my bag.

His team were going to a club function and I said if he fancied a beer later we usually ended up in Rumours. I then went into town with a few friends carrying the bag. We had a few days off and we were going to enjoy ourselves. Hong Kong has many bars and nightclubs and I think that night we drank in most of them. Late into the evening I asked the barman if I could put the bag behind the bar and I would pick it up the next day. He said it would be no problem and we carried on with our walkabout around Hong Kong with supporters who recognised us and wanted to chat or have a beer. Our group was growing larger with every bar we visited.

Needless to say, the night progressed into the early hours of the morning with lots of drinks consumed. I had a very sore head, but it was a worthwhile price to pay for a great night out. There was one slight problem. I called at the bar where I thought I had left my bag with Paul's boots and kit, but they said I hadn't left it there and so I had to take their word for it. I then had to try and remember which bars I had visited and that was not going to be easy. I got the phone book out then proceeded to recall the bars and nightclubs I went to. This took a while, but to no avail. To say I was disappointed is an understatement so if anyone in Hong Kong still has my bag, could I have it back please?

After playing a number of games for South China I found out just how superstitious the Chinese are when we lost two games in a row. The performances were good, but we lost to two late goals in both matches and the night before the next game the squad had to meet up at the stadium. This meeting was in the evening when we wandered onto the pitch in complete darkness. I asked one of the players what was going on and he said it was a ritual we had to go through to change our luck. The next minute I saw two staff from the club walk onto the field carrying a dead pig. I jokingly said: "I can't wait to see the size of the bread for this bacon sandwich!"

The thing was, they were all serious about what was going on so I did the same. After a small speech from a club representative on the halfway line, the squad then went towards one of the goals with the dead pig leading the way. We reached the six yard box where a few more words were said to the group. Then they rubbed the pig fat onto the posts and crossbar to bring luck in the next game. We were then given joss sticks which they lit. We shook them a few times and then said a prayer for the team to play well and win the next game.

The squad then walked around the pitch pushing the joss sticks into the ground to finish this part of the evening off.

We were then taken to a restaurant for something to eat. We sat down and I looked at the menu, only for a team mate to say: "It is taken care of."

The manager introduced me to the chef who said I could help pick the menu I thought: "Great, sweet and sour, and spare ribs." I followed him into the kitchen where the chef then gestured for me to look over a small wall which I did and I was shocked to see it was a pit full of snakes. I thought: "I'm not playing that bad!"

The manager said the chef wanted me to choose which snakes we were going to eat, but the only snakes I knew anything about came with ladders!

I stared at a few snakes for a minute or two as if I knew what I was doing then I picked two which the chef agreed were good choices.

I went back into the restaurant where a few of the lads were smiling, knowing that I had picked the snakes, and we sat down to eat. There were a lot of different dishes to choose from and the players began to help themselves. Then we were each given a small pigeon to eat. Obviously I wasn't used to this, but it was their culture and I didn't want to disrespect them by not eating the food.

Here we were, the night before a game eating snakes and pigeons. Would this change our luck? I'm not sure about that, but I do know that I slithered onto the coach and we did win the game next day.

Over the years I have heard many stories about George Best and his conquests, not only on the pitch, but also off it. It was at this time that George was rumoured to be seeing Mary Stavin who won Miss World in London in 1977. They were together in Hong Kong and made a stunning couple with the famous story going down in folklore about them. It is the one when George was in his hotel room with Mary when he ordered a couple of bottles of champagne from room service. The waiter came into the room, put the bottles on the table and glanced over to the bed where Mary was lying, – surrounded by thousands of pounds. As the waiter left the room he turned to George and said: "Where did it all go wrong George?"

He was clearly a world class player on and off the pitch!

Before we came back to England from Hong Kong in late summer I had a couple of months break with the family after the season had finished when we could spend a bit more time sightseeing. I wanted to take the kids to Ocean Park, the most popular tourist attraction in Hong Kong, but you had to get there by the Cable Car over Victoria Peak. The four of us got into the Cable Car with me sitting on one side with Christopher and Denise on the other with Gary. The car started going slowly up the mountain and I was talking to the kids to distract them from the height we were at and telling them we were going to see the fish, penguins and dolphins in the aquariums.

All of a sudden we came around the mountain to see a sheer drop to the rocks with a view of the South China Sea. They didn't care what height we were at and as I carried on talking, the kids started rocking the car from side to side and shouting: "Look Dad, it's swinging." They would then roar with laughter and it was as if we were at the funfair. I'm telling them to take it easy when I looked at Denise and she said: "They're only kids and enjoying themselves," but I was thinking it was a long way down to those rocks!

We all had a very enjoyable day at Ocean Park. The kids loved it but it had been a long day for them and I was hoping they would fall asleep on the way down for a smoother ride.

It had been a great experience for me living and playing football in Hong Kong, getting used to a different lifestyle and culture, and then playing against quality players from around the world. Hong Kong is a fabulous place which holds fond memories for me from my time spent there.

TINY CLUB THAT BOASTS OF THREE ENGLAND CAPTAINS!

I RECEIVED a phone call from John Duncan, ex-Spurs, but who was now manager of Scunthorpe United who wanted me to go on loan for a few months. Not long after, the phone rang again and it was George Telfer who was playing at Scunthorpe. Telf was an ex-team mate of mine at Everton and he said it would be great if I joined him there.

I decided to meet up with John Duncan and signed. They had some good players which included the goalkeeper Joe Neenan, Paul Moss, Steve Cammack and, of course, Telf.

All clubs have their characters and Scunthorpe was no different with Joe Neenan at the top of the list. He was a good keeper, a practical joker who was always up for a laugh and he never shut up. We lost the first game at York City, but then we had three home matches and it was a good opportunity to gain some points.

The first home game was against Stockport County. It was the first time I had played at the Old Show Ground. It finished goalless with both keepers playing well to deny the forwards on many occasions.

The second home game was against Colchester United. A few familiar names played for them in Kevin Bremner, goalkeeper Mike Walker, Ian Allinson and Roger Osborne who scored the winner in an FA Cup final for Ipswich Town.

John Duncan wanted to play attacking football with width and good movement from the forwards. He wanted us to get plenty of crosses in with midfield players making runs into the penalty area.

This is what happened with our goal after 19 minutes following a late run into the penalty area by Paul Moss. Mossy was a skilful midfield player who remained cool to put the chance away to make it 1–0. Joe Neenan made a couple of good saves, but Telf broke away in the 60th minute to hit a low shot past Walker to make it 2–0 for us. We let Colchester back into the game when Bremner scored after 64 minutes, but there were no more goals with the game finishing 2–1, a good win for us.

With me living in London and Telf in Liverpool, we had to stay in digs in Scunthorpe to save the travelling. Telf had been there for a number of months and knew the routine of the place. During my first week we sat down at the dining table on the Monday when George said: "She's a great cook and on a Friday she does Sausage Pie." His eyes lit up as he talked about her speciality dish. I'm a fussy eater and I didn't fancy this at all.

She was a lovely lady, but I wasn't quite as impressed with her cooking skills as George was. She was no Nigella Lawson and I mean cooking not looks! It got to the Friday and we were sitting at the table with George smiling in anticipation. The plates of Sausage Pie were placed in front of us and George said: "It looks lovely."

Within seconds there were sparks coming off George's plate, his knife and fork were moving that fast. I had one mouthful and it wasn't to my taste, but they had a dog that would sit by the table. He loved it and became my best friend every Friday.

The third game was against Rochdale and I knew a few of their team including Eric Snookes and, from my Everton days, Barry Wellings. It had been a few years since my Mum had watched me play, but she travelled over with our John and a few friends for this game. We played some good football and I saw a lot of the ball. It was an enjoyable match and we won it with an Andy Keeley penalty.

A few of the players wanted to go for a drink. I said I was meeting the family and the lads said they would join me.

One of the players was Ian Botham, the England cricket captain. He was not bad in the air, could hold the ball up well and had good skill on the floor. He came on as substitute in a few games when I was there. He's in the quiz question: Name three Scunthorpe players who have captained England? Answer: Kevin Keegan, Ray Clemence and Ian Botham.

Ian was a really good lad with no side to him. When we arrived at the pub I introduced him to my mum, my brother John and other friends. He sat in the company and signed the match programmes. I drank cider with him which he liked. We were having a great time and Beefy (I called him seven bellies) asked if I wanted to go back to his house for a drink and a game of snooker. I replied: "Does night follow day? Yes!"

He asked if our John and Telf would like to come as well. John he was buzzing, but Telf said he would like to, but he had told his wife that he was coming back after the game.

We tried working on Telf, but he wasn't drinking because he was driving. We chipped away for an hour, but he wouldn't change his mind. He apologised, but I think Telf was sensibly thinking of the consequences if he got into a session and then went home with his wife waiting at the front door! Sometimes, you have to have your sensible head on!

TRANMERE OFFER A CHALLENGE THAT WAS TOUGH BUT FULL OF FUN

WHEN I arrived back in England I was looking for a local team to play for. Having played for football clubs in Holland, London and Hong Kong, it was time to come home.

It was then I received a call from John McGrath, manager of Chester, who said he was interested in signing me and would I come over for a few days to train and have a talk which I agreed to.

John had been a big aggressive centre-half who took no prisoners and made his name at Newcastle United and

Southampton, but he was a totally different character off the pitch. He was an intelligent man, knew his football and had a good sense of humour. He was putting a team together with a young Lee Dixon at right-back where he would go on to play for Arsenal and England.

I enjoyed the training then went away to think about what I would do, planning to ring John back in a couple of days to give my answer.

The next day I received another phone call, but this time it was from Bryan Hamilton, my ex-Everton team mate and now manager of Tranmere Rovers who wanted me to go to Prenton Park for talks about a possible signing.

I went across to see Hammy who explained it was a young team with loads of potential. We then went on to discuss terms and then I signed later in the day. I had been a frequent visitor to Prenton to watch Tranmere play on a Friday night when I was at Everton so I knew it was a good and friendly club.

I remember my first day at training when I was introduced to the players by Hammy with Dai Davies, ex-Everton, also there. My training kit was laid out in the dressing room and I chatted with the players as I got changed. Most of them were Evertonians and one asked me if I ran around Croxteth Park when I was with the Blues.

I said that I used to run around the Lord Derby estate and 'Croccy Park' for a number of years for the build-up to pre season training. I told him I used to run through Croccy Park a lot and recalled that a lad was always sunbathing. When he stood up he was about 6ft 2ins with blond hair and looking bronzed in his shorts. He would wave and scream 'Ronny' at the top of his voice. I used to wave back at him and carry on running. "That was me shouting you," said John Williams, the Tranmere captain. We just started laughing.

I had extensive training through the week because Hammy wanted me to make my debut at Chesterfield on the Saturday which I did. We got off to a really good start by taking a 2–0 lead after 18 minutes with goals from Mark Ferguson and Mark Palios who is now the owner of Tranmere. They scored just before half time which was against the run of play and then surprisingly scored two more after half time to lead 3–2 in the 80th minute. With eight minutes left, Willo showed he was a goalscoring defender by equalising to make it 3–3.

It was an eventful debut for me with goals and good character shown by the team to earn a point.

The next game was my home debut against Blackpool who had many in the side who would go on to have good football careers such as Paul Stewart, Ian Britton, Colin Greenall, David McNiven and my mate to this day Billy Rodaway. We again started really well and went into another two goal lead after 11 minutes and could easily have had a couple of more goals before half time. Then, after 69 minutes, John Aspinall – who had scored after 11 minutes – got his second goal from the penalty spot to make it 3–0. That should have been game over, but Blackpool scored two late goals to make the scoreline look respectable, but we deserved the points and it was a good home win.

We played Blackpool on Boxing Day so, being the professional that I am, I never had an alcoholic drink on Christmas Day or after the Blackpool game because on the 27th December we played away to York City. This was normal for fixtures in our day, but there were no massive squads to rotate and you just picked your strongest line up and got on with it. You just had to shrug off the aches and pains and go through the pain barrier.

We knew it would be a tough game. Denis Smith was their manager who I had played against when he was a no-nonsense centre-half at Stoke City. There was a large crowd with a tremendous atmosphere and both teams wanted to win. The game finished 1–1 with Dave Philpotts scoring 15 minutes from the end. This was a good result for us because York would win the league at a canter amassing 101 points and with a goal difference of plus 57.

One of our lads knew the York striker John Byrne who asked if we fancied going for a drink in York after we got changed and the answer was a resounding yes.

We had a few drinks around York then ended up on a boat moored on the River Ouse that had a nightclub. What a night that was: The Pirates of York City!

We then played Reading before the turn of the year and then the 'derby' game at Chester City on the 2nd January. I've played in so many different types of conditions in games, but in this one it was blowing a gale from one goal to the other straight down the pitch and very difficult to play good football. It was no surprise it ended 0–0 and we had played four games in eight days.

The next game was at home to Torquay United and it was like an Everton reunion with myself, Dai Davies, Bryan Hamilton and Barry Wellings for Tranmere and Bruce Rioch as manager of Torquay. I had a lot of respect for Bruce which started in our Everton days. He was a tremendous player and man. I talked with him briefly before the game and said I would see him later.

We played well that day and should have been leading at half time but it stayed 0–0. In the second half we took full control and put in a really good performance, scoring three in 14 minutes through Mark Hilditch (2) and John Aspinall.

After getting changed I went to see Bruce in the away dressing room. I knocked on the dressing room door and Bruce shouted for me to come in. From the look on the players' faces Bruce had obviously given them a bollocking. Pointing to me, he then said: "There he is. The one I told you to mark and none of you could get anywhere near him."

Now Bruce can be scary if you don't know him and I just said :"We have all been here, but it's how you respond as a team and individually to a result like this so go out in your next game and give it your all, but we did fuck you, didn't we?"

I said the last part to get a reaction from the players and bring a smile to their faces which it did. In the Torquay line up that day was Keith Curle, later to play for Man City, Wimbledon and manage Chester City.

They were a cracking set of players at Tranmere with a few Liverpool based lads, including myself, John Williams, Dave Burgess, Mark Ferguson, Andy Lee and Dave Higgins.

Higgy was a centre-half, a young player at the time and a good lad. He was scouted playing Sunday League football, but he could be wound up. We had played at home on the Friday night and the usual routine was rallying the troops and seeing who was going back over to Liverpool for a drink. Higgy was complaining of a dead leg in the car which Willo was driving and I was joking with Willo about these hard case centre halves moaning about a dead leg.

I knew the owners of Rockford's bar opposite the Royal Court Theatre so I took the lads there and I ordered the drinks as we stood by the bar

After about 45 minutes I noticed Higgy was standing in a puddle of water. We asked him what was going on and he told us he had filled his right hand trouser pocket full with ice to try and numb the pain of his dead leg. Only Higgy!

The standard of the players in the league at this time was high and this included the managers also. We beat Mansfield Town at home 1–0. Steve Whitworth marked me as he did when I played for Everton against Leicester with ex-Bolton manager Ian Greaves as Mansfield manager. Then we drew 1–1 against Doncaster Rovers at Belle Vue with Billy Bremner manager and Glynn and Ian Snodin playing for Donny; then Peterborough United with John Wile, ex-WBA, and player manager of Posh with a certain David Seaman in goal with a young Gary Worrall in midfield and Ray Hankin and Alan Waddle the strikers.

We played at the County Ground against Swindon Town managed by Ken Beamish, ex-Tranmere with Jimmy Quinn and Andy Rowland, and drew 1–1. We had a good 3–2 win at Spotland against Rochdale who were managed by Jimmy Greenhoff, ex-Man Utd and Stoke.

I mentioned about the camaraderie that was in the squad between the lads and John Williams reminded me of a couple tales.

Willo said: *"This story started the night before when we played a game on the Tuesday and came back to Liverpool to visit a few bars and then we ended up in the Conti for more drinks with me looking for a bird. No luck there! We stopped off at a Kensington chippy on the way (our favourite Chinese) and I was driving and dropping everyone home. Marshall Burke was staying at your house, Ronny, because he was on loan from Blackburn and it saved him travelling home. Going to training the next day I would pick you up first and then the rest of the lads at the Mersey Tunnel entrance – Owen Brown, Ian St John Jnr and Dave Burgess. Going through the tunnel I had the usual problem. It cost 30p for the fee. Trying to get this off the lads was like getting blood from a stone with 5p here and 10p there. Another 5p materialised, but we were getting close to the booths now. You produced a chop suey roll out of your coat pocket, Ronny, with one bite out of it and calmly said: "I wondered where that had gone?" We fell about laughing.*

"On another occasion it was around Christmas time and there was snow everywhere so all the games had been cancelled. I decided to spend a large percentage of my time on Christmas Eve in your pub, Ronny, the Peel Hotel. At closing time you closed up, but we couldn't get a taxi so you had the idea that if we cut through the Ambulance Service Station onto Lower Breck Road it would save us some time. We got close to the Ambulance gate when the security guard stopped us. He recognised you, but nevertheless told us under no circumstances were we to be on the property. He wouldn't let us through the gate, obviously a Liverpool supporter.

"He told us to go all the way round which was about three quarters of a mile. I looked to the left and saw a wall about four feet high. I said to you: 'Fuck this, we'll go over the wall'.

"Being the super fit athletes that we were I knew he'd never catch us. I jumped up onto the wall and over I went. At the point of no return and flying through the air I realised the other side of the wall was about a 12 foot drop. Luckily I landed half on grass, half on concrete and bounced into a tree.

"The next thing I heard was you encouraging yourself to jump over the wall. I started to say 'don't do it' when you suddenly came flying through the air, hit the concrete and bounced off like a rag doll into a tree.

"I'd already started laughing before you hit the floor. After you untangled yourself and got over the shock, you said to me: 'Have you any more bright ideas?' It was then we got the next taxi and went straight home."

Thanks for those memories, Willo.

After we drew at Doncaster Rovers 1–1, we went on a

good run of nine league games undefeated and this co-incided with the start of the first Football League Trophy which was played in midweek, so it was thirteen games undefeated.

In the first round we beat Halifax Town 2–0. In a second round 'derby' game against Chester City we beat them 4–1 and I scored the third goal. In the quarter-final we beat Crewe 4–3 on penalties and in the Area Semi-Final we beat Burnley 2–0.

The team was playing well and we went into the home game with Chesterfield full of confidence, but it didn't go as we had planned. John Duncan had been my manager at Scunthorpe and he was now Chesterfield manager. We had scored three goals against them on my debut so he knew about me and wanted to stop me which they did. I was clattered after two minutes and should have come off, but stayed on. We lost the game and didn't play well.

The lads were saying in the dressing room that the defender had done me, and while Hammy was telling us where we had gone wrong I took my left boot off because my foot was aching. I removed my sock and looked down to see the damage. Now if anyone gets an injury, no matter how bad it is, an unwritten law is that you don't comment in front of the injured player. Owen Brown was sitting next to me and screamed out: "Oh my god, it's the worst injury I have ever seen." Nice one Owen.

I had nearly severed my Achilles tendon and Hammy asked why I never came off. I had not wanted to let the lads down and come off when we were losing, but it did make the injury worse.

Hammy then told me and the lads to have a shower and I then went into the treatment room for the doctor to have a look at the injury. The doc proceeded to put the stitches in and it's amazing how your team mates react when it is someone else getting the stitches and not them!

Twelve were inserted on the inside and fourteen on the outside, a good job by the doc. The injury was a real blow for me and it looked like I would miss the Northern Area Final against Hull City which was taking place on the 18th May.

I was doing everything that was asked of me in terms of treatment and training in the gym. The following Saturday I was in for treatment early at Prenton Park when the lads started to arrive for our game at Blackpool with 40 minutes to departure. I had finished my treatment and was walking down the corridor when Ray Mathias said to me: "The Gaffer wants you to do some exercises before we go to Blackpool." We went into the drying room where there was a mat, football, and a medicine ball.

Mathigo liked to train and it was a really hard thirty minute session. I did press ups at different points, but it was mostly abdominal exercises with me lying on my back and coming up to head the ball. It was one minute on, ten seconds rest, again and again. Then it was bouncing the medicine ball on my stomach for a minute with ten seconds rest and so on. At the end of the 30 minute session I thought I had gone 12 rounds with Anthony Joshua who could only hit me in the stomach!

I had intensive treatment and training to get me fit to play in the Area Final against Hull City at Boothferry Park and it worked, but unfortunately we lost to a team that included Brian Marwood, Steve McClaren, Billy Whitehurst and Alan Taylor. They were clinical on the night.

We were obviously disappointed, but we had arranged weeks before to travel to Wembley to watch Everton v Watford in the FA Cup final the next day.

Willo was the driver with me and Mark Ferguson acting as his co-pilots and we went early to check into the hotel.

We had arranged to meet up with a couple of lads in a pub called the Chequered Flag. It was heaving with Evertonians who were in good voice.

We started to get in the mood with the drinks really flowing and the atmosphere was tremendous. Willo was wearing a big crocodile hat with a tag attached. When you pulled it the crocodile would snap. The things you wear on Cup Final day!

I received tickets for behind the goal where the Evertonians were massed and Willo looked at me just before we kicked off and said: "I'm smashed." I think we all were, but I was going to enjoy the game.

Sharpy scored the first and when we started to celebrate Mark Ferguson was facing us with his back to goal. All of a sudden the crowd parted and he started staggering back down the terraces for about 30 yards. Then the crowd closed in and we couldn't see Fergy! About ten seconds went by before the crowd parted again then he started racing back up the terraces with a big smile on his face. We couldn't stop laughing.

When we came back for pre-season there were a few new faces (and old ones) that had joined the squad with Colin Clarke and John Clayton two good goalscorers, and Billy Rodaway a great professional with experience at a higher level.

The lads settled in quickly. I had known Billy for a long time and knew what a good lad he was, but let him explain, followed by some thoughts from other Rovers' personalities for which I am grateful...

BILLY RODAWAY:

"I first met Ronny in 1968 when I used to train with the older Liverpool Schoolboys team in which Ronny played. We came up against Manchester Schoolboys at Old Trafford and beat them 3–1. My Dad watched the game and said: 'That lad on the left wing looks a great player. He will definitely make the grade'. How true he was.

"Ronny and I both went our different ways with our professional football careers. I went to Burnley and Ronny went to Everton. Eventually we both ended up at Tranmere playing under Bryan Hamilton and Ray Mathias.

"They were both workhorses and you had to be fit. Ronny had no problem, but I struggled a bit. After one Friday night we ended up with our other team mates John Williams, Andy Lee, Dave Burgess and Dave Higgins having a drink in Liverpool town centre. Ronny met Jan Molby who at the time was injured for Liverpool. I was gobsmacked being with both of them and they were going on about when they played in Holland.

"When Ronny and I were both recovering from injury it was hard work. Bryan Hamilton and Ray Mathias ran us into the ground.

"Once again it was no problem for Ronny. He kept me going, saying 'Come on Billy, don't give in to these two bastards." We got through all the sessions and we were back playing sooner than we thought thanks to Ronny.

"We had a small group of players – Ronny, myself, John Williams (Greek God, loved himself), Andy Lee (another good looking lad) and Dave Burgess (the driver). Ronny was the organiser out of all of us. We had to be in early because Ronny organised the head tennis which he loved. He had great skill and technique and was always on the winning side.

"We also had a routine after training as all the pro footballers did in the 70's and 80's. We went to play snooker and had a few drinks again with Ronny being the organiser.

"I lived with my Dad at the time, waiting for my family to move back from Blackpool. It got a regular thing after training Tuesdays… snooker and then drinking. It would come to the afternoon and it would start getting a bit heavy because we were off the next day.

"I phoned my Dad to put my tea in the oven and said that I wouldn't be too long. He replied: 'You're not out with Ronny Goodlass again are you? No wonder your fucking career is going down the drain!' God bless Dad.

"I've got some great memories. It was a privilege to know you, Ronny, and play in the same football team. My dad was right. You were a top player, and a top man."

JOHN WILLIAMS, EX-TRANMERE ROVERS CAPTAIN

"In the pre-season of 1984 I was coming back from injury and Ronny was very inspirational to me. We became a tight group on and off the pitch. I can remember him telling me one day on an afternoon out that if you were going to have a few drinks, always make sure you are at the front in every way in training because Bryan Hamilton didn't just run us. He tortured us at Leasowe Beach and the nearby sandhills, his favourite haunt.

"Ronny was always on at me at being the best I could and I will always be eternally grateful. I remember great times at his house on Queens Drive with his beautiful wife Denise and family, enjoying our Sunday Roast. Plenty of Beatles and Roast Beef!"

MARK PALIOS, FORMER TRANMERE ROVERS PLAYER AND CURRENT OWNER

"I knew Ronny from the early days of our careers. We both cut our teeth in the Lancashire League, the proving ground for aspiring professional footballers in the North West. This was used by the A and B teams of the many professional clubs in the North West, a unique football geography of clubs that has produced so many players over the years.

"Clearly a major talent, Ronny came through that system and ended up playing for Everton at the same time as I began at Tranmere, so we played against each other many times before he eventually joined Rovers.

"Ronny came to Prenton Park after his top flight career had ended which included playing many years abroad. He had provided the cross for Bryan Hamilton's disallowed FA Cup Semi-Final goal in 1977 that has been the object of debate for many years on Merseyside. Bryan Hamilton was adept at building a competitive squad on a shoestring so it was no surprise when he brought Ronny to the club in the 1983/84 season.

"At the time he had built a squad which included a number of local lads who were all characters and the dressing room was a typical Merseyside mix in which Ronny fitted in well.

"The spirit was typified by one lazy, hot afternoon after training when John Williams, Mark Ferguson and Dave Burgess decided to kidnap another player's dog and hold it to ransom. The dog, in fact, belonged to the player's partner and she was seen as the barrier to her partner coming out 'to play' during afternoon get-togethers. As the story goes, they kidnapped the dog and then rang up from a public phone box, threatening that 'the dog gets it' if the player wasn't allowed to come out.

"The dog was made to bark down the phone. They followed this up by ominously driving up and down past the player's house, holding the dog up at the window. Whether the player was let out to play or not, I never found out, but that was the spirit of the dressing room at the time and Ronny was a natural fit.

"Ronny made his debut away at Chesterfield in the December – a game where I got on the scoresheet with John Williams and Mark Ferguson, two of the dog-nappers. He played most of the rest of the games, helping us to finish tenth in the league.

"As I said, Bryan was adept at building a squad and over the close season he brought in Clarke and Clayton who became one of the most prolific scoring partnerships seen at the club, grabbing over 50 league goals in a season in which we finished sixth.

"It was my last season at Tranmere as a player and Ronny left early on, having only played the first game. I would have liked to have seen him play with Clarke and Clayton and I've often wondered whether his supply from the wing would have helped take us into the promotion position that would have seen Bryan keeping his job."

BRYAN HAMILTON, FORMER TRANMERE ROVERS MANAGER

"My first job in football management was at Tranmere Rovers Football Club. They were in a poor situation financially which had a big effect, both on and off the field. When you are a manager it is important to have a good relationship with your chairman. I was lucky to have one of the nicest and most decent of men, Mr Harold

Thomas, as my first chairman.

"I had a squad of lads mostly from the North West and mainly from the Merseyside area. Many of the players had been with Everton and Liverpool as young players and had found their way across the Mersey to Prenton Park.

"There was a good mix of experienced and young players at the club who I really enjoyed working with. One player who found his way into the squad was one of my old teammates from Everton, Ronny Goodlass. I knew Ronny as a very talented and exciting player who could change the course of a game.

"He was also Liverpool born and bred and would have a feeling for the third team on Merseyside. I believed he would be a crowd pleaser with his dribbling skills and pace but importantly for me he would be great in the dressing room. He did not disappoint with his performances on the pitch and he was fantastic with the players.

"Ronny is a great character and the lads enjoyed his humour and I did hear he was responsible for some of their best social nights in the city. I lived on the Wirral and many of the players lived across the Mersey in the great city of Liverpool. Maybe it was just as well as I was not aware of all that took place, but later I did hear he was an inspirational leader who helped the team bonding.

"I am delighted that I was able to play with Ronny in the famous Blue shirt of Everton and that I was allowed to help extend his playing career at Tranmere Rovers.

"Ronny is one of the great characters in the game and

especially on Merseyside. I hope my small contribution will help him as he tells the story of his time in football and how he was the local boy who made good."

SURPRISED WHEN BRIAN KIDD SENDS S.O.S FROM BARROW!

I LEFT Tranmere Rovers to take up a tenancy in a pub called The Peel Hotel which was taking up a lot of my time. I was fully committed and so approached Bryan Hamilton to tell him I was leaving. He tried to persuade me to stay, but I thought it would be for the best.

After six months in the pub I decided to get it fully refurbished and this was a big job to undertake, ripping things out from top to bottom with designers and workmen all over the place. I was really busy.

I then received a phone call at home from Brian Kidd, the ex-Manchester United and Everton player who was now manager of Barrow, asking me to help him out. To put it in his words: "'We are in deep shit'!"

In his first seven games as manager they had drawn three and lost four and they had not scored a goal in any of those matches. We talked for about an hour before I said I would go up to Barrow to see him and have a chat.

I met Bill McCullough the club's owner/chairman and he was a really nice man who I liked and we hit it off straight away.

To help a mate out I signed on the 2nd February 1985. I made my league debut against Dagenham alongside two other new signings, right-back Benny Philips from Stalybridge Celtic and Andy Wharton from Chester City. You want to get off to a good start at your new club and it was a must win league game for the club, having not had a victory in ten games. We didn't get off to the best of starts when the referee, having seemed to initially award us free kick, gave Dagenham a penalty and booked our keeper Peter McDonnell. It was 0–1 at half time, not the score we envisaged before kick-off.

Kiddo had made other signings before I arrived at the club and these were Kevin Gorman, Kevin Keelan and Levi Edwards. We needed to score early in the second half to get back into the game which we did. It was a quality finish from Nigel Keen at an angle from the edge of the penalty area, his shot flying into the top corner of the net. Game on!

The goal was just what we needed to settle down the team and the crowd. If our first goal was good, the second was even better. Dagenham thwarted one of our attacks and cleared the ball 30 yards out, central to their goal. It found Kevin Gorman in midfield and he had a good first touch before smashing an unstoppable shot past the keeper before he could even move.

We wanted to keep this momentum going and were now well on top.

The local newspaper reported:

> *"Barrow continued to press forward and they used the speed and trickery of Ronny Goodlass to keep the pressure on the visitors who had to rely on breakaways to try and find an equaliser. With three minutes left Barrow made the game safe when Benny Phillips sent in a cracking shot that hit the post. The rebound fell to Colin Cowperthwaite who made no mistake from close range."*

It was a good win and we went on a six game unbeaten run.

The next game was my first away for the club at Kidderminster Harriers which I remember because I scored my first goal for the club and we won 1–0.

Kiddo and John Cook, his assistant manager, were building up a good camaraderie in the dressing room and the new signings were integrating well. Cooky was a good lad and there was great banter and plenty of laughs in the dressing room. It was needed because of where Barrow is situated and with a lot of long away trips all over the country.

Characters in the team included Keith Kennedy and Colin Cowperthwaite and togetherness was needed when we played Frickley Athletic. The club was formed to give Frickley Colliery miners a recreational outlet. We played the match during the miners' strikes and with the Colliery being the biggest employer in the town there was a lot of anger about. The football was a way of forgetting their problems for a while or so we thought.

The match was competitive which you expect, but the longer it went on the crowd were getting more involved, pressurising the referee and having a go at us for anything and everything as the tackles flew in.

The only downside was that Levi Edwards said he was getting racially abused which should never be tolerated and you could see it was affecting him. All you can do as a team mate is to be there to support him and to encourage him to get through the game as best he could. Near to the end, racial chants were now coming from a large section of the crowd and the Barrow lads clearly weren't happy.

We got a corner and the abuse from the crowd was constant with the V-sign and hand gestures prevalent from the Frickley supporters. I was standing by the bye line with Kevin Keelan, waiting for the ball to come back out of the crowd. We were talking and having a bit of banter with the fans when a big fella had a right go at Kevin. Now with all the racial abuse Levi was getting, the stick the players were taking and with this fella having a pop at Kevin, he had clearly had enough and turned to this fan, shouting: "Where are you going for your holidays this year."

Despite the abuse we had taken, it was a bit of a cynical comment while they were in the middle of strike action and unsurprisingly that supporter went ballistic, the crowd responded, and there was pandemonium as the final whistle went. Their supporters were trying to get over the wall onto the pitch. It was a good job the stewards were there. We made our way to the dressing room rather quickly.

You remember games for different reasons, but I will never forget this game at Frickley because it had everything.

We then played against Wealdstone at Holker Street. The squad reported early as usual for a brief meeting before inspecting the pitch. We glanced over to the tunnel to see the Wealdstone team also come out, suited up and wearing earphones to listen to their music. It was as if they were on a Sunday stroll. You don't mind a bit of confidence, but this was stretching it a bit and Kiddo's face said it all. He wasn't happy with their show of arrogance and he looked at me and said: "The state of them."

One of their players that day was a certain Vinnie Jones who would make a name for himself later in his career for some crunching tackles for Wimbledon as well as famously grabbing Gazza's meat and two veg!

We went back into the dressing room to get changed and listen to a few final instructions with a good result uppermost in our minds.

The pitch was heavy with Wealdstone frequently overstepping the mark with some of their tackles to keep the referee busy. We went behind to a Holmes goal which we didn't deserve and the referee wasn't giving us much protection. In the half time team talk Kiddo pulled no punches: "They have got stuck right into us and kicked Ronny for 45 minutes. If you don't go out and kick shit out of them, I will be waiting by that dressing room door when you come back in." Kiddo had a way with words.

We went out and got stuck in while playing some really good football and turned the game around. The crowd played their part and we beat them 2–1.

When we got back to the dressing room Kiddo was waiting by the door, but this time with a big smile on his face and congratulating us as we came in. The team had displayed great character and ability against a Wealdstone team that would win the FA Trophy in the May, beating Boston United at Wembley as well as winning the League by four points to gain the 'double'.

I had only been at the club for two months when Brian Kidd who had signed me said he was leaving which came as a shock. He went in early April when we drew 1–1 at Dagenham, becoming assistant manager to Tommy Booth at Preston NE, but that's football.

The Barrow supporters were a passionate crowd and gave great support to the club, but so did the Chairman/ Owner Bill McCulloch. He was a self-made man who worked hard all his life and knew Barrow FC was the hub of the community and he wanted to get Barrow back into the Football League. The team wasn't in the best of positions when we played Worcester City at Holker Street. The pressure was on for us to win because we needed the points to get us out of trouble.

I was standing on the halfway line waiting for Worcester City to kick off when I heard a voice in a deep Brummie accent say: "Alright there Ronny." I looked and noticed he had a Number 1 haircut. He gave me a half smile, but I was concentrating on the start of the game.

Again I heard "Ronny" and looked more closely. OMG it was Bernie Wright, my ex-Everton team mate, who had long red curly hair when I last saw him. He now looked like Yul Brynner, but more menacing!

It was a good team performance and we restricted Worcester's attacks. I scored to give us a 1–0 win. It was a very important result and Bill McCulloch was delighted. He said to me after the game: "That goal has kept us in the League and there will be a bonus in your pay packet at the end of the month." Bill was a man of his word!

Four days after this game we played Clitheroe in the Final of the Lancashire Junior Cup at Preston North End's Deepdale ground, but lost 1–0 after extra time.

We finished the season off with John Cooke as caretaker manager for the last three games.

The club appointed Maurice Whittle as manager in May 1985 and the first home game was against Frickley Athletic at home. You want to start with a win, but it ended 2–2. I scored one of the goals from the penalty spot. The next couple of months were not the best for the club with a run of poor results and another change of manager was made. Maurice was a good player and a nice man, but I think the manager's job in my opinion was thrust on him and he thought he would have to accept the offer.

That's a few changes in the position of manager in six months which was not good. When we played Northwich Victoria away, two of the former bosses were there to watch, Brian Kidd and John Cook.

We got the win we needed and I scored with a left foot drive into the roof of the net to give us a 1–0 win. After the game, Kiddo and Cooky came in the dressing room to say hello to the players. They were two good lads.

I decided to leave Barrow because it was difficult to run a busy pub with long hours travelling for training and also for the games. In my time at the club they had eight managers either full time or caretaker manager which is incredible.

Ray Wilkie, who took over in the March, tried to persuade me to change my mind. I liked Ray. He was a good manager and I liked his philosophy on football, but I wished him all the best for the future and was pleased to see that he brought success to Barrow.

JOE ROYLE CALL COMES OUT OF THE BLUE AND I'M HEADING HOME

RUNCORN Football Club were having a very poor season and they were in financial difficulties when Jimmy Smith, a very good friend of mine, was in talks with the Runcorn board about helping to turn the club's fortunes around by raising funds and helping on the football side. Jimmy had a vast amount of experience at non-league level and used to own South Liverpool where he had great success for a number of years.

Peter Barnes was sacked and I was approached to take

over as manager which I accepted. A lot of improvements and changes were needed, both on and off the field.

At the end of the season I was asked by the chairman to put together a five year plan to take the club forward.

I wanted to improve the playing squad, give youth players a chance, and set up a Youth Academy with teams of all ages. I also wanted to attract major sponsors and get involved in all aspects of the club. A meeting was arranged with the Runcorn board for me to present my five year plan. I was just leaving the house to attend the board meeting when the phone rang and Denise said: "It's Joe." I replied "Joe who?" and she shouted: "Royle!"

I closed the door and the conversation went like this: "Hi Joe," to which he replied: "Ronny, where are you going?"

I said: "I'm going over to Runcorn for a board meeting, why?"

Joe answered: "I want to offer you the job of Everton Youth Team Coach. Have a think about it," to which I replied: "I have thought about it. What time do you want me at Bellefield?"

Joe: "Monday at 8.30am," to which I said: "Okay, see you then."

I put the phone down with a big smile on my face, but I still had to go to Runcorn for the board meeting. When I arrived there all the directors were in the board room, waiting to call me in. When I entered the room there was one empty seat at the head of the board room table. I sat down and put my folder on the table.

In a formal manner, the chairman said: "'Thank you for attending, Mr Goodlass. Can you please tell the board about your plans for the club over the next five years."

I started with: "Thank you for giving me the opportunity to manage Runcorn Football Club, but I've been offered the job as Everton Youth Team Coach today and I've accepted."

I then said: "I will leave the folder here in case you want to look at my recommendations to take the club forward. I wish you every success for the future. Thank you."

There was complete silence as I got up from my chair and walked towards the door, the only noise being my shoes touching the floor. One door shuts and an even bigger one was about to open.

I was up very early on the Monday morning when I was going back to Bellefield for the second time as an Everton employee, but not as a player but as an Everton youth coach.

I walked through the gates just as I had when I was a 15 year old apprentice and felt exactly the same with a mixture of excitement and pride.

I went up to the dining room where a few of the groundsmen were having tea and toast. Then John Hurst came in. I had known Hursty from our Everton playing days. I then met first team coach Willie Donachie who I'd played against when he was with Manchester City.

We then went down to the coach's room where my training kit was on my peg, tops, shirts and shorts having my RG initials on them with socks, boots and trainers on the bench. That's when it hit me: "I'm back!"

Here are some parts of an interview I did with the Evertonian in August 1996, written by Paul Joyce, as I reflected on my new role. I told the magazine:

"Nothing has changed since I was here as a trainee. When I met the youngsters for the first time I was trying to get across to them that I had been a local lad who had supported Everton all my life, and that you can make it. Of course, not everyone is going to make the grade, so that is all the more reason to work hard during your apprenticeship. It passes you by so quickly. I can still remember the day I walked through the gate at Bellefield as a young pro. The club is about winning things. The kids now have a great opportunity and it is up to them to grasp the chance.

"At this stage they cannot afford to regret things. They mustn't get into a situation where they say to themselves 'If only I had done this or that'.

"The lads have impressed me with their ability already and the kids will be brought up playing the Everton way, so that if they do progress to the first team they'll know exactly what is expected. I think it is important to have local lads in the first team."

I was keen to have an early impact on those young players and the new influx of first year apprentices had some real quality in the group. Richard Dunne, Michael Ball and Danny Cadamarteri went on to have very good football careers.

Dunny came over as a 15 year old from Home Farm with his mate Paddy Drew who we also signed from the same club. I will mention Paddy again later. Even at 15 years old Dunny was a big powerful lad and Jimmy Gabriel, our reserve team coach, gave him the nickname 'The Honey Monster'. He would go on to play 80 times for the Republic of Ireland, captained them also and scored eight goals.

Like in my day, apprentices were assigned jobs to do for the first team and reserve team players concerning their training kit and boots. All the footballs had to be at the right pressure and bagged. They had to check that the senior players they were assigned to all had a complete training kit with boots and anything else that was needed. After all this was done, they could then go out as a group and train.

You had to have discipline and structure for the group or nothing would get done. Working as a team would put you in good stead as you progressed in your football career.

One morning their jobs were completed and we went out to train on the best area of grass at Bellefield that everyone called 'Wembley'. We started with a bit of ball work and then finished off with a five-a-side match. Everyone enjoyed playing on there. The lads walked ahead of me and Hursty, one carrying a bag of footballs.

Now nobody kicks a football until everyone has had a warm up. Paddy Drew had jogged past us to go on the pitch and then he emptied the footballs out of the bag.

I will tell you a bit about Paddy first, a really nice lad,

the joker in the group, enthusiastic with good skill and technique, but he could go from the sublime to the ridiculous in seconds.

As we turned the corner to go on the pitch, Paddy was running with the ball at pace towards one of the five-a-side goals. He then smashed the ball from six yards towards the goal. It thudded against the crossbar, sailed into the air, cleared the 15ft fence that surrounds Bellefield and smashed into one of the greenhouses in the back garden of a house on Eaton Road.

Everyone gasped with mouths open. Paddy was looking shocked and I thought Hursty was going to explode, while I was trying my best not to burst out laughing.

Paddy's punishment was to clean the toilets for a week, go around to the lady of the house and apologise. We paid for the glass and bought her some flowers and chocolates which Paddy gave her. He never got the footballs out of the bag again unless he had done his warm up.

The draw for the FA Youth Cup first round was a tie against Nuneaton at home and it was a good opportunity for our lads to play at Goodison.

FA YOUTH CUP FIRST ROUND.
EVERTON YOUTH 3 NUNEATON YOUTH 0

It was a professional performance from the lads. It's always going to be difficult when you are odds on favourites to win and Nuneaton were a determined team that made it difficult at times, but the quality came through, goals from Dunne, Branch and Jevons making it 3–0 to put us through comfortably in the end.

FA YOUTH CUP SECOND ROUND.
WEST BROMWICH ALBION YOUTH 1
EVERTON YOUTH 2

Manager Joe Royle, chairman Peter Johnson and first team coach Willie Donachie all attended the game at the Hawthorns which was brilliant for the young players.

It was a bright start from us and we were on the attack from the kick-off with pace and power throughout the team. This was shown when Danny Cadamarteri ran at pace and went past a couple of defenders before hitting a powerful shot from 20 yards into the top corner, a great finish. We were playing well, but just before half time and against the run of play West Brom equalised.

The lads came out after the break still positive to get on the front foot. We finally scored our second and winning goal with six minutes remaining. From a Michael Ball shot which rebounded off the keeper, Mark Quayle reacted quickest to score and take us into the third round against Bolton.

After the win the lads reminded me of what I had said to them on the way down to the Hawthorns. They wanted to watch a film that was funny and a bit risqué according to them, but I said no and that we should concentrate on the game. I added they could watch it on the way home if we won.

As soon as I got on the coach all the lads are shouting: "Ronny can we have the film on please." My positive response this time was greeted with cheers and clapping. There were televisions dotted all around the coach so everyone could watch it if they wanted to. About ten minutes into the journey home, I glanced at the TV and thought, OMG the driver has put a porn channel on by mistake!

I also forgot who was sitting next to me. It was Reverend Henry Corbett, the club's chaplain. I looked at him with a wry smile and Henry said: "Ronny that's life."

The players clearly enjoyed the film. I talked to Henry all the way home and I didn't look at that television screen once!

FA YOUTH CUP THIRD ROUND.
BOLTON YOUTH 1 EVERTON YOUTH 2

It was good to see Joe Royle and Willie Donachie there again. They always tried to attend our games when they could and they always took an interest in the development of the young players. Joe was looking at Branchy who had been involved with the first team, but Dunny was playing really well and he would make his first team debut in the coming months.

We were in control and dominated possession of the ball and created numerous chances, but didn't take any of them with Michael Branch the biggest culprit. We created the chances, but they took the lead from a breakaway after 30 minutes. The trouble with Branchy was that if he missed a chance he would take it too much to heart and he missed three real opportunities. At half time, Hursty and I both talked to him about forgetting the missed opportunities. He would never hide and would give you his all, but he just needed to relax a bit more and hit the target.

Michael Ball crossed from the right for Jamie Milligan to score and to put us level. We were finishing the stronger and with five minutes remaining good link up play between Branchy and Phil Jevons gave Jevo the chance to drill the ball into the far corner to make it 2–1.

Cad missed a good chance late on, but it was a good performance and result.

FA YOUTH CUP FOURTH ROUND. NORWICH CITY 1 EVERTON 1

We were drawn away again with Norwich, one of the favourites to win the trophy. They had Craig Bellamy and Adrian Forbes, two players with electric pace who would be a threat.

This was one of our best performances of the season against a good Norwich side and we restricted their attacks with very few shots at our keeper. We took the lead with a good footballing goal, Andrew West passing wide to Danny Cadamarteri who crossed for Branchy to head home, giving the keeper no chance.

We should have scored the second goal, but missed a couple of easy chances. Then Branchy had to go off with a hamstring injury and this worked in Norwich's favour.

They equalised with eight minutes to go with virtually their only chance of the game and it was a scrappy goal. We were disappointed not to win, but had earned a replay back at Goodison.

FA CUP FOURTH ROUND REPLAY.
EVERTON YOUTH 0 NORWICH 2

It was a disappointing result for us after we had played so well down at Norwich. We just couldn't turn all our possession into clearer chances and goals. Norwich were set up to hit us on the break and use the pace of Forbes and Bellamy, but the early goal they scored gave them something to hold onto.

There was no lack of effort from the players and they tried to the end, but that quality we had shown in other games was lacking and Norwich were clinical with the few chances they had. It was a learning curve for the players, defenders and attackers. We shouldn't have needed this replay, but wasn't ruthless enough.

THE CLUB was invited to play in a Youth Tournament in Turin which was being hosted by Juventus, known as 'The Old Lady' and the most successful team in the history of Italian football. They are my favourite Italian team and so I was looking forward to the tournament as much as the players.

This is a great opportunity for the lads to compete against the best youth football teams in the world and some the best players. There were sides like Argentinos Juniors, Colo Colo – the most successful club in Chilean football and youth champions – and of course Juventus.

As a coach you want to test yourself against the best

coaches in the game from the various top clubs while observing formations, team selections, and adapting to the different styles of play from other countries.

The opening ceremony was tremendous and when we played Juventus we all received Juve shirts and baseball caps which was a nice touch.

The weather wasn't the best when we played a very good Colo Colo, but I wasn't happy with our performance. They adapted much better to the conditions than we did, but it was no excuse that it rains in England and we play on heavy muddy pitches.

I told the players in no uncertain terms that some of them where treating the trip like it was a holiday and that had to change. It was learning curve for all of them, not least that they need to respect every team they play against and give the same commitment in every match.

You try your best to occupy the players when they are away and set up some site seeing trips. The hosts organise things and that is all good because you don't want the players to become bored. There are some things you don't plan and to this day the players still remind me of this incident and start laughing.

Ray Hall was head of youth development and was on the trip with me and he was stern with the players. They affectionately gave him the nickname 'The Dungeon Master' from Dungeon and Dragons.

The players had to look after their training kit, clean their own boots and on this occasion there were a few of them on the first floor balcony cleaning boots.

One of these was Paddy Drew, yes that same Paddy, and the lads were talking away when he accidently knocked the polish off the balcony onto Ray Hall's head below. The lads ran back into the room, leaving Paddy looking over the balcony, frozen with shock.

You could just hear laughing from the room and Paddy stuttering to get some words out. Ray looked a right sight, but luckily for Paddy he saw the funny side of it.

The next game was against Argentinos Juniors and I wanted to see a reaction from the players which I certainly got. It was a fantastic performance with passion, desire and a real attitude to win every tackle. The players wanted the ball in tight situations, even though some tasty tackles were flying in. We attacked and defended as a team with some tremendous displays, but Danny Cadamarteri was outstanding.

When I came back after the tournament, Joe asked me if any were ready for the first team and I said: "Dunny, Michael Ball and Cad."

Although we should have won against Argentinos, we drew 2–2, but I told them in the dressing room how well they had played and added that this was the standard they needed to sustain. It was good to see smiling faces again. Consistency is important at any level.

I mentioned earlier about playing against the best players and learning from them. I will name two of Argentinos players that day that would go on to have great careers in the game. Juan Roman Riquelme would make 51 appearances for Argentina, scoring 17 goals and was voted

Argentina 'Player of the Year' four times, playing for Boca Juniors and Barcelona. Evertonians will remember him at Villarreal. The other player was Esteban Cambiasso who would play 52 times for Argentina, scoring five goals. He played for Independiente, River Plate, Real Madrid and Inter Milan and had a season at Leicester.

Our final game was against Juventus, but it was marred by an unsavoury incident on the field. I couldn't complain about the hospitality that Juventus had shown and the tournament organisation. Games were fiercely competitive, but during this match Danny Cadamarteri was racially abused by Juventus players and reacted by lashing out before being sent off. We knew he shouldn't have reacted like that, but the perpetrator went unpunished.

Racism has no place in football or in any walk of life and it needs to be eradicated.

I approached the referee and the Juventus coach and made my feelings known. By the time I got back to the dressing room Cad had kicked the dressing room door in out of temper, but on my way out I said to the stadium manager: "Get the Juventus players to pay for the dressing room door." He didn't say a word as we got on the coach.

The players, including myself, learnt a lot on that tour, lots of good things and some bad, but it was a great experience for the whole group.

It was now transfer deadline day and we needed a couple of signings to strengthen the squad. Names were being bandied around as usual as the transfer window was ready to close. All the teams had finished training and the apprentices had completed their jobs so all the players had left Bellefield. I was having a coffee in the lounge upstairs with Hursty and Willie Donachie, waiting for news of any signings. We had heard that Joe was trying to secure the signature of SK Brann's Norwegian international striker Tore Andre Flo. As the day went on it appeared that Flo's team mate, defender Claus Eftevaag, might be part of the deal.

Joe came in the lounge and said the Flo deal was looking good, adding that he was going to have a chat with the chairman to include Eftevaag which would have been good for the squad. After about 30 minutes I looked out of the lounge window and saw Joe with Peter Johnson walking around the 'A' team pitch in deep conversation.

We knew Flo was on a Bosman free at the end of the season with Chelsea in the wings, but he had a £1.2million buy out clause and Joe wanted to pay it. He was trying to convince the chairman to do it now because we couldn't compete with the wages the London club would offer in the summer. Johnson wouldn't pay the fee and thought it better to take a chance and wait until the end of the season.

They started to make their way back into the building and a couple of minutes later the lounge door opened. It was Joe. He didn't come in, but just stood by the door and declared: "He won't pay the money. I'm resigning and he has got the manager he wants… himself! I'm off. Good luck."

We were obviously shocked and didn't see that one

coming. Joe quite rightly thought that he had been undermined by the chairman in not backing his judgement

There was a meeting the next day when Johnson said that Waggy (Dave Watson) would be coming in as caretaker manager until the end of the season.

We are all professionals and are expected to act that way which we did, but it was still sad to see Joe leave.

Flo would eventually sign for Chelsea, do well for them and score goals at Stamford Bridge and they would ultimately sell him to Rangers for £12 million. Whose decision do you think was right?

At the end of the season the first team squad plus the backroom staff were taken to Marbella for a week's break which the players and staff enjoyed. I could write a book about that trip alone.

A few days after we arrived back I received a phone call from Hursty saying he had left the club and up until then I hadn't heard anything about what might be happening to Joe's remaining backroom staff?

I then got a call off Michael Dunford, the club secretary, asking if I could meet him at Goodison Park the following day which I did. After the usual pleasantries, I received the news I didn't want to hear when he said: "You have been relieved of your duties."

This is what happens when a manager leaves a club, all the backroom staff follow, just like a union: "One out, all out."

Johnson later admitted he had got it wrong in not backing Joe which ultimately brought his own resignation, another owner making the wrong decisions and knocking the club back years.

The squad that season had long term injuries in major positions that didn't help the team and we needed new players, but for me Johnson didn't have the best board members around him to provide the right advice and guidance.

I thank Joe for giving me the opportunity to go back and coach at Everton. Along with Hursty and Willie, I left the club but had enjoyed every single minute of going back and coaching some quality young players. I was absolutely gutted when I left and while that's football, it doesn't make it any easier.

REV HENRY CORBETT
EVERTON FC CHAPLAIN

"I hear these words quite often now from youth coaches and managers, but the first time I heard this sentiment was back in the 1990s from Ronny.

"I don't just want you to be good footballers. I want you to be good people too', said Ronny in the Bellefield canteen.

"He was talking to the Everton apprentices, and I was so pleased and relieved to hear him say that. The situation was a session after training that I had suggested with a good colleague and drugs counsellor, Michelle. She had spoken at the Shewsy Youth club in Everton where I am a helper, and I knew she would be excellent at talking about illegal drugs, answering questions, coping with a group of lads whose minds might easily wander on to other subjects.

"I was pleased because it showed that at Everton we were a club concerned with what the lads were like as people not just as footballers and that is always the chaplain's concern and perspective. And I was relieved because Ronny's support as the youth team coach would help the lads engage with the session, which they duly did.

"I loved Ronny's concern for the whole person, and for many years he has continued that concern through his Health Through Sport programmes, helping and supporting young people, many of whom face difficult challenges, to become strong, caring, and thoughtful members of their communities and fulfil their potential."

TWO UNIQUE MEN WHO SUM UP A VERY SPECIAL FOOTBALL CLUB

YOU will have gathered by now that I'm an Evertonian through and through, always have been, always will be. When I was offered the opportunity to play for the Blues in 1969, it was a dream come true.

I have already reflected on my Liverpool Schoolboys and England Schoolboys days. I remember how I told all of the young lads at that level that if they had a choice and the chance they should sign for the greatest club in the world as far as I'm concerned – Everton.

One of them was as big a Manchester United fanatic as I was a Blue. His name was Mick Buckley. You should remember that United had just won the European Cup around this time, with stars like Best, Charlton and Law in their ranks.

I succeeded in convincing Mick that, as talented as these United stars were, Everton was the club that was going places. I kept saying that we had the best team on the planet.

Mick relented. I'm positive he would have signed for Manchester United. Instead, he came to Goodison with me.

We would both eventually have the honour and pleasure of rising from the youth team to the first team ranks. But in our first season, we were just starry-eyed apprentices, working in the dressing rooms and cleaning the first team kit and the boots.

Mick would always look at me as we got the brush out and I would keep telling him… BEST CLUB ON THE PLANET!

When we won the League Championship at the end of our first 1969/70 season with one of the greatest sides ever to walk out at Goodison Park, he was finally saying it back to me… DEFINITELY THE BEST CLUB ON THE PLANET!

I can't tell you how proud I was to be cleaning the boots of the players I had idolised from the terraces. It wasn't a chore. It was an honour to work alongside these Champions.

It was at this time that I first met Brian Labone who I have already mentioned in a previous chapter in relating to his remarkable personal relationship and partnership with Gordon West. Labby was our club captain, leader and greatest influence. All the usual banter went on with the first team players giving us stick and inspiring and terrifying us in equal measure, almost in the same breath.

But Labby would always give encouragement and say what a great job we were doing. He would always find time to sit with us and have a chat. We were not just in awe of him. We respected him for the way he treated us.

That's what a club captain should be all about, someone who makes an impact on everyone at the club.

I played with Labby in the reserves on many occasions and watched him play for the first team. What a class act he was. Brian was a great reader of the game, a good passer of the ball, a defender with superb timing when heading or tackling.

He won 26 England caps but should have gained more and I feel he should have had more recognition. Down the years when I was in Everton's first team and later when I was Everton Youth Coach, Labby was still a massive influence. Players would come and go, but he remained as the indisputable Mr Everton.

Even though his role at the club was now as a great ambassador rather than as a great captain, he still spoke with the same passion. I was now on the coaching staff myself, but still respected his words just as much as I did when I was cleaning his boots.

We were all devastated when Labby passed away, but his knowledge still amazes me. He seemed to have an instant recall about great games and famous Evertonians. He became the voice of the fans, possibly even the club's biggest fan.

But we remember him most as a great player and an inspirational captain. Brian Labone was a credit to football and genuinely the 'Last of the Corinthians'. He always gave me tremendous support and encouragement and took a real interest in my charity work and when I founded Health Through Sport. He immediately accepted my invitation to become our first Patron.

Youngsters are often looking for role models in sport but often they don't pick the right ones. I never had that problem. Brian was my captain and my role model. He is up there with the best of them in the game.

He was a great character, a lovely man and a great Evertonian. Earlier, I mentioned that I once called Everton the BEST CLUB ON THE PLANET.

That was because of giants like Brian Labone. Thanks for everything, Labby.

Of course, when talking about Everton immortals, I have to also mention the great Howard Kendall. I first met Howard when I joined the club in 1969 as an apprentice professional and watched him play in midfield as one of the Holy Trinity in that fabulous Everton 1969/70 Championship side. He went on to build a great team of his own in the mid-1980s and added to his success with two more top flight titles, the F.A. Cup, the European

Cup Winners Cup, plus four Charity Shields to become Everton's most successful manager.

I decided to arrange a tribute night for him in November 2014 and I couldn't think of anyone else who deserved it more than he did. I had always appreciated his help and support down the years. A special programme was published for the event and it featured quotes from former team mates Joe Royle and Colin Harvey and from former players Howard had managed at Everton such as Neville Southall, Kevin Ratcliffe, Graeme Sharp and John Bailey. It showed you just how highly regarded Howard was by his fellow professionals.

I also had a brilliant video produced by Ian Lysaght featuring Howard's football and managerial career which was shown on the night and the video finished off with a photo of his Dad which he loved.

Howard's half time team talk at Stoke City in the F.A. Cup in 1984 and his inspirational message to turn things around when we went in a goal down against Bayern Munich the Cup Winners Cup is now part of club folklore.

It is incredible the way Howard affected people. Despite everything he achieved, he was so humble and loved talking to people and answering questions.

It was a great night and everyone came because it was for Howard and it was just so nice to show him what he meant to us all while he was able to be there.

Afterwards, when all of the guests had left and the staff were clearing up in the main room, he came over to me and said: "I've had a fantastic night lad. Thank you so much."

He was thrilled at the honour of the tribute and with his Health Through Sport award. It summed him up perfectly, so polite and thoughtful. It meant a lot to him to know how much the fans loved him.

I was asked by the Winslow Hotel to do a Q and A with Howard and John Bailey after an Everton home game and asked if I would also be the MC. I got the event underway at 6pm and by this time the supporters had downed a lot of liquid and the place was packed.

It was lively with some good questions and answers. I then let a lad standing near the front ask his question. He asked: "'Why did you sell Gary Lineker our leading goal-scorer at the time?" Here we go, what would be Howard's reply be?

I handed the microphone across and he looked right at the questioner and said: "I sold Gary Lineker because I wanted to win the fucking league!" He received the biggest cheer of the night. You are still missed by so many mate, but you left so many fantastic memories.

Another of our great characters, although on a different level to Labby and Howard, was the inimitable and much-loved Andrew Edward King, to give him his full title. We knew him, of course, as Andy King, known by all and sundry as 'Kingy'.

Born in Luton, Berkshire, he signed as an apprentice for his home town club Luton and then joined us for £35,000 in 1976. He was another of those who simply could not live without Everton.

The fee, paid originally by Billy Bingham, was very good business by the club. He made his debut against Middlesbrough at Goodison, but we played at Derby County the following Wednesday and he really announced himself with two goals, one of them a bit special.

When he first arrived he was quiet with people forgetting that he came from a little village outside Luton and now he was at a massive club and living in a big city.

I got on with him straight away we enjoyed each other's company. I took him under my wing to show him around our lovely city and the introvert would quickly become an extrovert. He was a bubbly character, loved playing football and enjoyed going out and having a laugh. We affectionately gave Kingy the nickname 'Tithead' for the things he said and things he got up to.

Not long after Gordon Lee joined the club we went training on Ainsdale beach and he liked to create a good atmosphere between the players. He would split the squad into two groups to compete against each other in various games.

In one game, the first player had to run 25 yards out to a cone and write the first letter of a word Gordon Lee would shout out. The word had to be written neatly in the sand no spelling mistakes. The word then had to be underlined and all of this would be taken into consideration to decide the winner.

The losing team would have to do shuttle runs at the end of training as a forfeit. Kingy was in my team and he was the first player to run.

Gordon Lee shouted out the word – PHYSIOTHERA-PIST. Kingy raced out to the cone and wrote the first letter in the sand before coming back and touching the next player to go. He sprinted out to write the letter and came back and so on until the word was written and then underlined. My team started jumping around celebrating the win and winding the other team up about them doing the shuttle runs at the end of training.

Gordon Lee and Steve Burtenshaw, the coach wandered over to check the words of both teams. Gordon Lee declared Team B the winner and disqualified Team A, which was my team. We remonstrated about the decision and then we were called over to have a look.

Kingy had started the word 'Physiotherapist' with the letter F. 'Tithead' was born!

At the end of the 1977 season the squad was taken to Marbella for the week to wind down and relax after a hard season. Instead it ended up like a stag do!

On one of the days we went into town early, had some lunch and went around a few of the bars with supporters recognising us and joining us for a drink and friendly banter with the other customers. We never remained too long in any one bar and so a nice lunch became a pub crawl.

It was a good day with Kingy winding Latch up at every opportunity and the drinks going down very nicely. We stayed out for a few more hours and then worked our way back to our hotel for dinner. In the dining room the staff had laid out a long boardroom table for the squad and there were other guests dining. Everyone was in a good mood, but Kingy was still chipping away at Latch who told him to give it a rest.

The waiter took the drinks order and then we ordered our meals. As usual, when the meals arrived the conversation went quite with everyone tucking in. The only voice you could hear was Kingy's.

Everyone finished their starters and then the main courses got served, followed by more drinks. Now Latch is a placid lad and even with a few drinks in him it still takes something for him to lose his temper, but Kingy was sitting opposite and winding him up just one time too many.

Latch picked up his plate and said: "Kingy, shut up," and threw a full Spaghetti Bolognese over his head. Kingy, trying to get out of the way, fell backwards over his chair and landed under the table of a couple behind him.

With a hushed silence in the dining room, this was only broken by Kingy giggling under the table. He then came out with spaghetti sliding down his head and face. The lads, along with the couple, were laughing and Kingy said: "Good shot Latch."

That's when everyone in the dining room burst out laughing. We sent a few bottles of wine over to the couple, but they said they had enjoyed the side show.

Sometimes after games back home we would go into town where Kingy liked the nightclubs and places that served late. These were more like 'speakeasies' like the Black Cat off London Road with Pickwick's close by. The Tam O'Shanter pub, also off London Road, was a place you could go to have a late drink and I had known the manager Jimmy Cullen for a long time. He was a Blue Nose and brother of Pat Cullen who had the Bow and Arrow pub for many years.

We went in there one night and received a great welcome from Jimmy, as always. The music was on with everyone chatting and having a good time when a big fella by the bar said to Kingy: "You don't drink quickly like me, hurry up and I will buy you a drink."

Kingy said: "I drink fast and can drink faster than you." The big fella smiled and said: "No chance."

It was friendly banter and I claimed Kingy would beat this guy in drinking a pint the quickest. He smiled, thinking I was off my cake, but I had seen Kingy many times finishing a pint in one and a half seconds. I said: "He will beat you," and his mates said: "OK, let's have a bet on it."

I acted as the bookmaker and said it was £10 to bet at evens. Everyone bet on the big fella so we could lose a few quid if Kingy didn't do the business. Before the contest started, I got him a packet of crisps which he liked to eat. Bets all taken, we were ready… 3, 2, 1, go!

Kingy had downed the pint before the big fella had drunk half of his. The look on the faces of everyone was one of shock and disbelief, but it did happen. Kingy was challenged by another fella and the same thing happened, Kingy winning again, so I called a stop to it because no one would beat him and I wasn't going to carry him home! With the winnings, we bought everyone in the pub a drink so it finished off a great night.

This is the other side of Kingy. He was not just a tremendous goalscoring midfield player and someone who thought deeply about football and then went into management and scouting. He just loved football and having a laugh.

I will remember him as a great friend who played football with a smile on his face and loved life. The last time I saw him he was sitting on my table at the Everton Former Players Foundation Christmas party where we had our photo taken. After the dinner I went for a drink with him down County Road, just like old times. Andy King... always remembered.

Talking about great characters in football, I couldn't write a book without mentioning my great friend John Bailey. I first met Bails 41 years ago in the Yankee Clipper off Victoria Street when he played for Blackburn Rovers.

I was by the bar when he came bounding over to me and said: "Ronny, my name is John Bailey and I play for Blackburn Rovers."

He was and still is a bubbly personality and likes to have a laugh. During that first meeting, we had a few drinks. He is very good company and we have been great friends ever since.

I can always rely on Bails for his help and support at my fundraising events.

Oh and by the way what a good player he was for Everton – and I can genuinely say that as one ex-footballer to another without mentioning that famous FA Cup Final hat he wore in 1984 along with those Elton John glasses John Bailey, a complete one-off.

MY ALL-TIME EVERTON XI – AND WHAT A TEAM THEY WOULD HAVE BEEN

USING only the players you have seen playing for the Blues, have you ever tried to sit down and select your own personal all-time Everton XI? It's not an easy challenge and it certainly fires up an instant debate amongst supporters, but here we go with my own greatest fantasy team. You can argue with me about it the next time you see me!

NEVILLE SOUTHALL (GOALKEEPER)

This particular selection didn't take too much thought because this individual is not just my Everton No. 1, but also someone in my eyes who would find a place in my World XI. Howard signed Neville from Bury for £150,000 in the summer of 1981 and it has to rate as one of his top signings, if not his best!

Nev would have to compete with Jim Arnold in the first couple of seasons and was dropped after a heavy defeat against Liverpool at Goodison. He was then loaned out to Port Vale and showed the character to come back and claim the No 1 spot as his own before breaking all Everton appearance records.

I know from my time as Everton Youth Coach how hard Nev would train. He was first in and last out. After he had finished training with the first team he would come over and ask me on a number of occasions if he could join in with my training sessions. I was delighted because it showed the Youth players just how much hard work you have to put in to make the first team.

Neville liked to play in 5, 6, 7, 8 or any small-sided games that were available in training. He loved showing us his skill as an outfield player and he could play by the way!

He wouldn't hold back with some crunching tackles, but it toughened the lads up. Ask Richard Dunne, Danny Cadamarteri and Michael Ball. Nev's input made them more competitive and wanting to win.

When Neville was on the pitch, he had a presence and arrogance about him that all top players have. It says to the opposition: "You are not going to beat me!" More than that, it was a self belief in his own ability that pushed him on to become an even better player.

His accomplishments are there for all to see:

FWA Footballer of the Year award in 1985; named in the PFA Team of the Year in four consecutive seasons; played a major role in bringing success to Everton and won more honours than any other player in the history of the club. He holds Everton's appearance record, a top player and a top man.

TOMMY WRIGHT (RIGHT-BACK)

Just like me, Tommy signed for Everton as an apprentice and then came through our successful Youth system to make his debut in 1964.

He was quick, a good tackler, and used the ball well when he pushed forward to support the attack. I used to play against Tommy for the Youth and Reserve teams in practice matches, but these were played as if it was a League game so I can vouch for how good he was.

I liked watching his battles with Peter Thompson in the 'derby' matches and George Best once described Tommy as his most difficult opponent. I think that says it all.

Everton was Tommy's only club and he had to retire through injury in 1974, but had made 373 appearances, scoring four goals, and played twelve times for England.

He was named in the Gwladys Street Hall of Fame in 1996 and was deservedly made an 'Everton Giant' in 2016.

Tommy won the FA Cup in that never to be forgotten final in 1966, then was in the losing team that lost to West

Bromwich Albion in the 1968 FA Cup final, but won the League Division One title in 1969/70. He was a tremendous full-back whose career was sadly cut short by injury.

RAMON 'RAY' WILSON (LEFT-BACK)

Ray played 266 games for Huddersfield before he signed for us in 1964 and he had already won thirty caps for England by then, but there would be an even bigger prize that he would win two years later. He was not the tallest of defenders, but very athletic and a good header of the ball. Ray was very comfortable with the ball. He liked to overlap and could pass with either foot. Not many wingers ever getting the better of him.

He won the FA Cup in 1966 and then the biggest prize of all, the World Cup, as we beat West Germany at Wembley 4–2 after extra time.

Ray was in the side when we lost in the FA Cup final to West Bromwich Albion in 1968.

I would sum him up as a classy full-back, a great recovery tackler and a world class player.

BRIAN LABONE (CENTRE-HALF/CAPTAIN)

I have no hesitation in naming Labby in my team and making him the Captain. He had the respect of all of the teammates he played alongside. He was a great header of the ball, strong in the tackle, brave, a good reader of the game, and a role model for the younger players, skilful and a great motivator. He signed in 1957 and made his debut in 1958.

He was a one-club man who made 534 appearances in all competitions and was a massive Evertonian. He won the League Division One title in 1962/63 and 1969/70 and was in our FA Cup winning team against Sheffield Wednesday in 1966. He also played in the 1968 FA Cup final against West Brom.

Labby played twenty-six times for England which included the 1970 World Cup Finals where England reached the quarter-finals.

I once asked Tommy Smith, the ex-Liverpool player, who was the hardest individual he had ever played against and without hesitation he said Labby – and he meant it.

Being classed as a great player doesn't mean you are a great man, but in Labby's case this is certainly the case.

When I started my Health Through Sport charity I asked him if he would he be the first patron and he didn't even think about it. He just said: "Of course I will." Brian was a great supporter of my charity and I was so proud when he became our patron. We now present an annual Brian Labone 'Corinthian' award.

Labby received a serious Achilles tendon injury in 1971 and had to retire, a sad end to a great career, but he certainly made his mark at our club.

He was inducted as an Everton Giant in 2012 which I am sure Labby would have been so proud to have received. His most definitely was the 'Last of the Corinthians' – gone but not forgotten.

KEVIN RATCLIFFE (CENTRE-HALF)

Kevin was another player who came through the Everton ranks after he signed apprentice forms in 1977. He made his debut away to Manchester United when he was 19 years old.

In the early part of his Everton career he was in and out of the team and played at left-back, but wanted to play in the middle. He then formed a really good partnership with Mark Higgins before Higgy suffered a long term injury. Derek Mountfield stepped in and Kevin never looked back. His electric pace and reading of the game were his two main assets, but he was brave, liked a tackle and could leave his calling card on any forward. Having a left footer in a key position adds balance for any team and he was vociferous which you need from any leader. He played 489 times for Everton and was capped 59 times by Wales, mostly as captain.

Kevin was the most successful Captain in Everton's long history and won two League Division One titles, and the FA Cup. He also played in two other FA Cup finals and four Charity Shields and now he is in my all-time Everton team. That can't be bad Rats!

ANDREI KANCHELSKIS (FORWARD/MIDFIELD)

After his fallout with Alex Ferguson, it was a great bit of business by Joe Royle to get him to sign for Everton in 1995.He was a genuine world class player and on his day was unplayable. When he received the ball he was positive and wanted to go past defenders and use his scintillating pace, get shots away on goal and create chances for others. He had the skill, a tremendous shot with both feet and was one of the cleanest strikers of the ball I have seen.

That's how he got so much power into his shots. After training he would practice running with the ball at pace and hitting shots with his left and right foot for 30 minutes. I used to get the Youth team players to watch him and you can learn a lot from great players.

In that 1995/96 season he was out with a dislocated shoulder for six weeks, but he still played thirty-six games, scoring 16 goals and finishing leading scorer. This included two goals against Liverpool, the first a header and the second a shot he drilled in, both at the Kop End.

ALAN BALL (MIDFIELD)

After Dixie Dean, Bally was the greatest player to ever play for Everton Football Club in my opinion. We were youngsters when we watched him as he covered every blade of grass at Wembley in the World Cup Final against West Germany. He was just 21 and got the Man of the Match award when another player in his team scored a hat-trick.

It wasn't the case of would Bally be transferred from Blackpool that summer, but which top club would be lucky enough to sign him.

Many wanted him, but with a British record fee of £110,000 he signed for Everton and this was the start of a love affair that lasts to this day.

On his debut he scored at Fulham and we won 1–0. In his first 'derby' a few games later at Goodison we beat Liverpool 3–1. Bally scored two and was an instant hero.

Later in the season he scored at the Gwladys Street end to knock Liverpool out of the fifth round of the FA Cup, side footing in from a tight angle as we won 1–0.

He raised the bar for every player at the club with his enthusiasm, ability, passing, trying to win every ball, one touch football, and his energy. He could score goals, create goals and had this incredible will to win.

He played in that great 1969/70 Championship winning team and was part of the Holy Trinity midfield alongside Colin Harvey and Howard Kendall, the best midfield in our history.

In his first season he ended up leading goalscorer with 18 goals which is exceptional for a midfield player. The next season he scored 20 goals, absolutely outstanding again. Any striker would be proud of that return.

Bally played 251 times for Everton and scored 71 goals, but it's not how many times you play for the club that counts, it's what you do in those games and the impact you make on the club and the standards you set.

He won 39 of his 72 England caps playing for Everton and captained both club and country.

Bally leaves a lasting legacy of giving his all for the club, for his love of Everton and for being a winner.

As he said: "Once Everton has touched you, nothing will ever be the same."

COLIN HARVEY (MIDFIELD)

Another product of our very successful Everton Youth system, Colin signed on as an apprentice in 1960. In 1963, when Jimmy Gabriel was injured, Harry Catterick selected him to make his debut aged 18 against Inter Milan in the intimidating atmosphere of the San Siro Stadium and he didn't look out of place.

He was quick, skilful on the ball, a good tackler, his energy levels where second to none and his passing ability was there for all to see.

He was part of the legendary 'Holy Trinity' midfield and Evertonians dubbed him the 'The White Pele'.

He wasn't a prolific goalscorer, but he scored some very important ones.

I was there at Burnden Park, Bolton in 1966 when he scored the only goal of the game against Manchester United in the FA Cup semi-final, shooting in a low shot from the edge of the penalty area which took us to Wembley to play Sheffield Wednesday in the final.

Another goal that stands out was his fantastic solo effort against West Bromwich Albion at Goodison that clinched us the League title.

Colin made 383 Everton appearances, scoring 24 goals and helped us to win the League title in 1969/70 and the FA Cup in 1966. He was inducted as the Everton Giant for 2007.

KEVIN SHEEDY (LEFT MIDFIELD)

There have been a number of players to make the switch

from Liverpool to Everton down the years, but the last one before Kevin was Johnny Morrissey 20 years earlier. Howard paid £100,000 for him in 1982 and this would prove money well spent and a very astute signing. He was a tremendous player for both Everton and the Republic of Ireland. His great left foot could deliver a pinpoint cross or a defence splitting pass on a consistent basis.

He was lethal at free kicks and who can forget his twice taken efforts against Ipswich Town in the 1985 FA Cup tie. He scored the first one and then had to re-take the kick, scoring again by putting the ball into the opposite corner. Sheeds created many chances for his teammates, but he could also score himself.

He played 369 times and scored 97 goals which is excellent from his left side midfield position and gave a good balance to the team.

He won two League titles in 1984 and 1986, the FA Cup in 1984 and the European Cup Winners Cup in 1985.

He played 46 times for the Republic of Ireland and scored nine goals.

ALEX YOUNG (STRIKER)

Alex signed from Scottish club Hearts in a joint deal that also brought George Thomson to Goodison for £55,000. Alex was priced at £40,000, a steal! He was also my first idol as a player.

He made everything look so easy, from controlling the ball to beating a defender or passing the ball with either foot. He had elegance when running with the ball and a body swerve that would get him out of the tightest situations.

Alex wasn't the tallest striker, but he was an unbelievable header of a ball who generated a lot of power with the timing of his jumps.

His first touch was sublime and he had tremendous dribbling ability. Look at the goal he scored against Man United in 1967 at Goodison and it says everything about Alex's ability to dribble and score goals. Fantastic!

He wasn't all sweetness and light and could look after himself when needed and I have spoken to former team mates of his to verify this. Defenders certainly knew he was about.

His nickname was 'Tenderfoot' because he suffered so much from blisters so maybe that's why he glided over the turf.

Alex made 275 appearances for us, scoring 89 goals, and he assisted with countless goals for other team mates.

They say don't meet your hero because you may be disappointed, but I met Alex on a number of occasions and every time he never disappointed me. He was good company and an absolute gentleman. He was someone to respect and always had time for supporters.

Not many players get documentary dramas written about them, but Alex did and the 'Golden Vision' was directed by none other than Ken Loach, the award winning director.

Older generations of Evertonians will have seen this TV special. I would urge younger fans to watch this classic if you really want to know how much Alex meant to all Evertonians.

GRAEME SHARP (CENTRE FORWARD)

To complete my team selection I went for a centre-forward we bought from Dumbarton for a fee of £120,000 in 1980. Not many had heard of him when he arrived at the club, but by the end of his Everton career they certainly had.

Sharpy was a good target man who could hold the ball up under pressure to bring the midfield or wide players into the game. He knew when to lay the ball off for others or when to take the shot on himself. He was straight onto anything that came into the opposition's penalty area and would never give centre halves or keepers an easy time. If the service was good it invariably ended up in the back of the net.

He was brave and up for the fight and didn't hide. Sharpy always gave his best. Sometimes it's an unforgiving position when you are playing as a lone striker and the service is not good, but this is where your character comes in and Graeme had loads of that.

A really good header of the ball, he also had a good shot on him and could volley a great ball – especially into the Anfield Road net!

He made 425 appearances and scored 160 goals. Only Dixie Dean has scored more for the club and Graeme should be proud of this achievement.

A couple of his goals that supporters will remember

include the volley in the game at Liverpool, probably one of the best ever scored in a 'derby' game.

His goal in the FA Cup Final against Watford to make it 1–0, a low effort into the corner, was crucial in the ultimate 2–0 win that gave us the Cup.

THAT"S my team, but what about yours? My side could play football if you wanted that or battle with the best!

I would have loved to watch this side in its prime and what a force it would be with pace and power; an ability to score goals; great defenders; three world class players, and great character throughout. They are all winners and would play football the right way.

The School of Science is back.

It's easy this manager lark, especially when you can pick from a squad of legends!

BUILDING ON MY
FIRM BELIEFS ABOUT
HEALTH THROUGH SPORT

HEALTH Through Sport is a registered charity that I founded in 2005 to deliver football coaching to vulnerable and disadvantaged youngsters across Merseyside.

The outcome I was looking to achieve was based on the simple logic that every child matters, regardless of their background or circumstances. I want to ensure that youngsters – and others – can make a positive contribution to society and achieve economic wellbeing.

Health Through Sport is geared towards improving

fitness levels by offering advice on healthy eating and by organising trips around the country and abroad to help educate youngsters and broaden their horizons. We also have other initiatives that focus towards the rehabilitation of ex-offenders, people who misuse drugs and alcohol, and adults with mental health issues.

We are delighted to say that our projects across Merseyside are going from strength to strength and that more participants are gaining Football Coaching Level 1 and 2 qualifications. We have helped bolster their confidence and self-esteem through our football coaching courses, which have been authorised by Open Awards and which Health Through Sport is an accredited centre.

I'm proud with what we have achieved and the comments below from people I have had the pleasure of meeting and working with over the past 12 years help to inspire me as we drive forward with the charity's aims.

DARRYL LAYCOCK
CRIME PREVENTION CONSULTANT & MENTOR

Prior to meeting Ronny, I was a high-risk offender, subject to Multi Agency Public Protection Arrangement conditions. Not only that, I was a tier four offender, which is the highest risk there is and I was the most dangerous offender in Liverpool upon my release according to Greater Manchester Police and Merseyside Police. I was deemed a serious risk to known adults and this was due to my past.

I was a high-ranking gang member from Moss Side in Manchester. I am now a reformed character and I go into schools to deliver crime prevention events and try to deter the next generation of youths from going down the road I went down.

I met Ronny when he was running his health programme linked with probation. I played football and trained under Ronny for eight months and it was great. All in all, Greater Manchester Police and Probation are amazed at my transformation from high risk offender to a public-speaking ex-gang member.

GMP thought I couldn't leave my past offending behind. My transformation would have been impossible without Ronny's input. He taught me self discipline which I lacked due to my past. Not only did he give me this, he was also there to listen and advise me from an independent view, whilst helping me to tackle my mental health issues. To this day, over seven years later, I still value Ronny as a friend and he is always there at the end of a phone if I need his advice. I am now a self-employed mentor and crime prevention consultant and work alongside Xcalibre, which is the Greater Manchester Police gang policing unit. I also do work for numerous children's services throughout the UK and numerous probation services throughout the country.

I also provide training for children's care home staff and social workers. To date I have worked with over 48,000 school students and lectured to over 4,000 university students. I have seen a "Liverpool knife crime story" beat Donald Trump stories to headline on BBC News at Ten. I have advised Ross Kemp on his Sky series, advised on scripts for BBC drama series 'In The Dark 'and I am being featured in a docudrama on BBC2 entitled 'Gun No 6'.

I have come a long way thanks to the support of people like Ronny and Health Through Sport.

J.A DUNLEAVY
PROBATION RESIDENTIAL OFFICER

Ronny, the Health Through Sport team and staff from Southwood Approved premises help remove what can be the restricting and intimidating environments of approved premises and probation centres. They grasp the opportunity to effectively engage and communicate with the residents' group in a more relaxed and natural environment.

Ronny has managed to gradually introduce and instil core values such as discipline, communication, organisation, self-belief, teamwork and trust, all of which are vital skills that assist the residents as they embark on a journey of rehabilitation and successful social reintegration.

KURTIS BOURKE
BUILDING A NEW FUTURE

In 1998 I started to get involved with gangs and get into trouble. This led to crimes and I started going to prison in 2000 and was in and out of jail until 2011.

That was when I met Ronny Goodlass and started to listen to him about how to change my ways and my life. I wanted to get myself sorted out and become a better person and not waste any more time in life because I was not proud of myself at that time.

I had family problems and I was in care with social services and my head wasn't right. I got roped into crime, but my pattern started to change when I met Ronny and we discussed various things about where I wanted to go with my life.

This is when I went on the football coaching course which Ronny was running in partnership with the probation service to gain a football coaching Level 1 qualification. I am proud to say I have passed and am now looking forward to taking the Level 2 in the near future. I have been out of trouble for over two years and I now lead a better and healthier lifestyle. I would now like to help people similar to myself and turn their lives around. Everyone needs a second chance in life as I have with mine and an opportunity to come through on the other side. My next step is voluntary work in the community with football coaching to all ages.

I AM extremely grateful for all the above comments because they help to highlight the importance of my Health Through Sport charity. To raise much needed funds to continue our projects throughout the year I arrange two Sportspersons Dinners every November and May. I appreciate the support given by many ex-Everton players who attend and it is much appreciated. I will name the lads at the end of the book because there will be a long list and I have to mention my great friend Billy Ashcroft who also never misses. Although he played for Wrexham and Middlesbrough, he is a mad Blue Nose.

Dave Hickson, with his lovely wife Pat, absolutely loved attending our dinners. Everybody was always delighted to see them. I used to put Dave on the elevated Top Table with Pat on a table with friends. On one occasion, Dave had finished his three course meal with drinks and got up to head for the toilet before the guest speaker came on. We have pull-up banners on both sides of the Top Table promoting Health Through Sport and featuring our logo.

Dave started to go down the steps and leaned on the banner for support, thinking they were solid. He immediately went crashing to the floor. Dave was in his late seventies and we were all worried about him. He was taken to the toilet, but he insisted he was okay. He came back, but as a precaution the hotel had phoned for an ambulance to take him to hospital. The ambulance crew arrived with a stretcher and then Dave was wheeled through the function room. He was given a standing ovation by the audience and was sitting up waving as he left!

I have played with many ex-Everton players for the Ivor Scoles 'Over the Hill Mob' football team, people like Andy King, Roger Kenyon, Mick Buckley, John Hurst, John Bailey, and George Telfer to name a few, but I remember one game with Dave Hickson, the Cannonball Kid, at Long Lane, Aintree. The occasion stands out for me and sums Dave up.

We were playing in a charity match when the ball was

passed out to me by Andy King. I went past the full back and crossed from the bye line into the penalty area. As I looked up, the ball was heading for a position between their defenders and our attack.

Dave was one of our forwards attacking the ball with their centre-half also starting to close in at pace. The centre-half was 6ft 4ins and in his mid- twenties. Dave was 5ft 10ins and in his mid-60s. As the ball was getting closer to both of them, I could see the headlines in the next day's Echo: "Ronny Goodlass assists in getting Dave Hickson seriously injured."

The ball was head high when it reached them both and then BANG! Dave won the aerial challenge and as the ball flew into the top corner of the net they collided. I started to worry about Dave's wellbeing, but it was the centre-half who was pole axed and on the ground with Dave standing over him saying 'Are you ok son?'

He then wandered over to me and said 'great cross Ronny' before we strolled back to the halfway line chatting. That's why they called him the 'Cannonball Kid'. What a Man! We've lost him and we will always miss him, a remarkable character and an Everton great.

I arranged a Sportspersons' Dinner for Friday, 23rd November, 2007. It was another great night and a lot of ex-Everton players were supporting the event, including Dave Hickson. We drank long into the night as usual and everyone enjoyed themselves. I was on Radio Merseyside the next day to summarise on the Everton v Sunderland game at Goodison. We were live on air for 2pm when the programme would start. It got to about to 2.45pm when we heard from the producer that Dave Hickson had been taken ill in the reception area of the main stand and had been rushed to the Royal Liverpool University Hospital. I was very worried about him, but I knew he would receive the best treatment possible from the Royal. The game was tremendous and it finished 7-1 in our favour, but in the back of your mind I was wondering how Dave was getting on.

I kept phoning the hospital over the weekend to see if there was any change and Radio Merseyside kept the supporters informed of his condition through bulletins.

On the Monday morning I thought I would phone Dave's wife Pat to get the full prognosis, I asked how he was and she said: "He is in intensive care. He's got tubes everywhere, but he's improving."

We carried on chatting and then I heard Dave's voice. "Who is it?" he asked. "It's Ronny," she replied. Pat passed the phone to Dave and he said: "Ronny, what did you put in the wine on Friday at the Dinner?" I started laughing then said: "How are you mate?"

"I'm ok," said Dave. "I see the lads played well and won."

It was typical of Dave, thinking of Everton and not himself.

I have previously mentioned Ivor Scholes, a great character on the Liverpool amateur football scene and someone who got a lot of things right, but on a few occasions he got some things wrong as well. He had booked a coach to take his 'Over the Hill' football team, of which I was one, to Wembley for the FA Cup final between Everton and Manchester United in 1995. There were a couple of pick up points and along with a few other lads I was to be picked up at the Rocket by the M62. We were all there on time, but it started to get later and later with no sign of the team coach. Now was the time to start worrying.

A few of the lads were trying to contact Ivor to see what was happening when one of them came back and said we are not getting picked up and the coach was now cancelled. That came as a shock to me and eleven others. We were not happy at all, but my main concern was how we might now get to Wembley. The Rocket is a meeting point for a lot of the coaches, so I wandered over to a 'Happy Als' coach and asked the driver if there were any spare seats. He said 12!

It must have been written in the stars. I told the lads, boxed off the driver, and just as I was going to sit down at the front I heard someone shouting: "Dad!" I sat down, but kept hearing "Dad, Dad."

I looked at the back of the coach where I saw my 14 year old son Gary with his mates. I had now sorted tickets out for him, his mate and his Dad! Like father, like son, going to away games at a young age.

The day started off with what could have been a disaster, but turned out to be a great day with Everton beating Man United 1-0 thanks to a Paul Rideout header. To put the top hat on it, I went to the FA Cup Final with my son!

I have arranged a number of Sportspersons Dinners

over the years and held them at a few hotels across Liverpool with many top table and invited guests. I held a few at the Moat House in Paradise Street before it changed its name to the Holiday Inn. For one of the Dinners I invited Bobby Collins with his son and booked a room for them because they were travelling from Yorkshire. He sat next to me and we chatted all night about Everton and Leeds who he also played for. What an interesting and lovely gentleman he was. I mentioned I was a young lad who watched a game at Goodison between Everton and Leeds United when both teams were taken off to 'cool down' for ten minutes.

He was 5ft 3ins tall, but had a massive heart in that small frame with so much character. His nickname was the 'Little General'. My granddad thought he was great.

Brian Labone was on the Top Table and said a few words: "Bobby kept us in the First Division."

Bobby was sitting next to me. He was so quietly spoken and humble. He said "No Labby" but Brian – who was holding the microphone – was insistent replying: "Oh yes Bobby!"

The older members in the audience stood up and started clapping in agreement. Within seconds he was getting a standing ovation.

He joined Everton in 1958, made 147 appearances and scored 48 goals. He was strong in the tackle and an excellent passer of the ball, but most of all he was a leader and set his standards high. It was a surprise when he moved to Leeds in 1962 for the princely sum of £25,000, an absolute bargain for them. Later on in his Leeds managerial career, Don Revie would say he was the best signing he ever made. My granddad wasn't happy at all that we had lost the "Little General" when he still had so much to offer.

In December, 2016, a great charity - Beating Bowel Cancer - asked people to join in something called 'Decembeard' which meant you couldn't shave for all of December. You then asked family, friends and colleagues to donate any amount of money. I started a Just Giving page to raise funds, but it was also to help raise awareness and provide support to those affected by Bowel Cancer.

Like many others, I have had close family and friends affected by this terrible disease and with kind donations I was delighted with the £3,500 we raised. Thank you to everyone who donated. By the time the book is printed I will have shaved the beard off!

It was a good couple of months for me when I was presented with two awards.

The first was at the Gwladys Street Hall of Fame dinner which I attended on 10th March 2017 with many ex-players there to support the event. It was an excellent evening with the awards section at the end of the dinner and I received the 'Everton Pride' award, presented by my good friend and ex-team mate Bob Latchford.

The Health Through Sport Trustees and Patrons decided to present a new award called the 'Howard Kendall Achievement' award to honour the capabilities, values, and strengths of our great friend and supporter. Howard's wife Lily, who is a patron of our charity, was given the task of choosing a winner. At our next Sportspersons Dinner, held on the 11th May, 2017, I was both delighted and honoured when Lily announced me as the first winner. The second 'Howard Kendall Achievement' award winner for 2018 was Joe Anderson, Mayor of Liverpool.

I would like to mention George McKane. He does a great job for us at our Dinners with his camera, our very own David Bailey, but he has become a good friend to me over the years. He is a man of wisdom, a good heart, and is a mad Blue.

THE UNEXPECTED FOOTBALL 'SWERVE' THAT ACTUALLY SAVED MY LIFE

MY ROLE summarising games for Radio Merseyside over the past 22 years has been great. Following Everton I get to see all the matches home and away. This is my idea of royal blue heaven, but when I took up the job I didn't expect the real heaven to loom large on a long and winding journey to Leicester.

But first let me set the scene. Getting to the games is not always straightforward, although a lot depends on who is taking you. For long away trips, say to London, I usually travel by train, but if Radio Merseyside sports editor Ian Kennedy is covering the game, he insists on taking his car which is fine by me because he will do the driving and I can have a snooze on the way home.

Whether it's Crystal Palace, Southampton, Bournemouth, Brighton or Newcastle, Ian always drives, but one journey in particular will live long in the memory. It was the day we almost got killed going to Leicester.

It was the opening day of another challenging season and off we went. Ian, by the way, is a very good driver – in fact when I know Ian is driving I feel at ease because I know we will get there safely. However, on this particular sunny August morning, his driving skills were tested to the hilt.

We were on the A500 in between Stoke and Uttoxeter, doing about 60 mph, when we noticed a small lorry about 300 yards in front of us with a load of old tyres on the back. It turns out these tyres were not secured very well because suddenly one of them fell off and started bounding back towards us along the dual carriageway.

It was one of those sights you only see at a Grand Prix after a big smash – a stray wheel hurtling across the tarmac like a bouncing bomb.

This tyre just wouldn't stop and we both knew if it hit us head on through the windscreen we were 'gonners'. At one point it clipped one car and then bounced right across to the other side of the road.

Phew, it has gone into trees and the field, but no. It hit a tree and back it came towards us once again, flying from one side of the road to the other, seemingly with our name on it.

It was a surreal experience and I was fully expecting this bouncing bomb of a tyre to kill us stone dead. Ian managed to avoid swerving into the nearest ditch, and finally we saw it crashing into the hedge on the other side of the road. It took a few seconds before we realised it was all over. We were safe. We were ALIVE.

Surely, having cheated death, Everton would go on and record a famous victory to get the season off to the best start possible, but no. A 1–1 draw was all we got for putting our lives on the line. Typical!

Talking about Ian though, I've never seen anyone so obsessed with the old Little Chef restaurants. He just couldn't pass one – not without stopping for an Olympic Breakfast. There was one place in the middle of nowhere, somewhere on the way to Ipswich I think, and I swear when we walked in the waitress asked him if he wanted his usual table!

It broke his heart when the Little Chef outlets started to close. He knew where they all were, and it's with real sadness that he always points out: "There used to be one there you know."

On another trip with Ian we'd just completed a game between Ipswich and Everton at Portman Road. They seem to loom large in all of these stories. It's a long way there and back of course and Ian very rarely gets lost, but on this occasion he had to admit he didn't know where we were.

This was pre sat-nav, so you had to rely on your map reading skills. We were just outside Ipswich and I wound down the window to ask a local for directions. "We want to get to Bury St Edmunds," I said to this lad who was walking along the road. "I didn't know he was dead," he replied as quick as a flash.

He was no help, but what a great line!

I should say straight away that I don't just take my life in my own hands travelling with Ian Kennedy during the 22 years I have been a match summariser for Radio Merseyside. There have been many highs and lows while travelling the length and breadth of the country, and abroad. Here are a few more hair-raising stories.

Mike Hughes is a great lad and friend, but maybe after he reads this he won't be. He is not the best of drivers and always likes to leave early for games. I jokingly say to the family: "Light a few candles for me, Mike's driving today," and they also have a guessing competition to see what time he might pick me up.

We played Man Utd at Old Trafford one Sunday and the kick off was 4pm. I asked the family for their pick-up time guesses. The Premier League stipulates that the Media Room must be open three hours before kick-off, so it gives time for broadcasters to fix up their equipment to broadcast.

The family know Mike likes to leave early, so 12.15pm maybe 12.00pm? All wrong. He turned up at 8.30am and this was a record.

The roads approaching Old Trafford where empty,

nothing on them at all and so quiet that even the scarf sellers and hamburger vans where nowhere to be seen. We were driving to the media car park when a big white Transit van turns off Sir Alex Ferguson Way.

I assumed Mike had seen the van, but obviously he hadn't because he just kept going. It was getting worryingly closer. All of a sudden the van driver blasted his horn, loud and long. This was when Mike shouted out the immortal words that I will never forget:

"Where the fuck did he come from?"

I looked at him and replied:

"Sir Alex Ferguson Way!"

Another time we are playing away at the Riverside Stadium, Middlesbrough, and Mike picked me up for the start of the trip. We would be travelling via the M62, M1 North, A19 and A66 and had driven about 35 miles when there was a sign saying 'roadworks ahead'.

Mike said: "No problem."

He claimed he knew what route to take to get back on course for Middlesbrough. I said:

"Are you sure, Mike?"

And he confidently replied "yes."

Off we went chatting about Everton's form, team selection, would he make any team changes etc. I then started to read the newspaper, but we occasionally chatted and then I glanced to my left and saw a sign that read: HULL A63.

It didn't register to me straight away, but ten minutes later I looked up and there was the Humber Bridge! I said:

"There's the Humber Bridge"

And Mike replied: "I think I've gone the wrong way and a few extra miles."

The wrong way and a few extra miles! It sounded like a bit of an understatement to me.

Hull to Middlesbrough takes two hours and is 112 miles via the A1M. I'm glad to say we somehow got there before kick-off.

When travelling back from most Everton away games, we usually come along the M62 and take the Huyton/ Knotty Ash turn-off. On this occasion, as we turned off onto the slip road, he was driving on the hard shoulder.

I warned him: "You are on the hard shoulder."

"I'm not," replied Mike and it was then:

"You are."

"I'm not."

"You are."

"I'm not!"

As we came to the end of the slip road I shouted: "Watch that sign post," and he swerved off the hard shoulder and back onto the slip road. Luckily there was no traffic behind us and we carried on home. Tongue-in-cheek I said: "Tell Eve and Will (Mike's kids) that I saved their Dad's life today."

I now call that hard shoulder: "Mike Hughes Way."

Bournemouth is never a straightforward trip so we decided to take advantage of a flight from Manchester to Bournemouth Airport. The night before, I had a Sports Dinner for my charity Health Through Sport. Now anyone who has attended one of these knows how very enjoyable they are. They continue long into the night, a large amount of alcohol is consumed and it was sore heads all round the following morning. You don't get much sleep around these occasions.

I booked a taxi to pick me up at 5.45am to catch the 6am train from Lime Street to Manchester, the flight being 8.45am.

I don't think Ian Kennedy, Radio Merseyside's Sports Editor, had much confidence in me making the game when he realised my Dinner was the night before. Oh Ye of Little Faith!

This Bournemouth clash on 28 November, 2015, was an amazing game which Evertonians will remember for the wrong reasons. The final score was an eventful Bournemouth 3 Everton 3.

Romiro Funes Mori gave us the lead with a thumping header early on before Romelu Lukaku made it 2–0 with ten minutes left,

This is when the game started to change. They got one back and then, on 87 minutes, it was 2–2. We didn't see that coming, but it got even more interesting. Ross Barkley made it 3–2 in stoppage time and ran over to celebrate with the Evertonians. Some came on to the pitch to celebrate.

I remember turning to James Mountford and saying: "They'd better get off or they'll be spending the night in the clink." This is when James started laughing, but he had to compose himself quickly because the game wasn't finished yet. Bournemouth went up the other end and made it 3–3 with virtually the last kick of the game.

That match probably summed up in 90 minutes what it is like to be an Evertonian.

Matters didn't get any better – cue we couldn't get a flight back the next day, so had to get the train. Part of the subsequent journey was spent on a bus avoiding the track engineering works.

We love our job and we're privileged to do it, but sitting on a stuffy coach going out of Bournemouth station on a Sunday morning probably wasn't one of the more glamorous experiences of covering the games.

We found ourselves back on the South Coast three months later when the teams drew each other in the FA Cup, a 2–0 away victory for the Blues on Saturday, 20th February, 2016

As usual, with no regard for the travelling Everton fans, the TV companies decided to play this one at 5.30pm on a Saturday evening. Ross Barkley and Romelu Lukaku put us two in front in the second half and, unlike the previous visit, we didn't let this one slip and eventually made it to the semi-final.

But the one memory of this trip was the hotel we stayed in after the game. It entailed a drive to Bicester which is just off the M40 in Oxfordshire. The hotel was a small place in the middle of nowhere.

We got there about 11.30pm, but it might as well have been 3am as the place was awfully quite. The elderly gentleman on reception who checked us in couldn't have looked more disinterested, staring down at the piece of paper he was working on.

James said we wanted to check in. "Names?" answered the reception man, as though he was about to take a register.

"Mountford and Goodlass" James replied. There was a short silence. Hardly a "Welcome to our Hotel, you must both be very tired, how was your journey, can I get you a drink?"

None of these! He just gave us our keys. We had been keen to keep going on the road and get to the hotel as soon as possible, so we hadn't stopped to eat

"Are you still doing any food?" James enquired. He carried on writing on his piece of paper, then slowly raised his head. He peered over his glasses and had a facial expression as if he had smelt something extremely unpleasant. A sigh followed before he reluctantly said: "I can make you a cheese sandwich."

I was sure this was the brother of Basil Fawlty. It was hardly the most appealing of offers and where would he get the cheese from, the mouse traps in the cellar? We didn't want to take any chances so James ended up going to find a pizza shop.

We might have dodged a bullet there. And what super customer service skills. Needless to say, we haven't been back.

Premier League Leicester City were continuing to make history and their story that season just shows you that football dreams can come true as one of the teams that were favourites to be relegated drove on to become

Premier League Champions. As we headed to the King Power stadium, we knew all the roads to the ground would be very busy and that everyone in the city would want to be there. We left the car in the usual place allocated by the club and as we made our approach there was a carnival atmosphere already.

The media room was packed with journalists and camera crews from all over the world who wanted to report on this historic occasion. I had to get out of the room because it was so hot and I went up to the radio point from where I would be summarising the game. I had a really good view of the pitch and sat there drinking coffee and relaxing with three hours to the kick-off.

It was then that I noticed a man walking onto the pitch to make his way to the temporary stage that had been erected on the halfway line. I wondered who it was and as he turned I realised it was the fabulous classical singer Andrea Bocelli. He did a sound check and did two songs perfectly. What a start to the day.

Just before kick-off, he came out again with Claudio Ranieri escorting him and performed 'Nessun Dorma' and 'Time to say Goodbye' to a captivated crowd and one happy summariser!

It wasn't the best of games for us and with goals from Vardy after five minutes, King on 33 minutes, and Vardy again from the penalty spot. He would miss a second spot kick as they ran out 3–1 winners, with Mirallas getting a consolation goal for us in the 88th minute.

On the 12th May 2016, five days after this game,

Roberto Martinez was sacked as manager of Everton Football Club.

How long will it be before we are competing for the Premier League title or winning silverware?

It is twenty three years since my mate Joe Royle and his very good team won our last trophy. That is much too long a period for a club like ours.

Joe's players were more than just the 'Dogs of War'. Andrei Kanchelskis and Anders Limpar were quality wide players and played some entertaining football. Dreams can come true but let's turn hope into reality.

I always liked going to Leeds United to do games for Radio Merseyside. They are passionate supporters, the club has a good history with tremendous players down the years, and there has always been a great rivalry with Everton. In this particular fixture there was a lot of commitment from the players, but not much creativity on show and Nick Barmby, playing for Leeds, was booked for diving in the first half. The game was similar in the second half and with 16 minutes left Wayne Rooney came off the bench. Within six minutes he had scored a sublime goal.

Wayne picked the ball up 30 yards out with his back to goal. He turned past Bakke easily and ran towards Radebe before dropping his shoulder and speeding wide to the edge of the area from where he drilled a right foot shot past Robinson inside the far post. Live on air, I said: "He's turned Radebe so much that he's had to pay to get back in."

The reaction from the supporters was one of delight

because it would be our first win at Elland Road in the league for 51 years. At the time I knew Wayne had loads of potential and was a very special young player who could become a great player. What he has achieved in the game is exceptional… England captain, record England goalscorer, and also a local lad from 'Croccy.' Well done Wayne and good on yer! Once a Blue, always a Blue.

At the next game at Goodison, I was in my usual place doing commentary when the head steward wandered over and said: "You owe me £120." I looked at him mystified and said: "Why?"

"I was lying on the couch listening to you summerising the Leeds United game on the radio. You said Radebe had to pay to get back in. When Rooney scored, I started laughing so much that my foot kicked the lamp on the table and it smashed on the floor."

We then started smiling. His wife wasn't happy, but we had won 1 − 0 at Leeds, something which made all Evertonians beam.

Occasionally I do the hospitality lounges at Goodison, but also at away games. This time I got a phone call from Leeds United's hospitality team and they asked me if I would do a 'Q & A' with Peter Lorimer in some of their lounges, an invite I accepted. Peter was a very good player for Leeds and played in their heyday. This was the game Wayne scored his goal. They met me in the media room before the match and we were first taken to a lounge with 350 people, all Leeds supporters.

The compere asked me how I thought Everton might

get on and who I thought would be a player they needed to watch. I said we had a good chance to win, which was greeted with a few groans, and that the player to watch was Wayne Rooney, who had scored the winner against Arsenal and was doing well.

They wanted to know any stories of Leeds against Everton. I told them one that occurred during a period when Everton and Leeds had two great teams and were always battling for titles and cups. The game in question was another Elland Road sell-out.

These clashes featured two great teams giving it there all, not an inch given, and tackles flying in left, right and centre. The pitch was muddy and slide tackles were going in everywhere.

Howard Kendall won a tackle in midfield and then turned with the ball, only to be met by a tackle from Norman 'Bites Yer Legs' Hunter. BANG! Howard fell to the deck poleaxed and there was a melee involving both sets of players. Brian Labone was the Everton captain and in the thick of the action with a crowd of players standing around Howard.

Norman wandered over to stand near Labby and asked: "How is he?" Now Labby had a great sense of humour and with a sad look on his face, he turned and said: "Norman, he's dead!"

The shocked look on Hunter's face was there for a few seconds before Labby smiled and said: "I think he'll be okay." What a relief for the Leeds man!

Stories over, I moved to my radio position for the commentary. The only regret I had that day was when I had finished the phone-in. I didn't have time to go back into the hospitality lounges to tell them: "Wayne Rooney? I told you so!"

Everton had a midweek game at Chelsea. I was on the commentary team with Gary Flintoff. We gave Radio City's Daniel Mann, now with Sky Sports, a lift down to London. We were all staying at the Millennium and Copthorne Hotel at Stamford Bridge.

After the game we went to the hotel bar to have a nightcap. I ordered our drinks and another of the media lads joined us, announcing it was his birthday. He was keen to celebrate and ordered Jack Daniels all round. We had been drinking San Miguel so these were chases which we knocked back as we wished him all the best.

I wasn't being greedy, but I then got 'doubles' for everyone because it was his birthday. The drink was going down very nicely with the company relaxed and having a laugh.

After about an hour of this, Dan started talking Russian so I knew he'd had enough. He said he was going to bed and we agreed to meet the following morning for breakfast.

Next day, we saw Dan outside, looking forlorn. We went to sit with him and his colour was changing by the minute. You could say he was 50 Shades of Grey!

We went in for breakfast which is always excellent. Dan made an attempt to eat before we all set off home in Gary's car with Dan in the back, still looking very pasty. We had been travelling for about 15 minutes when he suddenly had to wind his window down and he gave Gary's light blue Vauxhall Meriva a more abstract look down the side of one of the back doors. The poor lad looked awful and it looked like a scene out of 'Little Britain'.

We stopped at a petrol station for Dan to go the toilet and get cleaned up, after which he said he needed a drink and something to eat. I said to him: "Dan, just get some water to rehydrate yourself and something light to eat because of your upset stomach."

He came back with the biggest packet of crisps I'd ever seen and fizzy drinks. How long would it take on the journey home for us to see those crisps again?

I couldn't talk about my time at Radio Merseyside without mentioning the legendary Alan Jackson. Jacko was at Radio Merseyside for more than 30 years and was an enormously popular sports presenter and an excellent interviewer. He would play devil's advocate when hosting the phone-in and certainly had his own way of doing things. He would read back the starting X1's of teams containing 12 names. There was a period when Jacko had a "man on the inside' who knew the starting X1's before we did? It went something like: "Ronny, I've heard there's no Tim Cahill tonight." I would reply: "Are you sure Alan, we've not heard anything at this end."

He would continue: "Well, that's what my source tells me," the cue for ten minutes of speculation as to why Cahill might not be starting. Then I would interject with: "By the way Alan, Gary has just been handed the team news," and Jacko would build up the tension still further by declaring: ""Well, Gary, you'd better give us that team news, and let's see how David Moyes has shuffled things round in the absence of Tim Cahill."

Then Gary would say: "Well Alan, Tim Cahill starts in midfield." Our eyes would look up to the heavens!

Jacko's phone-in show was legendary. He would say: "Call 709 9333, especially if you're on a mobile coming back from the game. Dave is on the line from the Dingle."

Dave: "Hi Alan, I want to ask Ronny his view on Tony Hibbert's performance tonight? '

Jacko: "Dave that's a very good question. Ronny, Dave has called in with a really good question about Tony Hibbert, but just let me ask you. Where is Everton's threat from the left this season?" I would just sit there bemused. "Well Jacko… " and off I'd go with my thoughts on something that had nothing to do with the fan's question.

I will always remember Jacko for his sports forum programmes with invited guests who would discuss a number of sports. It was in 2001 when the British Open Golf Championship was being held at Royal Lytham St. Anne's Golf Club. The panel consisted of golf experts, a professional golfer, a journalist – and Jacko.

The programme would be running smoothly with Jacko asking the questions in his usual relaxed manner about the Open Golf until he made a significant faux pas.

He went round the panellists asking who they thought would win the Open. One said 'Tiger Woods', another 'Ernie Els', 'Bernhard Langer' and so on.

Jacko then said: "Do you know who I fancy? Payne Stewart.'

There was complete silence for about five seconds when one of the panellists gingerly said: "Payne Stewart died in an airplane accident two years ago."

Jacko, being the professional he was, didn't bat an eyelid. He just carried on and said: "What about Justin Leonard then"

He was definitely one of a kind!

My radio travels now took me abroad for Everton's first game at Benfica's Estadio da Luz, the Stadium of Light. It ended with our heaviest defeat in Europe 5–0. They played excellent on the night.

With the second game against Benfica being held on Thursday 5th November 2009, we would need fireworks in the penalty area to get back on track and qualify. It wasn't to be with Benfica again running out winners, but this time 0–2. This was a very good Benfica team with David Luiz, Julio Cesar and goal scorer Saviola.

Before the game I was in the reception at the ground before going up to the radio point to summarise on the action. I was chatting to Peter McFall, the Everton photographer, when all of a sudden a large entourage came into the reception area. I soon realised what all the fuss was about. In the midst of it all was the iconic Eusebio.

I said to Peter: "As a young lad I watched him play against North Korea at Goodison in the 1966 World Cup when they came back from three down to win 5–3 and he scored four of the goals. Peter asked if I wanted my photo taken with him. As the great man walked past, Peter beckoned Eusebio to have his photo taken with me. Shaking his hand, I introduced myself: "My name is Ronny and I used to play for Everton."

I explained to him and his translator that I was in the stadium when he scored four goals for Portugal against North Korea in 1966 and I said he was fantastic.

Peter took our photo I thanked Eusebio and then he walked to the lift to go to the boardroom which was on the first floor. I made my way to the stairs to go to the media room. As I reached the first floor the lift doors opened and out walked Eusebio. He saw me and said "Ronny" and I replied "Eusebio, how are you?" with him and his entourage smiling. Obviously he had only just been talking to me downstairs, but the looks on the faces of the people by the boardroom was priceless.

I said to Eusebio who was now my best mate: "Safe journey home and enjoy the game."

He was an absolute gentleman and a world class footballer.

Because I'm football crazy I once agreed to be manager of the Wavertree Legion football team on a Sunday and we had some good players like our John, Georgie Stranack (the Garrincha of the Sunday League), Billy 'Maldini' Bolland and the legendary Currie family from Lodge Lane that had so many characters in one family. I had three of them in my team – Eddie Currie, Alan 'Peanut' Currie who has sadly passed away, and Peter Currie. They were a great set of lads on and off the field. The camaraderie between the lads was great and they were always ready to help each other out, like when someone forgot their boots. Peter Currie came into the dressing room one day and said he had no boots and asked: "Can anyone lend me a pair?"

One of the lads shouted "what size?" to which Peter replied: "From a size 7 to an 11!"

Eddie and Peter came to my house to repair some roof tiles and they had a break for lunch. Denise was making them some sandwiches and they were sitting in the front room. I shouted: "Do you want some salt and pepper?" Eddie replied: "Just threaten them with the salt!"

Don't you just love Scousers!

MICK ORD, THE FORMER MANAGING DIRECTOR OF RADIO MERSEYSIDE

"As a blue from boyhood it was a real honour to be asked to write some words for Ronny's book. I've known him for 20 years during which time he has been working as BBC Radio Merseyside's main Everton summariser. What always impressed me about Ronny - and I know I'm not alone here - is that he tells it like it is. No flam or spin just honest opinion and analysis gained from years of experience as a player, coach and Blue Nose.

"Unlike certain other ex-pros who summarise at Premiership games on TV and radio, he isn't controversial for the sake of it, and doesn't hide his opinions in case he upsets anyone at the club.

"That's all we ask for as football fans - whichever team

you follow. That's what we expect from our team and also our media, and hopefully our friends. Those values of honesty and integrity shine through this book. What more can you ask for?

"'It's one of them' - as Ronny USED to say in his early days as a radio match summariser.

"It certainly is."

PROUD TO LAUNCH 'BALL OF FIRE' AWARD IN HONOUR OF A LEGEND

WHAT Alan Ball lacked in height he more than made up for in skill, determination and stamina. His boundless energy and drive helped Everton become the best team in the league in 1970 and gloriously when in 1966 England were the best team in the world. The 'Ball of Fire' award we now present every year at our big Health Through Sport dinner aims to honour somebody recognised within the community as having outstanding qualities; someone who set goals and strove to achieve them by being steadfast and loyal; someone who cared for others and was loved in return; someone for whom nothing was too much trouble; someone who appreciated the value of working hard, and someone who could be called a friend by all who knew them.

I had always wondered why nobody has honoured Alan Ball with an award in his name. What he achieved for club and country, in my opinion, deserved more recognition than he received, so I came up with the idea of the annual 'Ball of Fire' award, to be given to a deserving person in the community. I approached the family for their approval and they wholeheartedly agreed for me to go ahead and to keep their Dad's name alive.

Our first recipient was presented with the accolade in November 2007 and in early 2014 I decided to hold a tribute night to Bally and to invite his family and ex-Everton team mates, including Joe Royle, John Hurst and Derek Temple, to celebrate his life and football career. I had a video produced with action from his Everton and England playing career and we heard stories and quotes from many ex-players. I organised the tribute night for Bally on the 9th May 2014 and it was a sell out, which shows you what Evertonians thought of him.

This is what Keely, his daughter, said on the tribute night: "I speak on behalf of my brother Jimmy and my sister Mandy when I say we are delighted that Ronny has dedicated a tribute night to our wonderful father Alan Ball MBE.

"This tribute night falls on what would have been the

eve of his 69th birthday. In April this year it has been seven years since he died very suddenly of a heart attack, so being invited to this very special night to celebrate his life is a real honour for us as a family.

"As most people know we lost our beloved mother Lesley in 2004 to ovarian cancer which our very strong family unit found very difficult to deal with. After 40 years of marriage to his best friend and soul mate, when she died part of my Dad died with her. He was never the same without her and I know that we all felt comfort that when he died she was up there waiting for him.

"My Dad achieved so much in his life. In 1966 he was crowned the world's greatest when England won the World Cup and he was voted Man of the Match. He was 21 years of age. His career took him to lots of different football clubs including Blackpool, Arsenal and Southampton, but I know for a fact that the one closest to his heart was the football club that paid a record transfer fee of £110,000 for him, Everton Football Club.

"He famously said: 'Once Everton has touched you nothing will be the same'. He meant that from the bottom of his heart. Dad was totally in love with the game of football. It was his absolute passion. He was a great ambassador for English football not only on the pitch but also for his endless work for charity. As you can imagine for all three of us children there is a big void in our lives.

"Losing both our parents at such a young age has been too hard to bear at times, especially as we have six children between us that were either too young to really remember them, some not even born. However, we have done everything to keep their memories alive and all the children know everything about their Nanny and Granddad Ball. That is why nights like this mean so much to the Ball Family. It helps to carry on life without them.

"Winning the World Cup for England in 1966 has made him part of English history and Jimmy, Mandy and I couldn't even begin to explain how proud we are of him. What is most important to us is how proud we are of him as a Father and Grandfather. He and our mother were the most loving and supportive parents any children could ask for. They were simply the best and we miss them so very, very much.

"A massive thank you, to you, Ronny, and to everyone who has come to this very special night, celebrating the life of a very special man, our Dad Alan Ball MBE."

Thank you Mandy. I'm just so proud to have been involved with this initiative.

During the evening, I presented Keely and Mandy with an iconic photo of Bally. Jimmy couldn't be there because he was coaching in America, but I gave one to the girls for him. The photo is of Bally, carrying a ball and leading the lads out against Leeds United at Elland Road on the 23rd October 1971. The captain, with that steely look, was striding out in blue shirt, white shorts and amber socks. The words next to him: 'Once Everton has touched you, nothing will ever be the same'. The photo and words still make the hairs on the back of my neck stand up, just like when I hear the Z Cars theme.

The photo was on the front of the Evertonian magazine. I phoned Ken Rogers, who at that time was Executive Editor of the Trinity Mirror Sport Media company producing it, to ask if I could have three copies. I explained it was to present one to each of Bally's children. Ken, the former Liverpool Echo Sports Editor, immediately said yes. I was very confident he would help. Not only is he a great friend of mine, he's also a mad blue!

I have many stories about Bally, but this is one of my favourites and when I told it to his son Jimmy, he loved it.

I wanted to watch Everton so much as a young lad that I started hitch hiking to games and it was with my two amigos, Brian Blythe and Tommy Hassett. One game we wanted to see was Everton playing at Burnley on the 28th January 1967 in a third round FA Cup tie and we decided in the week that we were going to go. We arranged to meet by Croxteth Hall Lane early Saturday morning and get to the English Electric factory on the East Lancs Road where there would be a high volume of traffic, giving us a better chance to get a lift and head towards the M6.

We clearly thought this hitch hiking was a doddle. We tried to get a lift, but after 15 minutes we were still there. Then 30 minutes had gone by and we started getting a bit cold. After 45 minutes we were starting to think we were never going to get a lift. Then all of a sudden a car pulled up about 20 yards away and we all raced towards it. The passenger door opened and a voice inside said: "Where are you going to?"

I shouted out 'Burnley '. The reply came back: "I'm not

going there, but I will take you as far as I can."

I jumped in the passenger seat and Brian and Tommy got in the back. We started moving away and the driver said: "Why are you going to Burnley?" and I said: "To watch Everton play." He said: "I'm going to the game later. Who is your favourite player?"

I immediately said 'Alan Ball 'and Tommy said 'Colin Harvey.'

I asked the driver: "Who is your favourite player?" and he replied: "Alan Ball, he's the best in the world, but I would say that wouldn't I because I'm his Dad!"

There were now four heads in the front of the car. Brian and Tommy sprung from their seats and their heads were now poking through the gap between the passenger and driver's seat.

He could have been anyone, so we started asking him numerous questions and giving him the third degree. It was the Scouse in us! Then I asked him what job he did he said: "I am a manager. Go to the glove compartment and take the brown envelope out and open it. "

I did and it was a telegram saying that a flight had been booked in the name of Alan Ball Snr. I showed it to Brian and Tommy. This was, without doubt, Bally's Dad.

When he finally dropped us off, he told us which way to go and to take care of ourselves. We were made up because it was not too far to Burnley and we had been given a lift by Alan Ball's father.

The three of us thanked Mr Ball for the lift and we got out of the car and he drove away with a wave. As we watched the car disappearing into the distance, I said to the lads: "It's a pity we didn't keep that telegram to show everyone and prove we got a lift off Alan Ball's Dad."

Then Tommy said: "Do you mean this one?" He was holding up the telegram!

The three of us just burst out laughing and started to walk. Burnley here we come. After the game we went around to the Players' Entrance to try and see any players. Out came Alan Ball, Lesley (Alan's wife) and Bally's Dad.

He saw us right away and said: "You're the three lads I gave a lift to this morning." With me being the youngest, it was on me to ask: "Can you give us a lift again Mr Ball?"

"Sorry lads," he said. "I can't, the car is full and we are going the other way. See you again and take care".

By the way we drew the game 0–0 but in the replay on the 31st January we beat Burnley 2–1 with the Golden Vision, Alex Young scoring twice.

Some days, when I had finished my jobs early, some of the first team would be up in the lounge relaxing after training. As I was leaving Bellefield Bally would always ask me if I wanted a lift home. He would drive down Croxteth Hall Lane to get onto the East Lancs Road, but he would take me home first and park outside our house. I would carry on the conversation because I used to love listening to him talking football with his knowledge of the game being second to none.

We would sit in his Plymouth Barracuda car with my mates and neighbours walking past. I would acknowledge them with a nod, a smile and a look of 'Yes, it is Alan

Ball sitting next to me!' The Plymouth Barracuda car was certainly a show stopper, but it was Bally they were really looking at.

I would ask him about the team they were playing against in the next game and how they planned to beat them. I'd suggest the opposition had a strong midfield, but he'd say: "We've got a stronger one." He would then explain how Everton would dominate the game.

I would then go on about the strikers, defenders, the keeper, and then Bally would say: "Ronny, we are playing tomorrow and I don't want to be late for the kick off."

It was time to get out of the car and go into the house, a case of: "Here endeth the lesson for now, until the next time."

I always love travelling around the country watching Everton, but enjoy certain grounds more than others. St Mary's, Southampton was one I always looked forward to because I would see Alan Ball there. Bally was a summariser for Radio Solent, similar to what I do for Radio Merseyside, and sat behind me to comment on games. When he saw me he would ask how I was and how the family were doing. Then it would be straight into Everton FC matters, who was playing well or not so good, which players they might be interested in buying and so on.

He wanted to know everything that was happening at 'his' club.

We would still be chatting away when the producers of the show would tell us we were about to go on air. It was always interesting to hear Bally's philosophy on football.

He was honest and never held back. I would have some team sheets on the table and ask Bally if he would sign them for my kids. "Certainly." he would reply.

I would say: "The first one is to Christopher, please" and then give him another "To Gary, please." I'd hand him a third "To Stacey, please."

He would smile and say: "How many kids have you got now?" I'd say: "We are nearly finished now... "To Mark, please – and I have four kids now."

Bally would reply: "Then you've bought a television, have you?"

"We would both start to laugh, two Blue Noses together, revelling in our club and our families. To this day I still have those team sheets. He was different class as a football player and as a man, always living up to his famous quote: "Once Everton has touched you, nothing will ever be the same again."

That has certainly been the case for me.

I was so proud to accept the job of narrator in the successful 'Ball of Fire' play co-written by Kenny O'Connell and Bobby Parry. There were long hours of hard work in rehearsals to get everything right for the opening night at Liverpool's Lantern Theatre. It was a sell-out and so well received by the audience. The play was also staged at the Epstein Theatre, New Brighton's Floral Pavilion, the Brindley in Runcorn, the Atkinson in Southport and the Royal in St Helens. The audiences were tremendous and created an excellent atmosphere. A large number of the Ball family attended at the Epstein, including Keely and

Jimmy (Bally's children), his sister, brother and some of his grandchildren. They all loved it, an excellent stage play telling the real story behind the great man.

Well done to Kenny and Bobby for writing the play which was performed to a very high standard by a talented cast with the excellent Margaret Connell as Director. It was a pleasure to be part of it. Now all break a leg!

'BALL OF FIRE' CO-WRITER KENNY O'CONNELL

As a fifteen-year-old Everton fan in 1970, I watched Alan Ball lifting the league championship trophy. I always followed Bally's football career and the inspiration for the stage play emerged after I read his autobiography "Playing Extra Time". I was thrilled to hear Ronny would take the part as narrator.

He did a fantastic job in 'Ball of Fire'. He used his skills as a radio presenter and we incorporated one of his Radio Merseyside phone-ins into the stage set. Ronny engaged in some great banter with a caller that brought the house down.

'BALL OF FIRE' CO-WRITER BOBBY PARRY

Securing Ronny Goodlass as the 'Ball of Fire' show's narrator was an honour. He grew into the role and made it his own after only a few shows. It really was a joy to behold. I just sat there in total awe that our work was being played out on stage with people hanging on to every word.

Ronny added charisma and a lot more for which we

will be forever grateful. It's great being around him, because of his energy and his larger than life personality, and I wish Ronny every success in whatever he does, especially with this fantastic book.

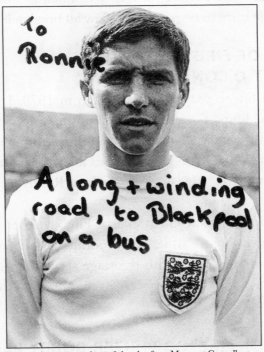

Presented to cast members of the play from Margaret Connell – a photo of Alan Ball with a line from the script. This was my line.

THE SHOCKING ALLARDYCE ERA OVER! NOW LET'S GET IT RIGHT

I HAVE to end this journey through my football lifetime with some thoughts about the modern Everton and where the current regime is taking us.

The 2017/18 season was awful with so many changes… Is this the start of a new successful era?

After Ronald Koeman had guided us to seventh place the previous year to set us up with Europa League football there was a real optimism around Finch Farm. With £140m having been invested in the summer of 2017, the supporters were looking forward to a successful campaign. Steve Walsh, Director of Football, arrived at the club with a big reputation. Would his recommendations to Koeman bring in the quality of player needed to take us to the next level?

In the first six fixtures we had Man City, Chelsea, and Tottenham away with Man Utd at home. These were difficult games, but it was still a poor start to the season considering the substantial investment that had been made by the club.

The pressure was building on Ronald Koeman to turn the club's fortunes around quickly, but after just two wins in eight games and a 5–2 hammering against Arsenal at home he was sacked.

He had been at the club for 16 months, but was on a three-year contract, believed to be worth £6m per annum so this would be another massive pay out to a sacked manager in less than two years. We were 18th in the Premier League.

David Unsworth was appointed as caretaker manager with help from Joe Royle which would give time for Farhad Moshiri and the board to look for a full time manager, whoever that would be!!

If results improved quickly, Unsy might have retained the job, but after a 5–1 defeat at home to Atalanta, followed by a 4–1 defeat at Southampton, things were clearly not right. The Saints setback was one of the worst performances I had ever seen by an Everton team and against a side that was out of form and struggling to score goals.

Unsy was in charge for the last time against David Moyes' West Ham at home and I was delighted he ended on a high with a resounding 4–0 win. We were now 13th in the league table.

The next day Sam Allardyce signed as manager on an 18 month contract.

Farhad Moshiri told Everton's AGM in January 2018 that he came to the decision "after reading Allardyce's autobiography."

That is mind blowing. I might send a copy of my book to all Premier League owners and major shareholders, you never know!!

Now Allardyce's remit was to keep Everton in the Premier League which he certainly did, but I am still adamant that there were at least three poorer teams than us in the top flight.

Allardyce never understood the club from day one and he didn't endear himself to supporters while he was here.

He claimed every positive result for himself, telling anyone who would listen that it was his team selection, tactics or substitutions that led to the win or draw. It was a different story when we lost. He would avoid taking any responsibility for a defeat, claiming "he never passed the ball to the opposing team!"

Certain games stand out for me which epitomise his tenure as manager. One of these was when we played at Burnley who hadn't won in 12 games. Cenk Tosun scored his first goal for the club with a good header from a Walcott cross which was headed on by Seamus Coleman.

We were leading 1–0 at half time. Then, as Allardyce was walking back to the dressing room, he grinned as he past the supporters with a look of arrogance that didn't go down well at all with the fans. Then Burnley turned the scoreline after the break to win 2–1 and we slipped to a fifth consecutive away defeat.

Then, as if the day couldn't get any worse for the supporters, Allardyce was seen smirking on screen when asked about their reaction at the end.

I also remember when we played Watford who were in a very poor run of form and hadn't kept a clean sheet in the previous seven league games. It was a poor first half with very few chances and similar in the second when suddenly there was movement on the Everton bench. Who was coming on to get us that vital goal? Morgan Schneiderlin, a defensive midfield player, was standing by the touchline and the phrase "what we have we hold" came to mind!

Then, after 79 minutes, Troy Deeney scored for Watford. It was his first goal from open play in 27 matches. Only then was Schneiderlin told to sit down and a striker was brought on instead.

Allardyce was still talking about his plans for the following season, but the game at West Ham finally brought home to Farhad Moshiri that the manager had to go and not many Evertonians were going to shed a tear on his sacking.

Everton have a great away support with their allocation of tickets selling out very quickly for every away game and West Ham was no different.

It was Everton's 500th Premier League away game.

It was played on the 13th May 2018 at the London Stadium with an attendance of 56,926. Could we at least put in a good performance and get a positive result to finish the season off and send our supporters home in a happier mood? The answer to both questions was a resounding no.

We had to watch some dire games in 2017/18, but this was up there with the poorest of them. It was lacking in passion, enthusiasm, direction, quality… I think I'll leave it there if you've got the picture!

It could have been six but it ended up 3–1. We were second best in every department.

We know it's a result-oriented business, but a total lack of entertaining football home and away was not what the supporters wanted to watch. There was a lack of shots at goal and in some games none at all.

Three days after this game Allardyce was sacked and his back room staff soon followed. Then Steve Walsh, Director of Football, was sacked. The next managerial appointment would be vital to take the club forward. Before this happened the appointment of Marcel Brands from PSV as the new Director of football took place in the May and he came with a good reputation on the continent. His first task would be to select a new manager to work with him on buying and selling at the club.

Mr Moshri wanted Marco Silva as his first choice again, but this time he got his man who signed a three-year contract. Silva has appointed his own back room staff.

There is a lot of hard work ahead for both him and Brands to strengthen an unbalanced squad with quality signings while recouping as much as we can on players who are not good enough to take the club forward, enabling us to reinvest the transfer fees into the squad.

We need to get the Bramley-Moore Dock stadium project sorted as soon as possible and we cannot miss out on this fantastic opportunity to move to a new stadium situated on the 'Banks of the Royal Blue Mersey'. What a sight that will be and it must be done if we are to compete on a regular basis with the present top six. Look at Tottenham as an example of what can be achieved.

The departure of CEO Robert Elstone, movement at boardroom level, then the appointment of a new CEO has hopefully set us on a positive road – and how the supporters crave some long overdue success.

SPECIAL THANKS TO

KEN ROGERS

Like many others, I regard Ken as one of the finest in his field whether it be in journalism, his many books, or even his ability to produce a successful play about our famous district, a man of many talents. He has been a great friend and confidante of mine for many years. Thanks for all the encouragement and guidance you gave me while I was writing my book.

JOE ROYLE

I'm grateful to Joe for writing the Foreword. He was a great player, manager and friend. I have always been able to rely on his support and I will always appreciate the opportunity he gave me to become Everton Youth Coach. He is a 'Top Man' and one of the true good guys.

THOMAS REGAN

I've had a number of commissioned paintings from Thomas for my Health Through Sport charity dinners and they have always been of the highest standard. That's why I approached him to design the cover of my book and I'm very pleased with the outcome.

EVERTON FC

Matt McPeake, the Everton scout who signed me. Bruce Rioch, Ken McNaught, Mike Pejic, Dave Jones, Bryan Hamilton, Duncan McKenzie, Alan Wilson, Stan Osbourne, David Poppleton, Rev Harry Ross, Richard Kenyon and his marketing/media team, Tony Sage, Carena Duffy and Henry Mooney.

DARREN GRIFFITHS

Everton Media & Publications Manager and a good mate of mine who I have known for many years. I see him at all the Everton games. He is a big supporter of my charity and when we meet up we always discuss the game over a glass of orange juice!

NAC BREDA

Ruud Jansen, Ria, Ben, Marissa Maas, Addy Brouwers, Netty Brouwers, Tim Meeus, Theo Dierickx and Jan de Jong.

ADO DEN HAAG

Piet de Visser, Lex Schoenmaker, John van Zweden and Aad Mansveld.

FULHAM FC

Tony Gale, Ray Lewington, Drew Heatley and Ken Coton.

TRANMERE ROVERS FC

Mark Palios, Bryan Hamilton, John Williams and Billy Rodaway.

SCUNTHORPE UNITED FC

James and Phil Moody.

BARROW FC

Phil Yelland and Ralph Sheppard.

RADIO MERSEYSIDE

Mick Ord, Ian Kennedy, James Mountford, Alan Jackson, Mike Hughes and Gary Flintoff.

HEALTH THROUGH SPORT TRUSTEES

Chairman Mike Dalton, Rev Henry Corbett and Edward Bowman.

HEALTH THROUGH SPORT PATRONS

Joe Royle, Lord John Grantchester, Lily Kendall, Simon Britton, Tony Byrne and John Blain.

CONTRIBUTORS

Keely, Jimmy and Mandy Ball, Mick Ord, Henry Corbett, Darryl Laycock, Kurtis Bourke, John Dunleavy, Kenny O'Connell, Bobby Parry and Brian Blythe.

RESEARCHERS

Kenny Pritchard, Richard Gillham, Brendan Connolly, Gavin Buckland and Billy Smith.

SPONSORS

Frank Bird, Trish Campbell, Lesley Taylor, John Blain, Jamie Rowland, Dave Harper, Kings Construction and Kevin O'Connor.

REGULAR ATTENDEES AT THE SPORTSPERSONS DINNERS

Joe Royle, Derek Temple, John Hurst, John Bailey, Graeme Sharp, Derek Mountfield, Tony Kay, Barry Horne, Mark Higgins, Larry Carberry, Kenny Pritchard, Billy Baker, Billy Ashcroft and Billy Rodaway.

TRIBUTE NIGHTS HELD IN HONOUR OF

Alan Ball, Howard Kendall, Joe Royle, Derek Temple, Tony Kay, John Bailey, Derek Mountfield, Kevin Sheedy and Neville Southall.

ALAN BALL 'BALL OF FIRE' AWARD

Winners include: Rhys Jones, Colorectal Unit Royal Liverpool University Hospital, Sandra Rothwell, Jeanette Stockton, The Irish Toffees, Kurtis Bourke, David Fehily and Liam King.

BRIAN LABONE 'CORINTHIAN' AWARD

Winners include: Dave Hickson, Ken Rogers, Rev Harry Ross, Clatterbridge Hospital, Richie Gillham, George McKane and Richie Rooney.

RONNY GOODLASS
CAREER STATISTICS

EVERTON
1969/70
Lancashire League 'B' team - 18 apps, 8 goals.
Lancashire League 'A' team - 10 apps, 7 goals.
FA Youth Cup - 3 apps.
Lancashire Senior Cup - 2 apps (beating Man United 1- 0).

1970/71

Lancashire League 'A' team - 28 apps, 12 goals.
Everton FC were Lancashire League 'A' team
Champions.
Lancashire League 'B' team - 2 apps, 1 goal.
FA Youth Cup – 2 apps, 1 goal.

1971/72

FA Youth Cup - 4 apps, 2 goals. Reached quarter-final.

1971/76

Reserves -149 apps, 24 goals.

1975/77

First Team - 51 apps.
League - 35 apps
League Cup - 9 apps including three League Cup Finals.
FA Cup - 7 apps including 2 FA Cup semi-finals.

NAC BREDA (HOLLAND)
1977/79

League - 57 apps, 7goals.
KNVB Cup - 5 apps, 2 goals including two- legged
quarter-final defeat to PSV Eindhoven 3-2 on aggregate.

ADO DEN HAAG (HOLLAND)
1979/80

League - 34 apps, 4 goals.
KNVB Cup - 4 apps, 1 goal including quarter-final

defeat to PSV 4- 3 on aggregate after winning the first leg 3- 1.

FULHAM
1980/81
League - 22 apps, 2 goals.
FA Cup - 1 app.

SCUNTHORPE UNITED
1981/82
League - 9 apps.

SOUTH CHINA (HONG KONG)
1982/83
League - 20 apps, 2 goals.
Hong Kong Cup - 1 app, 1 goal.

TRANMERE ROVERS
1983/85
League - 21 apps.
Football League Trophy - 4 apps, 1 goal.

BARROW FC
1985/87
League - 49 apps, 4 goals.

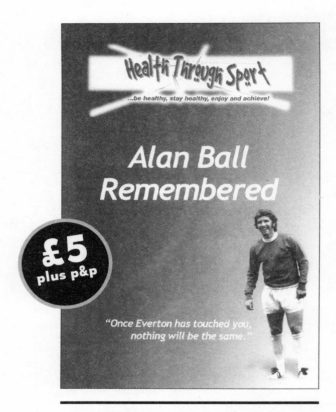

Alan Ball Remembered

£5 plus p&p

"Once Everton has touched you, nothing will be the same."

This dvd features a selection of Everton greats including Howard Kendall, Joe Royle, Graeme Sharp and Ronny Goodlass reminiscing about Bally's commitment, determination and skill whilst playing in one of 'the greatest Everton sides'. In 2006, Bally returned to Liverpool to present one of his final after-dinner speeches. Fortunately the occasion was filmed... so sit back and enjoy one of Everton and England's greatest players talk about his boyhood dreams of winning the World Cup and a glittering career that saw him play across three decades.

Available from **healththroughsport.co.uk** and **St Luke's Church** before Everton home games.

All proceeds to the Health Through Sport charity.